POETRY AND IRELAND SINCE 1800:
A Source Book

WORLD AND WORD SERIES
Edited by Professor Isobel Armstrong, University of
Southampton

POETRY AND IRELAND SINCE 1800: A Source Book

Edited by
MARK STOREY

ROUTLEDGE
London and New York

First published in 1988 by
Routledge
11 New Fetter Lane, London EC4P 4EE

Published in the USA by
Routledge
in association with Routledge, Chapman & Hall, Inc.
29 West 35th Street, New York NY 10001

© 1988 Mark Storey

British Library Cataloguing in Publication Data

Poetry and Ireland since 1800 : a source
    book. — (World and word series).
    1. English poetry — Irish authors —
History and criticism
    I. Storey, Mark II. Series
    821' .009   PR3767

ISBN 0-415-00331-8
       0-415-00332-6 pbk.

Library of Congress Cataloging-in-Publication Data

ISBN 0-415-00331-8
       0-415-00332-6 pbk.

Printed and bound in Great Britain by
Biddles Ltd, Guildford and King's Lynn

GENERAL EDITOR'S PREFACE

The *World and Word* series, as its title implies, is based on the assumption that literary texts cannot be studied in isolation. The series presents to students, mainly of English literature, documents and materials which will enable them to have first-hand experience of some of the writing which forms the context of the literature they read. The aim is to put students in possession of material to which they cannot normally gain access so that they may arrive at an independent understanding of the inter-relationships of literary texts with other writing.

There are to be twelve volumes, covering topics from the Middle Ages to the twentieth century. Each volume concentrates on a specific area of thought in a particular period, selecting from religious, philosophical or scientific works, literary theory or political or social material, according to its chosen topic. The extracts included are substantial in order to enable students themselves to arrive at an understanding of the significance of the material they read and to make responsible historical connections with some precision and independence. The task of compilation itself, of course, predetermines to a great extent the kind of connections and relationships which can be made in a particular period. We all bring our own categories to the work of interpretation. However, each compiler makes clear the grounds on which the choice of material is made, and thus the series encourages the valuable understanding that there can be no single, authoritative account of the relationships between world and word.

Each volume is annotated and indexed and includes a short bibliography and suggestions for further reading. The *World and Word* series can be used in different teaching contexts, in the students' independent work, in seminar discussion, and on lecture courses.

Isobel Armstrong
University of Southampton

Contents

Contents

Preface

This volume contains a number of documents from the 1830s to the present, all of them concerned with the particular and peculiar problems of writing poetry in Ireland. Many of these articles and essays are not easily accessible; some, such as those by Yeats, are merely representative of a much larger and more varied body of thought, which can be pursued readily enough in various collections of his prose. My aim has been to present, so far as is possible within certain obvious constraints, the several strands of an argument about the nature of a poetry that seeks to establish itself as distinctively Irish; there are clearly mergings and overlappings, anticipations and echoes, affirmations and denials, unresolved contradictions and ambiguities. I pursue some of these in the Introduction, which is offered neither as a comprehensive historical survey of ideas — still less of events — nor as an account of the development of Irish poetry, but rather as a series of pointers to the recurrent issues in the debate.

It might be thought that the picture is limited by the concentration on poetry; certainly the argument centres also on fiction and drama. I would merely plead here that many of the early contributors to the debate are talking about literature in the widest sense; also, that it is precisely drama that sparks off the particular debates at the turn of the century, and that ten years later it is impossible to disentangle Yeats's enterprise from his support for the Irish Theatre, and especially for J.M.Synge. But my starting point has been, in particular, the efflorescence of poetic activity in Ireland in the last 20 years; it seems to me impossible for us to understand what has been happening there unless we see it, as so much in Ireland, in its historical context. These documents are at least part of that context. Many poets, it is true, have not written much in the way of theory, or statements of practice; their own work acts as its own commentary. Others have written at length in autobiographical terms. Yeats, Austin Clarke, Louis MacNeice, Patrick Kavanagh — all have left invaluable material of this kind, matched by something like Frank O'Connor's *Backward Look* (1967). For various, I hope obvious, reasons, I felt unable to include any of this material here.

The poems, of course, from Moore, through Yeats, to Clarke, Kavanagh and beyond, provide both the basic material and the basic context. I have had to take the poems, along with so much else, as read: they provide the reason for this collection of

1

documents, and it is to them that I hope any reader will ultimately turn.

My thanks go to many people, including the students at Birmingham with whom I talked about some of these matters during a series of seminars on 'Irish poetry since Yeats': these are some of the documents we all felt we needed then. But my larger gratitude is to all those I knew in Belfast from 1970-76. It would not have made sense for me to discuss these things at all if I had not lived and worked there when I did, which is not to say that yet another Englishman should be writing about Ireland; it is merely to hope that my friends will excuse this dipping of toes in waters not my own.

Acknowledgements

Extracts from W.B.Yeats, *Essays and Introductions*, are reprinted with the permission of Michael B. Yeats, Macmillan London Ltd and A.P.Watt Ltd; also of Macmillan Publishing Company © Mrs W.B.Yeats 1961; extracts from *W.B.Yeats's Uncollected Prose*, ed. Frayne and Johnson (1970,1975), are reprinted with the permission of Michael B. Yeats, Macmillan London Ltd and A.P.Watt Ltd. Extracts from Patrick Kavanagh, *Collected Pruse* (1967), are reprinted with the permission of Martin, Brian and O'Keefe. The essay by Thomas Kinsella, 'The Divided Mind', from Seán Lucy (ed.), *Irish Poets in English* (Cork, 1973), is reprinted with the permission of the author.

Acknowledgements

[faded, largely illegible text]

Introduction

The cosmopolitan is a nonentity — worse than a nonentity;
without nationality is no art, nor truth, nor life, nor anything.

Turgenev[1]

Whenever an Irish writer has strayed away from Irish
themes and Irish feelings, in almost all cases he has done
no more than make alms for oblivion. There is no great
literature without nationality, no great nationality without
literature.

W.B.Yeats[2]

I

There is something almost perversely defiant about the placing
of Michael Hartnett's poem, 'A Farewell to English', at the end
of the *New Oxford Book of Irish Verse* (1986). Thomas Kinsella's
anthology is anxious to make a central point about the continuity
of the Irish tradition, and one senses a shared scorn for what
Hartnett dismisses as the 'celebrated Anglo-Irish stew'. None the
less, few enough of the other modern writers represented in the
New Oxford Book have taken such an unambiguous farewell of the
English part of what is a highly troubled tradition. The answer
that Seán Lucy gave, in 1973, to his own question, 'What is
Anglo-Irish Poetry?', hints at the nature of these contradictions:

> on the one hand...a complex and developing relationship
> between two traditions, two cultures, two languages; and
> on the other, it is the story of a search: it is part of the quest
> of the English-speaking Irish for an identity, the reshaping
> of English to express the Irish experience.[3]

That quest, that search, dominates Irish poetry from the late
eighteenth century onwards, and it characterises the poetry of
Ireland since Yeats. What is striking about the recent burgeoning
of poetry in Ireland is the way in which so many writers address
themselves to the problem of their origins, their roots, where they

5

belong: few of them can forget for long Stephen Daedalus' self-dedication to 'silence, exile and cunning'. Heaney's plangent description of himself as 'lost,/Unhappy and at home'[4] has a wry truthfulness about it, that glances sideways at his contemporaries, and back to that seemingly endless, dark Irish past.

One of the most ambitious poems from Ireland in recent years has been John Montague's *The Rough Field* (1972), in which he attempts to set the present in the context of a particularly daunting past; he concludes, with some sobriety, that the glory and the dream — in the Wordsworthian sense — have gone; that however much he might circle around the question of home, he can never get back there. Exile has been forced upon him, rather than chosen. This preoccupation haunts (and that seems to be the appropriate word) much modern Irish poetry. Even Austin Clarke, the major Irish poet since Yeats to redefine a peculiarly Gaelic inheritance, concludes his 'Return from England' (*Ancient Lights*, 1955) with a teasing, self-tormenting question:

> When I had brought my wife
> And children, wave over wave,
> From exile, could I have known
> That I would sleep in England
> Still, lie awake at home?

Home provides few easy comforts for the Irish: as Clarke's question implies, home itself is not readily defined, especially if you are Irish. The recollections of Louis MacNeice's sister present the problems of exile from a different perspective, underlining the tensions within Ireland itself:

> [Connemara] became for us both a 'many-coloured land',
> a kind of lost Atlantis where we thought that by right we
> should be living, and it came to be a point of honour that
> we did not belong to the North of Ireland. We were in our
> minds a West of Ireland family exiled from our homeland.[5]

The renewed 'Troubles' from 1968 onwards have served to emphasise and exacerbate the underlying tensions: definition — self-definition — has to be seen not merely in terms of Ireland against England, but the North of Ireland as against the South.

There is no doubt that there has been a release of Irish poetic energy in the last 20 years. It has had some odd effects, certainly, and judgments have been warped by passion's ardour. Against *The Wearing of the Black* (1974), Padraic Fiacc's distinctly odd and uncomfortable anthology, we can set the more sober claims of Frank Ormsby's *Poetry from the North of Ireland* (1979), and the typically enigmatic *Faber Book of Contemporary Irish Poetry* (1986), where Paul Muldoon gathers eight poets, excludes himself, and dispenses with an Introduction. An index of the complications that have set in since Clarke is provided by Derek Mahon's poem 'Afterlives', which seems a formal echo (deliberate or not) of Clarke's poem, and yet whose greater precision and detail locate it firmly in the political realities of the 1970s.

> And I step ashore in a fine rain
> To a city so changed
> By five years of war
> I scarcely recognize
> The places I grew up in
> The faces that try to explain.
>
> But the hills are still the same
> Grey-blue above Belfast.
> Perhaps if I'd stayed behind
> And lived it bomb by bomb
> I might have grown up at last
> And learnt what is meant by home.

It is impossible to read recent Irish verse without a strong sense of these sharply felt details (hence the unsatisfactory nature of something like Craig Raine's detached 'Flying to Belfast, 1977'). The difficulties of recognition in the face of change — personal, cultural, historical — are recurrent themes. Seamus Heaney's solace when confronted with Tollund or Grabaulle Man is a pained realisation of the equation of home and lostness. In 'Traditions' he asks again the famous question, 'What is my nation?', and provides us with Bloom's answer, 'Ireland, I was born here. Ireland.' Of course we know, and Heaney knows, that things aren't that easy. If he got few thanks in some quarters for *North* (1975), and the personal move South that it partly mirrored, that was a reflection of others' expectations rather than his own limitations. He picks up and develops Montague's image of the circle, nudging around the problem of being Irish, exploring what is possible, and what art — particularly Irish art — can make

7

possible. To that extent Heaney seems an appositely modern writer, alert to his role as artist, desperately seeking the right voice, listening for the right sounds, or, to use his own characteristic metaphor, making the appropriate soundings. So that, whatever home is, in terms of place and personality, it is also, in the last resort, the form you adopt as a poet, the cloak you wrap around yourself, the mask you put on. There might, as Yeats suggested, be 'more enterprise in walking naked', but to be naked in Ireland is, as Yeats learnt, usually to be cold. The chill titles of Heaney's early volumes imply that he is prepared to confront the cold; but the paradox of 'Exposure', the concluding poem of *North*, is that he is an 'inner émigré'. Part of his exposure would seem to be that he has not dared to expose himself enough ('a wood kerne/Escaped from the massacre,/Taking protective colouring/From bole and bark'). The subtext to *North* is a despairing one: Britain's colonisation of Ulster has taken away her strength, just as the famous wrestler Antaeus, who survives, Heaney-like, when he lies flat on the ground, is lifted high in the air by the arrogant Hercules. But out of such apparent defeat, Heaney makes artistic virtue. *Field Work* (1979) signalled a new start, which was continued in *Station Island* (1984). Personal and local concerns are sanctioned and illuminated by a literary tradition that embraces, amongst others, Wyatt, Spenser, Dante, Wordsworth and Robert Lowell, and by a recourse to myth that is reminiscent of Yeats. And it is Yeats whom Heaney quotes in 'The Harvest Bow': '*The end of art is peace*'. In 1979 that had a particular significance. It is a reminder that all Irish writing worth its salt finds its bearings in relation to the explorations conducted by Yeats throughout his long poetic career, at a time when the relationship between art and political and national life was of central importance. Yeats, in his turn, could only talk of his ideals for Ireland in the context of a long debate that had begun a hundred years earlier.

II

Thomas MacDonagh's *Literature in Ireland* was published posthumously in 1916 after his execution for his part in the abortive Easter Rising. He comes in some ways to represent the perfect, tragic fusion of literature and politics in Ireland. His book still has its historical interest, particularly for his attempt to define what he called a distinctive 'Irish Mode' which would set Irish verse apart from English. One of the ironies — one of many — is that MacDonagh could well have found a model for this 'Irish Mode' in the work of Thomas Moore, the early nineteenth century lyric poet vilified by Hazlitt for converting 'the wild harp of Erin into a musical snuff-box'.[6] Moore is not, nowadays, often thought of as a poet in the Irish tradition at all, and his appearance in anthologies tends to be a grudging one. But if MacDonagh stands for the great extreme, Moore is one of the first to represent the alternative, the Irish writer who leaves Dublin to find an audience and a market in London. It is precisely because he was a commercial success, and a hit in the society salons, that he is worth attending to.[7] The stream of *Irish Melodies* that he produced, set to music by John Stevenson (1808-34), have become something of a landmark in this strange and contorted history: 'The harp that once through Tara's halls', 'Let Erin remember the days of old', 'Oh blame not the bard' — such songs were more than the languishing ditties we associate with early Byron (a staunch admirer, incidentally); Moore was not merely turning out album verses that went well to music. He was consciously addressing himself as an Irish poet to an English audience (anticipating a similar role adopted by William Allingham),[8] performing a balancing act with which most subsequent Irish poets have become familiar. There can be no doubt about Moore's intentions, as he spelt them out in a letter to the composer: he was out to reclaim the country's songs from the

> service of foreigners. But we are come, I hope, to a better period of both politics and music; and how much they are connected, in Ireland at least, appears too plainly in the tone of sorrow and depression which characterises most of our early songs... The poet... must feel and understand that rapid fluctuation of spirits, that unaccountable mixture of gloom and levity, which composes the character of my countrymen, and has deeply tinged their music.[9]

Two important notes are sounded here: the melancholy nature of much of the material — a point seized upon repeatedly by later writers, especially Englishmen such as Matthew Arnold — and the connection between politics and music. The extension from music to poetry is easy to make, especially for Moore, who sees the two as inextricable: for him, music was 'the source of my poetic talent, since it was merely the effort to translate into words the different feelings and passions which melody seemed to me to express'.[10]

For Moore, then, the songs were an expression of national identity, although quite what that meant in practice was not so clear nor so easily defined. That he should be worrying at the problem in an ambiguous fashion (he was by no means the last to do so) owes a lot to the historical and cultural circumstances. The two events that sandwiched his departure from Ireland were the 1798 rebellion and the 1800 Act of Union. But such blunt facts had, and have continued to have, a real and symbolic significance that became interwoven with the imaginative history of the country. Moore was himself acquainted with some of the United Irishmen, including Robert Emmet, whose death prompted the elegiac 'Oh breathe not his name...', and Edward Hudson, the flautist; in 1796 the first volume of a collection of Irish folk music was published by Edward Bunting, who had four years earlier attended the Belfast Harp Festival, where he heard and transcribed many of the old songs; Hudson and Moore, at Trinity College, Dublin, played through these songs in Bunting's collection, and it was Emmet who exclaimed, upon hearing 'Let Erin remember the day', 'Oh that I were at the head of twenty thousand men, marching to that air.'[11] Bunting's collection gathered around itself a host of emotional and political aspirations, which had already been sparked off by the publication, in 1789, of Charlotte Brooke's *Reliques of Ancient Irish Poetry*, a volume that was more than a piece of apparent antiquarianism; if it caught the vogue of much of the late eighteenth century for the medieval and the quaint, it echoed in particular Bishop Thomas Percy's *Reliques of Ancient English Poetry* (1765), and even more importantly established a genuinely Irish tradition in answer to the bizarrely popular Ossianic fabrications of the Scotsman James Macpherson. Macpherson had claimed that all the Ossianic myths, Fionn and the Fionna, were in fact Scottish, and had nothing to do with Ireland; he produced something that was bogus and synthetic, and yet strangely appealing to those on the mainland in the grip of the cult of sensibility. The Irish were less impressed. They felt, as Moore felt about the songs he knew, that they had been denied and deprived. Brooke and Bunting were signs that things might be put right; gradually the antiquarian movement grew more confident, and historians addressed themselves to the question of a national identity that could be recaptured through history. If the Act of Union seemed like a British attempt to close the Irish problem once and for all, it was quite clear to many in Ireland that this was just another utter miscalculation; a political battle might have been lost, but the war was not over. And so it is that the apparently innocuous Tom Moore, singing his sad songs in London, becomes not so much a rallying point for dissent as an indication of the ways in which national feelings will force their way through to the surface. And it is important to register the fact that his popularity owed much to what was in effect the domestication of potentially troubling themes. He was not the last poet in Ireland to touch on the ambiguous nature of an appeal to the Gaelic past, whilst at the same time making oblique reference to the turbulent Irish present.

III

It was the precise nature of that appeal that lay at the centre of an intriguing debate which was to take place in the pages of the *Dublin University Magazine* in the 1830s. In an attempt to offer translations of the old ballads to a wider public — and thereby touching on one of the basic irritants, the general ignorance of Gaelic — James Hardiman edited, with a small team, the *Irish Minstrelsy* (1831). This might have joined all those other well-meant attempts in the dustbin of history were it not for the attentions of Samuel Ferguson, who wrote four lengthy articles on the topic for the *Dublin University Magazine* in 1834 (no.1). Ferguson himself (along with many other figures in this drama) is something of a paradox. He was a Northern Protestant and loyalist who went from Belfast, to Trinity College, Dublin, to London; he became a barrister in 1838 and later, by marrying into the Guinness family, became part of the Anglo-Irish Ascendancy. A career of perfect rectitude was rewarded by a knighthood in 1878, and in 1881 the Presidency of the Royal Irish Academy. For Ferguson, the Act of Union made good sense: he would have none of the questionings of a Moore, let alone an O'Connell. But his antiquarian knowledge and interests — he knew George Petrie, the archaeologist, and James Mangan, the poet and translator — led him to his own brand of cultural questioning, perhaps best manifested in his 'Dialogue between the Head and the Heart of an Irish Protestant', which appeared in the *DUM* in 1833. The problem was how to be a true Irishman, what in fact that meant, when already on a political level the gap between Catholic and Protestant was wider than ever. He himself had nothing but contempt for the 'Priestcraft of Popery', but in his 'Dialogue' he is able imaginatively to enter the entrenched positions of both sides: the Protestant's 'birthright' is 'the love of Ireland', whilst the Catholic declares, 'I know not whence my blood may have been drawn but...I feel and know that I am the heart of an Irishman.' The Catholic heart, we could say, is almost given its radical head, but the Protestant head knows where such dangerously radical tendencies will lead. It is Ferguson's imaginative sympathy that allows him to indulge in his cultural optimism: beneath the political, religious division lies a unity that will in fact make sense of the Act of Union; there is no need to take the separatist path of Wolfe Tone, or of O'Connell. On the cultural level there is no need to believe with Hardiman that the Gaelic tradition is exclusively Catholic. On the contrary, Ferguson can show the crucial connections between the apparently distinct traditions, the Anglo-Irish and the Gaelic: to this end he insists on accuracy in translation, on attention to the facts, on a scrupulosity of scholarship which he finds sadly wanting in Hardiman's team. Whatever the political motivation, we can see how Ferguson is aiming at a refinement of Moore's notion of national identity. Mere gesturing to the past was not enough: Ferguson seems to recognise the dangers — especially for a Protestant — of loose and mawkish sensibility latching onto a dreamy vision of the Gaelic heritage. Not for nothing did Yeats later pay him the compliment of regarding him as a key figure in the development of a national consciousness.

The essays constitute a remarkable performance. They are both a celebration of Hardiman's achievement, and a demolition of his claims to scholarship; they urge reconciliation and unity, whilst scoffing at the Catholic rabble; they combine learned debate with almost knockabout point-scoring; they espouse all the rigours of research whilst indulging in a type of rhetoric that manages to blur the very issues Ferguson hopes to clarify. The first essay is an extraordinary example of the level at which Ferguson is prepared to pitch the debate, in his desire to get beyond the conflict between Protestant and Catholic, to make 'the people of Ireland better acquainted with one another'. In the pages of the ultra-conservative *DUM* Ferguson's audience is proclaimedly the 'Protestant wealth and intelligence of the country', and it is perhaps an indication of his almost innocent *naïveté* that he can still hope to have so much of his cake and eat it. There is no doubt about his views on the present troublesome Catholics, 'the perverse rabble', but he insists on a deep sympathy with the 'poor Papist' the world over; he is determined to show how little the modern Protestant knows of his forebears. As he goes on to say, the 'Protestant's idea of a mere Irishman, even of the sixteenth century, is still an ill-defined and dour delineation of fancy. The very costume is uncertain...' Only by learning what that 'mere Irishman' was like can we begin to understand what it means to be an Irishman in the 1830s. Out of Ferguson's tortured argument three points in particular emerge: first, he is only too conscious of the underlying violence of Irish history; secondly, he argues against the dangers of what he calls Clanism, which carries with it another danger that is anathema to a loyalist, that of anti-Anglicism; thirdly, in his attempts to define the *je ne sais quoi* of Irish balladry, he characterises the desire and despair of these songs as 'the pathetic'. This foreshadows what Matthew Arnold is to say when he tries to define the nature of the Celtic imagination, which in turn is to have a profound influence on Yeats and the whole of the Irish Literary Revival.

IV

It was another Protestant, this time from Dublin, who was to continue and extend the line of argument begun by Ferguson. Thomas Davis is remembered for his rather frail political ballads, and for his founding, with C. G. Duffy and J. B. Dillon, of the *Nation* newspaper in 1842. This organ provided him with a mouthpiece until his early death in 1845. Whereas Ferguson had been able to keep relatively aloof from the political upheavals of his day, Davis's significance stems partly from his active embroilment in politics and in his attempts to educate the people; there is a world of difference between Ferguson's almost Byzantine rhetoric and the calls to action of Davis (whatever their shared aim of cultural unity). There is a sense, in Davis's essay, 'The History of Ireland', that things are stirring; the language is that of revolution, with Ireland a slave, struggling to free herself from her chains (no.2). Whereas Ferguson had spoken of the dangers of turning against the English, Davis emphasises the nature of English oppression: Irish suffering is a concomitant of English crimes; the relationship between past and present now extends into the future, and in the process shifts from the cultural to the political realm. The cry is 'Ireland for the Irish... We want to win Ireland and keep it.' But to this end it is not enough merely to have or to voice noble sentiments; we must study, for we cannot be a nation without a knowledge of the country's history. Significantly, though, the study itself is no longer a place of shelter. 'Disciplined habits' and 'military accomplishments' go hand in hand as the 'pillars of independence'. This is fighting talk, the more interesting because it is both undeveloped and not fully conscious of itself in the way that, say, Pearse's is later to be: it is as though the words announce themselves, divorced from their connotations. For the most part, Davis is content to operate on a humbler, more practical level.

One of his obsessions is what he calls 'Our National Language'. It is the logical culmination of an argument that has been developing from Charlotte Brooke onwards. As Davis points out, once you impose a language on a people, things begin to go awry; identity is lost; language becomes mere 'arbitrary signs' without any of the crucial links with the actual past. The cry for liberty then becomes linked with the cry for the nation's language, and the logic appears to be impeccable: unless we hold on to our language, we remain a conquered race. But Davis is naïvely honest enough to admit that things are not quite so simple: he has to acknowledge that already the language has begun to disappear, that in fact the national language will not be resuscitated. He shifts his ground by saying that even if we can't keep the language, we can at least keep the literature. He knows that it is mere wishful thinking to imagine that the Irish language will be introduced into the national schools in the East of Ireland; all he can hope for is some kind of gradual preservation and extension. Rather quaintly, he hopes that the upper classes will begin the process, helped along by a newspaper.

If much of this seems half-baked, the explanation could well lie in Davis's own confusion as to what was actually possible. There is a circularity and lack of substance in his arguments which render them less persuasive as rhetoric than as historical curiosities. But in his brief years of activity he made of himself — as so many Irishmen did — a legend that counted for more than the reality. That legend (celebrated most memorably by Yeats in 'To Ireland in the Coming Times' — 'Know, that I would accounted be/True brother of a company/That sang, to sweeten Ireland's wrong,/Ballad and story, rann and song... Nor

may I less be counted one/With Davis, Mangan, Ferguson...')
centred on Davis's attempts at a definition of Irishness in a context
that was both cultural and political, that extended from the ballad
to what should be taught in schools; Davis's optimism was not
necessarily grounded in anything very firm or demonstrable, but
it was an optimism that allowed those who came after him to
believe things could in fact change, that whatever Auden was to
say on Yeats's death, poetry could make things happen. Davis's
own poems have not worn too well (less well than some of
Mangan's translations), but that is scarcely the point. He became
a rallying cry. When the whole question of Irish literature and
language and identity was thrown up again in the 1890s, all eyes
were cast back to the earlier part of the century. Moore, Ferguson
and Davis (along with Callanan, Mangan and Allingham) had
set out the terms of the debate.

V

If there was something heroic, romanticised and idealised about
the *Nation*'s view of Ireland and its possible future, the Famine
of 1845-7 was a devastating reminder of a reality to which England
was ready to turn a blind eye. Nearly a million died, another
million emigrated; talk of the Irish peasantry and the Irish
language could, on one level, seem mere empty sentiment. But
to some the need to cling on to these ideals was stronger than
ever: what might have started as gentlemanly antiquarianism
soon became angrily political. The Repeal Movement of
O'Connell had failed, much to the sorrow of Young Irelanders
like Davis; in its stead came the more radical and revolutionary
Fenianism of men like John Mitchel. England was trying to make
up its collective mind about Ireland, and consistently failing to
do so: Gladstone soldiered on with Home Rule, but the disgrace
of Parnell in 1890, and his death the following year, effectively
splintered what unity there had been. It is hard not to feel the
shadow of Parnell and his death falling over the literature and
politics of Ireland for the next twenty-odd years. When Yeats
received the Nobel Prize in 1923, he was to declare, 'The modern
literature of Ireland, and indeed all that stir of thought that
prepared for the Anglo-Irish war, began when Parnell fell from
power in 1891. A disillusioned and embittered Ireland turned
from parliamentary politics; an event was conceived; and the race

began, as I think, to be troubled by that event's long gestation.'[12]

For poetry, Yeats becomes the crucial figure. The personal, the political and the aesthetic become intertwined in a startlingly dramatic way. On the personal and political front, Yeats fell under the spell of John O'Leary, one of the Old Fenians who had, in Yeats's eyes, the virtue of being above the factionalism that developed in the nationalist movement, especially around Parnell and his opponents. O'Leary represented an arrogant anti-democratism which eschewed violence, and which was initially attractive to Yeats because it also embraced a nationalism that had nothing to do with the church, and even approached his own growingly mystical sense of a country's being. O'Leary's return to Ireland in 1885, after imprisonment for treason in England and years of exile in France, was a symbolic moment for more than Yeats. He became a central figure for a host of eager young nationalists. His two pamphlets of 1886, 'What Irishmen Should Know' and 'How Irishmen Should Feel' assumed an almost scriptural authority: attention was refocused on the tenets of the Young Irelanders and the *Nation*. It was in 1886 that, as Ellman has put it, Yeats 'came of age poetically';[13] in March he published his first specifically 'Irish' poem, 'The Two Titans, a Political Poem', and, much more importantly, began the *Wanderings of Oisin*, picking up O'Leary's emphasis on the importance of Gaelic mythology. O'Leary had introduced Yeats to the works of Davis, and to the Young Ireland Society; he also brought him into contact with the major literary activists of the day — Katherine Tynan, Douglas Hyde, and, most notoriously, Maud Gonne. One of the important literary influences was Standish O'Grady, author of two works which furthered the notion of the heroic ideal heralded in Ferguson's epic poem *Congal* (1872) — *History of Ireland: the Heroic Period* and *Cuchulain and his Contemporaries* (1878); *The Story of Ireland* followed in 1894. O'Grady's importance for Yeats, when linked to that of O'Leary, is clear: there was a similar lament for the Ascendancy, a similar notion of betrayal. It was perhaps in response to O'Grady's thinking, and certainly in response to Parnell's death, that Yeats threw himself into the founding of various literary societies at the beginning of the decade — The Irish Literary Society of London (1891), the National Literary Society in Dublin (1892) — and the various dramatic ventures which culminated in the founding of the Abbey Theatre in 1904.

A parallel movement gained a momentum of its own with the establishment of the Gaelic League. Whereas many, including

Yeats, had given up the notion of a revival of the Irish language as simply impracticable, Douglas Hyde, Michael O'Hickey and others firmly believed that a sense of the nation's culture depended on a knowledge of its language. Hyde's translations, *The Love Songs of Connaught* (1893), are in many respects remarkable, and a fitting monument in themselves; but as a document his Inaugural Lecture in 1892 as President of the National Literary Society is perhaps of more historical importance (no.5). 'The Necessity for De-Anglicising Ireland' demonstrates an astute awareness of the anomalies of the Irish position, 'imitating England and yet apparently hating it'; the Irish are caught between their own country and the Empire to which they are supposed to announce loyalty. It is, Hyde argues (echoing Thomas Davis), impossible to have a sense of national identity without a national language, and the 'reproach of West-Britonism' is likely to stick the more insistently. What had been half hinted at in the revival of interest in the Gaelic past at the beginning of the century is now openly declared: 'we must strive to cultivate everything that is most racial, most smacking of the soil, most Gaelic, most Irish, because...this island *is* and will *ever* remain Celtic at the core...' But after the initial enthusiasm, the movement seemed to lose its impetus. Hyde was obviously aware of its nationalistic tendencies, but spoke of giving out medals as though the whole thing were little more than a school competition; in 1915 he resigned as President when he thought the political implications of the movement had swamped the cultural. At this distance it seems odd that he should have been able to hold the two things so separately in his mind; but just as politics and literature seem invariably to be intertwined in Irish history, so the Irish have developed the knack of being schizoid about the union (let alone the Union) when it suited them. However, one of the central planks of Hyde's policy had altered the nature of the debate; by focusing specifically on the language question, he had challenged many of the spurious notions that accumulated around the idea of the Celtic Twilight, and he had helped to further a desire for precision which had tended until then to be an elusive element in the debate.

There was always some uncertainty as to what the Gaelic League had achieved: even the single-minded Pearse could declare, within three months, that 'the Gaelic League is a spent force' and that 'the Gaelic League will be recognized in history as the most revolutionary influence that has ever come into

17

Ireland'.[14] D.P.Moran, who founded *The Leader* in 1900, acknowledged the 'revolution that the Gaelic League has worked', and pointed to the fact that 'the nineteenth century had been for Ireland mostly a century of humbug' (no.13b). The novelist George Moore, who started his career in the hope that he would incorporate into English fiction both the realism of Zola and (encouraged here by Arthur Symons) the symbolism of Mallarmé, was adamant about the importance of the national language (no.13c). 'The restoration of the language is the nation's need'; but his stirring talk of the nation's soul is slightly undercut by his recognition (again echoing Davis) that there might be practical problems: 'our desire is to make Ireland a bi-lingual country — to use English as a universal language, and to save our own as a medium for some future literature'. If this seems a fairly safe hostage to fortune, given its vagueness, there is an element of pure farce about Moore's peroration, and we have to disabuse ourselves of any idea that he is indulging in Swiftian irony. Against this failure of nerve we should set Charles Gavan Duffy's argument (no.5) that the threat to the nation was a moral one: the last virtues of 'purity, piety and simplicity' were in danger, in face of the onslaught of English, American and European 'literary garbage'.[15] George Sigerson was bold enough to claim that but for the influence of Irish literature, Shakespeare would have produced neither *A Midsummer Night's Dream*, nor *Macbeth*, nor *The Tempest*; nor would Spenser have been 'saved'. But for all his misty-eyed romanticism, he announced a truth that was to be echoed by Yeats: 'If our nation is to live, it must live by the energy of intellect, and be prepared to take its place in competition with all other peoples.'[16] This was not something that all members of the Gaelic League could have subscribed to.[17]

AE's (George Russell's) place in the debate is interesting. In many respects he seems a perfect exemplification of the Celtic twilight at its most sentimental and airy-fairy; he plays a prominent part in the Literary Revival, perhaps more influential even than Yeats in terms of the writers he fostered and gathered around himself. On the one hand he embraces a mysticism similar to that of the early Yeats (Madame Blavatsky and her Theosophical Society in Dublin held both men in thrall for a while); on the other hand, as early as 1897, he is acting as a field representative for the Irish Agricultural Organisation under Sir Horace Plunkett. He thus saw the Irish problem from two very different perspectives. His literary activities were extensive —

poems, pamphlets, journalism, and, just as important, drama.[18] As often in the literary history of Ireland, drama provides the stage for the acting out of passions and loyalties. The strange confluence of Arthur Symons, Edward Martyn, George Moore, Lady Gregory, and J. M. Synge led to a series of plays which struck at the heart of the Irish question and assaulted the sensibilities of the Dublin middle classes. Yeats's play *The Countess Cathleen* was performed in Dublin in 1899, and typically raised the hackles of those who thought it undermined all decent notions of nation and religion. His next play, *Cathleen ni Houlihan*, was even more provocatively anti-English; AE's *Deirdre* was performed at the same time. In the book of essays that appeared in 1899, *Literary Ideals in Ireland*, edited by John Eglinton, AE put this gloss on Yeats's intentions:

> To sum it all up, Mr. Yeats, in common with other literary men, is trying to ennoble literature by making it religious rather than secular, by using his art for the revelation of another world rather than to depict this one. (no.11)

That other world had a fascination for AE, which meant that even in his moments of patriotic nationalism he took a line that was often at one remove from reality. He kept returning to the idea of the ancient Celt, which in turn led him to believe in Ireland's eventual emergence as a 'rural civilization'. In *The National Being* (1919) he defined nationality as

> a state of consciousness, a mood of definite character in our intellectual being, and it is not perceived first except in profound meditation; it does not become apparent from superficial activities any more than we could, by looking at the world and the tragic history of mankind, discover that the Kingdom of Heaven is within us.

In practical terms this led AE to espouse a kind of poetry that was naïve and simplistic, and to encourage poets like Padraic Colum and James Stephens, who shared his vision of rural beauty and immortality. But in fairness to AE, it should be pointed out that in one of his essays in *Literary Ideals in Ireland* he touches on the conflict between nationalism and cosmopolitanism; he is aware, as is Yeats, that a European tradition has a strength which it is increasingly difficult to counter and the great writers, 'Tolstoi and Ibsen', are 'conscious of addressing a European audience'. For a sense of nationality to survive in this context, it has to believe in itself, to believe that its 'peculiar ideal is nobler than that which the cosmopolitan spirit suggests'. AE thinks such a belief tenable in Ireland, where nationality is 'beginning to be felt, less as a political movement than as a spiritual force'.

> To reveal Ireland in clear and beautiful light, to create the Ireland in the heart, is the province of a national literature. Other arts would add to this ideal hereafter, and social life and politics must in the end be in harmony.

AE's life was to end in disappointment and disillusionment; his dream of harmony was not fulfilled. But in 'Nationality and Imperialism' (1901) he seems to achieve a truth that goes beyond rhetoric and which might act as some kind of bridge-head between the concerns of the Gaelic League and his, and Yeats's, own mysticism (no.13a).

AE had spoken as though there were only two paths to go down: the one that refuted nationalism, and the one that embraced it. No embrace could have been warmer than that bestowed by the three poets who have come to represent Irish literary nationalism in its most violent form — Pearse, MacDonagh, and Plunkett. They took the logic of the Gaelic League several steps further than the wildest imaginings of Sigerson or Duffy or Hyde. The ruthlessness of the logic emerges in Pearse's ability to weld pagan and Christian traditions in his ideal of inspiration for the Irish:

> Colmcille suggested what that inspiration was when he said, 'If I die, it shall be from the excess of love that I bear the Gael.' A love and a service so excessive that one must give all, must be willing always to make the ultimate sacrifice — this is the inspiration alike of the story of Cuchulain and the story of Colmcille, the inspiration that made one a hero and the other a saint.[19]

The old notion of heroism is back, literally, with a vengeance. Yeats and AE were thought to be lacking because of a mysticism that was decidedly pagan; for Pearse and his followers mysticism had to be married to a specifically Catholic vision. This allowed for the flowering of an ideal of purgation, of self-sacrifice in the cause of nationalism. As Pearse said at his trial, 'To refuse to fight would have been to lose, to fight is to win, we have kept faith with the past, and handed a tradition to the future.'[20]

The Easter Rising was a tragic reminder of the interconnectedness of art and political life. Thirty years earlier (in the very same year that O'Leary had mourned the fact that Ireland had 'never yet produced a great poet')[21] Yeats had said that 'Irish singers, who are genuinely Irish in language, thought or style must, whether they will or no, nourish the forces that make for the political liberties of Ireland.'[22] What this could well mean in practice was demonstrated when Pearse, MacDonagh, Plunkett and the rest offered themselves as martyrs to the cause. As Pearse's poem 'Renunciation' puts it:

> I have turned my face
> To this road before me
> To the deed that I see
> And the death I shall die.

Cuchulain and Christ merge in ways that were to make Yeats uncomfortable. He pondered in his verse on the connection between the incendiary *Cathleen ni Houlihan* (1902) — in which Maud Gonne took the leading role — and the Easter Rising; *Responsibilities* was the significant title of his 1914 volume. He wrote in 1916, 'I count the links in the chain of responsibility, and wonder if any of them ends in my workshop.'[23]

VI

Yeats had to find his own identity, and his sense of a national identity, against this tumultuous, shifting and confusing background. Ironically, he moves between Dublin and London, finding, as Ellman has observed, paradoxical support for his nationalist notions in the milieu of the Rhymers' Club, and yearning, in Ireland, for some of the artistic purity he missed when surrounded by his own countrymen.[24] His poetry itself, of course, is the important thing, and it is possible to chart his move from a fervent, engaged nationalism, combined with his own brand of magical romanticism, to the isolated position he adopts as the poet-cum-prophet, addressing the few from his lofty and privileged tower. This is not the place to pursue Yeats's complex career as a poet. However, his self-consciousness as to what he was doing is manifested in the large body of his prose writings, all of which act as a sustained commentary on his work. Some of the major issues emerge in the pieces in this volume.

There is something appropriate about the title of Yeats's early piece, 'Hopes and Fears for Irish Literature' (1892), hinting as it does at the dangers inherent in the youthful optimism he senses in Irish literature (no.6). If the basic contrast is between an English (and European) tradition at its sunset, and an Irish one in all the vigour of a new, even Blakean, dawn, there is another contrast between what needs to be said, and how it should be said — between, in fact, life and art. Yeats shows himself and Ireland caught in the muddied waters of the English Romantics, addressing himself to the problems faced by Keats and Wordsworth, and then again by Arnold. Significantly, the aesthetic ground can only be cleared by reference to the European tradition. Yeats's own experience had, of course, taken him to the extreme baptism of the Rhymers' Club in London, and it was there that he had seen the effects of a creeping European decadence: whatever its attractions, he had tried to counter this aestheticism with something more serviceable — he had to 'show the dependence...of all great art and literature upon conviction and upon heroic life'. Whilst he could see the attractions of what he saw then as the perfect but closed world of the French symbolists, he came to abhor the idea that 'Poetry is an end in itself.' Returning to Ireland he found in poems ranging from Ferguson's *Congal* to MacCarthy's *Ferdiah* a tradition that was 'the expression of conviction, and...the garment of noble emotion'. But already the counter-arguments present themselves: that almost Arnoldian celebration of action (in Yeats's terms, 'youth' and 'energy') is darkened by a Keatsian warning about the 'most utter indifference to art, the most dire carelessness'. It is all very well to have noble sentiments, but the poet must expect to pay the price of expressing them — a price that involves pain and solitude. Yeats quotes Wilde to the effect that 'we are a nation of brilliant failures'. For all the initial optimism of this essay, Yeats espouses a caution that touches on the central problem for Irish writers: 'conviction' is a word that rings through his essay, but so too does his insistence on the need for care and knowledge. The seeds of a national literature require vigilant tending.

Yeats develops some of these ideas in a talk he gives in 1893,

'Nationality and Literature' (no.8). Typically, he is aware of the need to talk in terms of a wide European context and perspective, stretching back to Greek epic. His point is that in all literatures, there is an epic, or ballad, period, and a dramatic period, followed by a lyric period; it is in the first two periods that nationality establishes itself, whereas lyric poetry explores feelings that have ceased to have any recognisable nationality. 'With this advancing subtlety', writes Yeats, 'poetry steps out of the marketplace, out of the general tide of life and becomes a mysterious cult, as it were, an almost secret religion made by the few for the few.' There is a pervasive irony in all this: the perfect flowering of a nation's literature ('Everywhere the elaborate luxuriance of leaf and bud and flower') — picking up his image of the seed and the tree — entails a transcending of national boundaries. Whereas epic and drama remain confined within particular countries, lyric poets are 'citizens of the world, cosmopolitans... for the great passions know nothing of boundaries'. Not for the first time, Yeats is somewhat stranded: he realises the dangers in granting to cosmopolitanism the virtues others are to see in it. For the drift of his argument is that Irish literature is still in its epic or ballad period — 'All that is greatest in [our] literature is based upon legend' — and he intones the familiar roll-call — De Vere, Ferguson, Allingham, Mangan, Davis, O'Grady. He insists that there is indeed a 'distinct school of Irish literature...and its foundation as such is in the legend lore of the people and in the National history'. But there is the paradox that in order to fulfil their national aspirations, the Irish should look beyond their geographical and historical boundaries. 'We must learn from the literatures of France and England to be supreme artists, and then God will send to us supreme inspiration.' This was not the kind of thing Thomas Davis had had in mind, nor, for that matter, the Gaelic League.

In his thinkings about the problem of a national identity and a national literature, Yeats had up to this point circled around the question of what that identity might actually mean for Irish writers; much of his writing depended on the rhetoric of a 'new dawn', on his appeal to legend, and to particular poems that represented what he thought was most promising in an embryonic tradition. In 'The Celtic Element in Literature' he broadens the scope of his argument, and, in so doing, tries to tackle head-on the image of the Celts that had prevailed since Renan and Arnold (no.10): Renan's work had been significant partly because of his breezy readiness to talk about the spirit of place and people in a grandly generalising manner. The Celts were pure and noble, but threatened by the invasion of modern civilisation. All their purity and nobility could not save them from their own failings, especially their 'invincible need for illusion'. The qualities of imagination, mystery and sadness are all very well, but they lose some of their charm in the face of such a catalogue of disasters. Arnold's long piece *On the Study of Celtic Literature* (1867) was an elaborate extension and qualification of what he called Renan's 'beautiful essay'; he wanted to emphasise the sentiment of Irish literature, the style and the magic. Yeats was alert to the dangers of these famous statements of what constituted the 'Celtic element', and his own essay is an attempt to 'restate a little Renan's and Arnold's argument'. It is not as persuasive as Yeats might have hoped, because he is unable to escape from the terms of the argument as set out by his predecessors. Yeats, like Arnold, is fascinated by the idea of a 'natural magic', and proceeds to show how it is, in fact, 'the ancient religion of the world'. Such a formulation lands him in considerable trouble: he has become a victim of the very rhetoric he has decried in others. None the less, we have to register the emphasis he places on legend, and how he relates the various Celtic legends, especially his own favourite, Oisin, to other European legends. He speaks of a 'new fountain of...Gaelic legends being opened', and it is in this that he would locate his idea of the 'Celtic movement'. Whatever his earlier doubts about the aesthetes and the symbolists, he now avers that it is the symbolical movement which is the 'only movement saying new things'. In *The Trembling of the Veil* (1922), he was to write, 'Nations, races, and individual men are unified by an image, or bundle of related images, symbolical or evocative of the state of mind, which is of all states of mind not impossible, the most difficult to that man, race, or nation; because only the greatest obstacle that can be contemplated without despair rouses the will to full intensity.'[25] It is as though we can see Yeats, in this early essay, feeling his way towards that later, much more confident assertion. Whilst he is trying to expand upon earlier ideas and intuitions, there is a sense of his falling foul of his own best intentions. There is certainly some irony in his celebrating the fact, in 'The Literary Movement in Ireland' (1899), that the Celtic movement was about to become part of Irish thought, and simultaneously urging the need for intellect as well as rhetoric. Only two years later he was to begin 'Ireland and the Arts' with the glum declaration, 'The arts have failed'. All that optimism acquires, in retrospect, a hollow ring.

'Ireland and the Arts' (no.12) has its special place in Yeats's series of *apologias*: it is addressed to those who believe, as he declares he himself did when young, that 'art is tribeless, nationless, a blossom gathered in No Man's Land'. As the Greeks looked to their own past, so should the Irish, especially as that past is exemplified in the legends of the Irish; Yeats, as so often, cannot avoid the mystical, but he acknowledges the difficulties, the possible criticisms. Whilst an Irish reader will see the obvious affinities with Thomas Davis, and with the Young Irelanders, an Englishman might regard such talk as 'parochial' (anticipating the charge that Patrick Kavanagh was to cope with in his own idiosyncratic way in the 1950s). Yeats immediately draws a distinction between the Davis tradition, and his own insistence on the avoidance of popularity: interestingly, he quotes Whitman in support of his Keatsian vision of the artist making 'his own journey towards beauty and truth'. Almost echoing Wordsworth, he argues that the artist has at some point to assert himself, to deny the humility that might in another phase of the argument have suited him, and to move away from the idea of pleasing the public taste. It is here that Yeats talks most interestingly of the related problem of voice, of style, and he admits that he needed time to move away from the influence of the European tradition; even when he was writing on an Irish theme, the style was wrong; but now his style has 'been shaped by the subjects I have worked on'. As he puts it, he is out from under Shelley's shadow, 'now I think my style is myself'. In addressing himself to the concerns of his country, with all the rigour that we might associate with the high Romantics of the European tradition, he has found a voice that is appropriate to those concerns; and in so doing, he has found a voice that is his own. He talks, in fact, of artists 'finding themselves' once they turn to the local and the particular, to what is Irish (Robert Gregory is held up as an example). There is a fine balance in this essay between the needs of the country and the needs of the artist; it was a conflict that Pearse and MacDonagh, in their more fervent belief in a national literature and identity, were not to countenance. Yeats's later essay, 'Poetry and Tradition' (1907) shows him confident enough to make distinctions between different kinds of nationalism, even if at the same time he finds himself expressing an increased sense of disillusionment (no.14).

'Romantic Ireland's dead and gone,/It's with O'Leary in the grave.' Yeats pays tribute, in 'Poetry and Tradition', to that 'romantic conception of Irish Nationality' represented by O'Leary, a conception that stretched back not only to Davis, but to Grattan, and to a whole tradition of European idealism. Yeats could not bear the thought of standing at O'Leary's grave, surrounded by Nationalists of so many different colours. He goes on to chart what he, Lionel Johnson and Katherine Tynan took upon themselves as a result of O'Leary's influence. There was, of course, the political aspect, more suited, in Yeats's view, to Johnson's gifts; he himself, 'more preoccupied with Ireland', 'found [his] symbols of expression in Ireland'. But what emerges from his statement of initial optimism is Yeats's divided response to the developing political situation. He could not sustain Maud Gonne's passionate belief in 'Mother Ireland with the crown of stars about her head'; what had started out, under O'Leary, as grand and ambitious, became petty and vindictive. The political backbone of O'Leary's thought was the very thing that got in the way of the poetical ideals. Things had not been very different early on: Yeats had not been afraid to criticise fiercely any Irish literature that was badly written, that 'owed its position to its moral or political worth'. In this, he had had the full support of O'Leary. Yeats had, none the less, believed that something wonderful would happen, even in the face of Lionel Johnson's scepticism. Yeats's point is a saddened one. 'I do not think either of us saw that, as belief in the possibility of armed insurrection withered, the old romantic Nationalism would wither too, and that the young would become less ready to find pleasure in whatever they believed to be literature.' He touches here on the apparently tenuous connection between politics and literature, for all the affirmations to the contrary; the dawn he had spoken of in earlier essays and speeches had proved to be a false one. The fury, the frustration, the despair of 'Easter 1916' are anticipated in his diatribe against the complacent lower middle classes. The artist is, once again, the 'protesting individual', with little or no audience. The poets had failed to create the taste by which they should be enjoyed.

VII

It was perhaps appropriate, if ironic, that one of the most moving tributes to Yeats on his death in 1939 came from that most English of poets, W.H.Auden.[26] For by then Yeats had become the elderly Irish senator, but, more importantly, the Irish literary man of international standing. It was not that he had solved all the problems, but he had confronted most of the questions, and in so doing, left those who came after him with a freedom that had not been previously available. 'Since Yeats', writes Seán Lucy, 'Irishmen writing in English have been able to choose freely just how much or how little of either English or Irish poetry they consider relevant to their own poetic vocations.'[27] But if Yeats had apparently made all things possible, his shadow was to fall heavily on his successors. Austin Clarke is the prime example of a writer who feels the need to forge again his own particular Gaelic chains, to assert his own Irishness as against that of Yeats (he had been omitted from Yeats's *Oxford Book of Modern Verse* (1935)). It is by no means an easy task, and Clarke's is a peculiarly hard-won, personal triumph. As John Montague declares, with some justification, 'he is our first completely Irish poet in English'.[28]

Other writers had latched on, before Yeats's death, to the realisation that a narrow nationalism would be self-defeating. As James Stephens said in 1922, 'we shall *talk* like Irishmen, or we are done for: we shall *think* like Europeans, or we are done for' (no.15). The pull of the past held too many dangers for the Irish: writers in Ireland had to look to a future where there was little guidance. Pound's modernist injunction, 'Make it new', acquires a particular cultural overtone in Stephens's appeal to the Irish to put the past behind them, to put on one side the pale imitations of English, American and European writing, and start afresh. This sense of a new dawn (it echoes Yeats, but has a different ring to it) was rung out by the editor of a new journal, *The Bell*, in 1941. Sean O'Faolain declared that none of the 'old symbolic words' could be used:

They are dead as Brian Boru...Roisin Dubh, Fodhla, Cathleen ni Houlihan, the sounds of light and the risings of the moon... All our symbols have to be created afresh, and the only way to create a living symbol is to take a naked thing and clothe it with new life, new association, new meaning, with all the vigour of the life we live in the Here and Now. We refused to use the word Irish, or Ireland, in the title. We said, 'It will plainly be that by being alive.'

Our only job was to encourage Life to speak.

The Bell was intent on encouraging a sense of infinite possibility, where there would be no problems because no questions were left to be asked. 'Ireland' would become synonymous with 'the whole world'. And yet O'Faolain's appeal is also to a naïve sentiment which even manages to belittle Pearse; Joyce's exile is reduced to moisture in the corner of the eye:

> Men and women who have suffered or died in the name of Ireland who have thereby died for Life as they know it, have died for some old gateway, some old trustled lagfield in which their hearts have been stuck since they were children. These are the things that come at night to tear at our exile's heart. These are the true symbols. When Pearse faced death it was of such things he thought — the rabbits on the sloping field at Rosmuc, the field lit by the slanting sun, a speckled ladybird on a blade of grass. That is Life.

Such images appealed not at all to Louis MacNeice, the major Ulster poet this century to build his work on the tensions of being an Irish exile in England (and, as I hinted earlier, an Irish exile in Ireland).[29] Nor did they appeal to Patrick Kavanagh, who has become something of a talismanic figure for present Irish writers, particularly Seamus Heaney.[30] Kavanagh's poetry is remarkable for its early insistence on the importance of the local and the particular. He picks up some of the early warning notes of the nineteenth century on the dangers of provincialism, and draws a distinction between this, and the parochialism (such as that of a Moore or a Joyce), which he admires and cultivates.[31] He argues that all great civilisations are based on parochialism (no.16). This recognition of the local habitation and its name has its obvious appeal for writers who want to assert their identity without engaging with what Kavanagh calls the 'thorough-going English-bred lie' of being Irish. It would be true to say that Kavanagh's own poetry has an unevenness that gives the lie to some of his own claims: he would no doubt have answered that he didn't claim much anyway. But he has become the representative figure for those who face both the North-South divide and also that other cultural gap between the metropolis and the province. With his devil-may-care iconoclasm (and of course a clutch of truly remarkable poems) Kavanagh, no doubt unwittingly, opened the way for more recent Irish writers who were trying to define their own parish, looking anxiously over their shoulders to the past, across the water to England and Europe, or across the Atlantic to America.

The quantity and quality of Irish writing in recent years is astonishing, and to list the major figures here would be superfluous. But it is one of the contentions of this volume that such abundance owes at least something to the continued debate as to what poetry was possible, given that place and those circumstances. This is not to say that everything in the garden is lovely; that Ireland has become some kind of poet's paradise. Far from it. But the very heat, even venom, of the present debates on Irish literature seems to me an indication of its basic health and strength. There may be local back-biting, elevation of inferior talent, exaggerated claims made on slender evidence, just as good writers are diminished, if they do not suit the prevailing fashion: it has always been thus. Beneath such surface fripperies, however, is the sense that poetry matters, as it has always mattered in Ireland. Roy McFadden wrote in 1949, in an editorial article in *Rann*, something that has a passing echo of Yeats:

> We shall not find a unified movement in our poetry until we have achieved a pattern of living which we can call our own (something very different from a political programme); and the achievement of that pattern is as much the responsibility of the poet as of anyone else.[32]

It could be said that poets as diverse as Heaney, Mahon, Longley, Montague, Kinsella, Paulin and Muldoon have recognised that responsibility, both in their poetry and in what they have said about poetry. Nor does it seem coincidental that one of the best critical books of recent times, specifically devoted to poetry, Edna Longley's *Poetry in the Wars* (1986), should come from the North of Ireland. Her Introductory essay concludes:

> In 'Nineteen Hundred and Nineteen' and the related later sequences ('Meditations in Time of Civil War', 'The Tower'), [Yeats] dramatises a twentieth-century crisis of faith: for humanity and poetry. That his strategy is not really to 'lament' but to engage, exposes the spirit of resistance latent in poetry. The dialectic between poet and man of action in 'Meditations in Time of Civil War' enacts

29

a more explicit recovery of artistic nerve. By identifying with a besieged man-at-arms, former tenant of the tower, Yeats establishes poetry as at least a marginal stronghold 'through long wars and sudden night alarms'.

Thomas Kinsella, in 1973, might have spoken of the 'Divided Mind' (no.17); a symposium on the arts in *The Irish Times* the following year (the famous year in which the power-sharing Executive in the North was brought down by the Ulster Workers Council) talked of a 'Clash of Identities'. But the Dublin critic Seamus Deane, in his remarkable *Short History of Irish Literature* (1986), matches Edna Longley with his insight, even if it is derived from a different perspective:

> [Irish literature] is, in many ways, a specifically modern literature bred out of the most dishevelled and improbable circumstances. By now, it is neither Gaelic nor Anglo-Irish writing which is central. The conciliation between the two, although by no means complete, is sufficiently advanced to allow the use of the phrase 'Irish writing' without fear of its being misunderstood or recruited to any particular group or sect. That, at least, is one symptom of a fundamental and hopeful change.[33]

Notes

1. This was one of the epigraphs quoted by Lady Gregory in her volume *Ideals in Ireland* (1901) (see no.13).
2. 'Browning', in *Letters to the New Island* (New York, 1934), pp. 103-4; originally published in the *Boston Pilot*, 22 February 1890.
3. 'What is Anglo-Irish Poetry?', in Seán Lucy (ed.), *Irish Poets in English* (Cork and Dublin, 1973), p. 15.
4. 'Tollund Man', *Wintering Out* (1972).
5. Elizabeth Nicholson, 'Trees Were Green', in Terence Brown and Alex Reid (eds), *Time Was Away* (Dublin, 1974), p. 14.
6. *The Complete Works of William Hazlitt*, P.P. Howe (ed.) (21 vols, London, 1930), vol. 7, p. 234.
7. See Robert Welch, *Irish Poetry from Moore to Yeats* (Gerrards Cross, 1980).
8. See Terence Brown, *Northern Voices: Poets from Ulster* (Dublin and London, 1975), pp. 42-54.
9. *The Letters of Thomas Moore*, W.S. Dowden (ed.) (2 vols, Oxford, 1964), vol. 1, p. 116.
10. *Memoirs, Journals and Correspondence of Thomas Moore*, Lord John

Russell (ed.) (London, 1853), vol. 1, p. 60.

11. *Memoirs, Journals and Correspondence of Thomas Moore*, vol. 1, p. 58.

12. 'The Bounty of Sweden', in *Autobiographies* (1955), p. 559.

13. Richard Ellman, *Yeats: The Man and the Masks* (London, 1949, rev. edn 1961), p. 51.

14. Patrick Pearse, *Political Writings and Speeches* (Dublin, 1922), p. 91.

15. *The Revival of Irish Literature* (London, 1894), p. 12.

16. 'Irish Literature: Its Origin, Environment and Influence', in *The Revival of Irish Literature*, p. 114.

17. J.M.Synge's 'Letter to the Gaelic League' of 1907 spells out his own extreme form of disaffection: 'The Gaelic League is founded on a doctrine that is made up of ignorance, fraud, and hypocrisy' (quoted in *Collected Works*, Alan Price (ed.) (London, 1966), vol. 2, p. 399).

18. See Richard J. Loftus, *Nationalism in Modern Anglo-Irish Poetry* (Madison and Milwaukee, 1964), ch. 5.

19. Pearse, *Political Writings and Speeches*, p. 38.

20. Quoted in Loftus, *Nationalism in Modern Anglo-Irish Poetry*, p. 163.

21. John O'Leary, *What Irishmen Should Know* (Cork, 1886), p. 8.

22. In his footnote to a review of 'The Poetry of Sir Samuel Ferguson (II)', in the *Dublin University Review*, November 1886 (reprinted in *Uncollected Prose*, J. Frayne (ed.) (London 1970), vol. 1, p. 100).

23. Quoted in Peter Costello, *The Heart Grown Brutal: The Irish Revolution in Literature from Parnell to the Death of Yeats* (Dublin and New Jersey, 1978), pp. 2-3.

24. See Richard Ellman, *Yeats: The Man and the Masks* (London, 1949, rev. edn 1961).

25. *The Trembling of the Veil* (London, 1922), p. 80.

26. 'In Memory of W.B.Yeats'; this is the poem which contains the words 'For poetry makes nothing happen', and then qualifies it: 'it survives, / A way of happening, a mouth.'

27. Seán Lucy, *Irish Poets in English*, p. 18.

28. John Montague, *The Faber Book of Irish Verse* (London, 1974), p. 35.

29. MacNeice is at the centre of Terence Brown's book, *Northern Voices* (referred to above); there are two important essays on him in Edna Longley, *Poetry in the Wars* (Newcastle upon Tyne, 1986); a selection of his *Literary Criticism* has just appeared, edited by Alan Heuser (Oxford, 1987).

30. See especially Seamus Heaney on Kavanagh in *Two Decades of Irish Writing*, Douglas Dunn (ed.) (Cheadle Hulme, 1975), pp. 105-17.

31. See Michael Allen, 'Provincialism and Recent Irish Poetry: The Importance of Patrick Kavanagh', in *Two Decades of Irish Writing*, pp. 23-36.

32. Quoted in Terence Brown, *Northern Voices*, p. 221.

33. The irony of bringing Longley and Deane together in this fashion will not be lost on either of them, nor on those who have followed the debate surrounding the *Field Day* pamphlets, nor on those who peruse the literary columns of the *Irish Times*.

1

Samuel Ferguson, from the
Dublin University Magazine, 1834

Sir Samuel Ferguson (1810-86) was a Belfast Protestant who by 1881 had become such a respected figure in the antiquarian world that he was elected President of the Royal Irish Academy. His Lays of the Western Gael *(1865) were followed by* Congal, An Epic Poem in Five Books *(1872). His influence on Yeats was profound, and in fact Yeats's first published review was of Ferguson's poetry. The four long essays Ferguson wrote in the* Dublin University Magazine, *reviewing James Hardiman's* Irish Minstrelsy *(1831), a compilation of old ballads, represent one of the first serious attempts to come to terms with the problems of the country's literature.*

I

Oh, ye fair hills of holy Ireland, who dares sustain the strangled calumny that you are not the land of our love?

> Sweet land of the bee-abounding hills,
> Island of the year-old young horses,
> Soil of the heaviest fruit of trees,
> Soil of the greenest grassed pastures,
> Old plain of Eber, harvestful,
> Land of the ears of corn and wheat,
> Land of heroes and clergy,
> Baubá of the golden-haired damsels,
> Land of blue running pure streams,
> And of the gold-rich fortunate men,

Who is he who ventures to stand between us and your Catholic sons' good-will? What though for three centuries they and we have made your valleys resound with the clang of axe and broadsword, ringing on chain-mail and plate armour, or with the thunder of artillery tearing their way in bloody lanes, through column and solid square, or with the discordant clash of pike or bayonet, and the vollied rattling of more deadly musket thinning the contracted lines, till wing and centre shrunk into one undistinguishably-embattled band at nightfall? What though in times long past they startled your midnight echoes with our groans under the knife that spared neither bedridden age nor cradled infancy, neither man nor woman, nor the child in the mother's womb; what though in sacred vengeance of that brave villainy, we fattened two generations of your kites with heads of traitors; what though the thick dregs of that sanguinary intoxication are still poured forth by Discord's Ganymedes, and still quaffed savagely in many a misty glen and black bog of your mountains. — What then? It was for love of you that we contended, for possession and enjoyment of you that we trampled down our rivals on your bosom; and now that the nuptial knot is tied and consecrated between us, nothing save the sword of an Alexander shall dissolve that Gordian consummation! But who would be the jealous Turk to say, that those amorous Irishmen, whose love has been as constant as our own, and more legitimate by ages of possession, should not be admitted to all the privileges of a national panogamy? May we never again behold the Curragh of Kildare if we would be that sordid tyrant for all the wealth and power of the British empire. The only emulation between us shall be in the honest endeavour of each to benefit and protect the common object of our affection; and, scorning the rancour of low rivalry that would contend with misrepresentation, detraction, or suppression, we will be the first to tell to the world what genius, what bravery, what loyalty, what pious love of country and kind has been vindicated to the mere Irish by Mr. Hardiman, in his collection and preservation of their national songs. Mr. Hardiman's collection is truly a boon to the Irish reader. But the Irish reader is, in general, a being who exercises little influence on the book market; for, however highly he may appreciate the service done him, he must confine the expression of his thanks to the few who have been hitherto supposed to sympathise with a poor scholar, a Papist and a Connaughtman. Much as the announcement may mortify some who would usurp the exclusive right to Catholic good-will, we declare ourselves one of the number of those who can feel for, and sympathise with, the poor Papist, whether drudging on the wharfs of London, or eating limpets and sea weed on the rocks of Erris, or toiling homeward from the harvest of rich Britain, lying poorly in barns or ditches by the wayside, or herded like one of a drove of swine on the wet deck of a collier; or, when he has returned, sitting perhaps on the bleak hill side, and looking back, with wife and hungry little ones, on the roof he has been forced to relinquish at the bidding of a cruel landlord; nay, to the most distant dens of squalid and savage barbarism, where burnings, housebreakings, rapes, assassinations, are to the ruffian conspirator familiar as the glass he drains; and to the very files of the marching marauders, as they line the road by which their victim is expected, we are not ashamed to declare that we can extend our indignant commiseration, and are not yet hopeless of obtaining the grateful confidence of an undeceived and rescued people in return. We will not suffer two of the finest races of men in the world, the Catholic and Protestant, or the Milesian and Anglo-Irish, to be duped into mutual hatred by the tale-bearing go-betweens who may struggle in impotent malice against our honest efforts, even though the panders of dissension should be willing to pay out of their own pockets — as some, who may look to their backs and shoulders, have done — for the satisfaction of setting us by the ears. But let it first be our task to make the people of Ireland better acquainted with one another. We address in these pages the Protestant wealth and intelligence of the country, an interest acknowledged on all hands to be the depository of Ireland's fate for good or evil. The Protestants of Ireland are wealthy and intelligent beyond most classes, of their numbers, in the world: but their wealth has hitherto been insecure, because their intelligence has not embraced a thorough knowledge of the genius and disposition of their Catholic fellow-citizens. The genius of a people at large is not to be learned by the notes of Sunday tourists. The history of centuries must be gathered, published, studied and digested, before the Irish people can be known to the world, and to each other, as they ought to be. We hail, with daily-increasing pleasure, the spirit of research and liberality which is manifesting itself in all the branches of our national literature, but chiefly in our earlier history and antiquities — subjects of paramount importance to every people who respect, or even desire to respect themselves. Let us contribute our aid to the auspicious undertaking, and introduce the Saxon and the Scottish Protestant to an acquaintance with the poetical genius of a people hitherto unknown to them, as being known only in a character incompatible with sincerity or plain dealing. The present century will not answer the conditions of our enquiry. We will look nearer to times when they who had high treason in their hearts had arms in their hands, and honest defiance on their faces — when the game of nations was played boldly and won fairly — when victors and vanquished could afford to seem what they really were, and genuine feeling found utterance undisguised, in the passionate sincerity of exultation or despair. We will leave the idiotic brawler, the bankrupt and fraudulent demagogue, the crawling incendiary, the scheming, jesuitical, ambitious priest — that perverse rabble, on whom the mire in which they have wallowed for the last quarter of a century, has caked into a crust like the armour of the Egyptian beast, till they are case-hardened invulnerably in the filth of habitual impudence, ingratitude, hypocrisy, envy and malice; so that it were but a vain defilement of aught manly or honorable to advance it against such panoply of every foul component — we will leave them to their employment of reproach and agitation, and sing the songs of men who might well rise from honourable graves, and affright the midnight echoes of Aughrim or Benburb with their lamentations, if they could know that their descendants were fools enough to be led by such a directory of knaves and cowards...

II

The thrushes are singing, the dews glistening, the cuckoo is calling from the grove, the rail replying from the meadows, and a crop, which by the blessing of God, will ere long, fill the granaries of Ireland with food for many millions, is gushing from the moist earth, like an exhalation. We write in early May, for May is the month of lovers — love is the subject of our labours, and to all who love we dedicate the vernal conception. May is the month of lovers, whether their path be in city or solitude, bright in sunshine, or lustrous in moonlight, or dim in the still radiance of the stars. May breathes the inspiration of desire from all the fresh bosom of the impregnated earth; May sheds the animation of hope from all the clear depths of the buxom and enamoured air. God bless the happy hearts, that even now thrill with Heaven's holiest influences, in the breasts of many fond and innocent young creatures, walking or wandering by one another's sides, over the fair face of this delightful island; for on such a bright May morning when were the valleys of our country not sanctified by the presence of true lovers? Under many an odorous hawthorn, and among the dews of many a daisied meadow, are youths and maidens even now exchanging vows, to be ratified, ere long, before the altar, in unions which shall yet brighten a hundred hearths with the glad faces of free and happy generations. Alas! a thousand springs have smiled on the same scenes of love and promise; but, of their thousand winters, few, few have scowled in vain through the closed lattice on secure or free firesides.

Year by year, if we could obtain a retrospect of the scene before us, with its ascending succession of yearly change, our eyes, which now rest delighted on as fair a valley as ever yielded its increase to the hand of man, bright with the dwellings of as honest and as happy a people as ever sowed, reaped, or consumed the fruits of earth, and, we again, thank God, smiling with the promise of as rich a harvest as ever filled the barns and bawns of Ireland — our eyes resting delighted on such a scene would, we say, ere they had contemplated it under the receding change of half a century, shrink back, appalled, at the spectacle of smoking ruins, trampled corn fields, discoloured waters, and fugitive and famishing families, houseless — lawless — hopeless. Shift back the scene another two or three half centuries. Fewer corn fields there are here to trample; fewer cottages to burn; but the stream of blood flows freely as ever. Musket and cannon still mingle their dreadful noises with the clash of steel, and the victorious troops still shout the same huzzas which followed the rebellious rout from Ross and Antrim; but, mingling with the British cheer are war-cries long unheard upon our hills, and fighting, foot to foot, with the trained soldiery of England, are men, the recollection of whose very costume is lost among their descendants. See the wild Irishmen — how the chain mail still glances on their breasts — how the long glibbs are still tossed on their mantled shoulders! — mark that stirrupless lancer, how he dashes at the ponderous man-at-arms. He bears one stave like a javelin, whirled high overhead; another fills his left hand, with the tasselled reins; his sword is in its sheath till these are cast; his rear-rank man sways a broad battle-axe — the last — he of the galloglasses. — See the kern with the matchlock; how he blows his fuse in the face of a field-piece. — Hark to the war-cries of Claneboy, Iveagh, and Clanbrasil. — *Farrah! Farrah! Lamh dearg aboo! Aengus more aboo! Lamh laidir air uachdir! — Faunat aboo!* shouts Mac Sweeny of the ships; *Bataillach aboo!* cries Mac Sweeny of the battle-axes —

Huzza! Huzza! replies the British line; and down go kern and carbineer, galloglass and trooper, tanist and captain, in the reeling struggle. Again shift back the scene till the roar of the artillery is heard no longer, and the only smoke of battle is the steam of reeking men and horses; and over the same valley, now all uncultivated, yet green in deep, delicious pasture, we see the ancestors of the same men who vainly strove with British discipline at Kinsale and the Boyne, now still more vainly striving with one another, for the possession, perhaps, of the unconscious brutes scared from their grazing ground beside, perhaps of the grey ruin crumbling on the hill above; or, it may be, as it often was, for the mere lust of inflicting pain, and the mad glory of fighting. A horrid sight! They hack one another with brazen knives; they pierce one another with flint-headed arrows and the barbed blades of javelins; they torture the dying; they mangle and insult over the dead. Woe to the conquered! Wives and little ones, old men and maidens mingled in common massacre, expire among the ruins of the huts or the unavailing defences of their earthen rampart. No sulphurous canopy here to hide them from the eye of day; but all on the open plain, where summer dust never soiled a daisy, do the heroic savages exult before the face of heaven, while bards and Seanachies contend in glorifying the brave atrocity! Alas! how soon have we forgotten that love was to have been our theme! How soon has the sad necessity of Irish history drawn us into the strife, and cruelty, and desolation, and despair, by the modifications of which alone can we compare the different aspects of early Irish society — a society which has differed little from the days of Henry to those of George, save in degrees of violence or misery. But let war and famine do their worst, love is immortal and the same; and the valley before us, with all its successions of disfigurement and desolation, has never missed its May tribute of sighs and songs. The flowers of our forest are hard to weed away. Seven hundred years of disaster, as destructive as ever consumed the vitals of any country, have each in succession seen our people perishing by famine or the sword in almost every quarter of the land; yet at this day there is neither mountain, plain, nor valley that is not rife with generations of the unextinguishable nation; long may they walk upon our hills with the steps of freemen! long may they make our valleys ring with the songs of that love which has thus made them indomitable in defeat and ineradicable in a struggle of extermination!

These are the songs before us — songs such as the speakers of the English language at large have never heard before, and which they could not see and hear now but for the pious labours of a man who, however politically malignant and religiously fanatical, has yet done such good service to his country in their collection and preservation, that for her sake we half forgive him our own quarrel, and consent to forego a great part of its vindication.

Those who have known the melodies of Ireland only in association with the delightful lyrics of Moore, will, we fear, be startled to find them connected with songs so marked as these are, by all the characteristics which distinguish the productions of rude, from those of refined society. Moore's Melodies, indeed, present a combination of the most delightful attributes of music and poetry, unattainable otherwise than by uniting the music of a rude age to the poetry of a refined one. The hardships, dangers, and afflictions which must have crushed the heart of the musician before it could so shed its whole life-blood of passion into the absorbing and almost painful pathos of an Irish melody, must have been too destructive of all security to have admitted even an approach to that devoted leisure which alone could qualify a writer for success in finished poetry. The contrast between the native songs and the lyrics of Moore is indeed strangely striking — as strange as uncouthness can present in juxtaposition with politeness, but still no more than that which may be admitted to have distinguished the *Merus Hibernicus*, from the modern Irish gentleman. We will look in vain for the chasteness, the appositeness, the antithetical and epigrammatic point, and the measured propriety of prosody, which delight the ear and the judgment, in a song by Thomas Moore, among the rude rhymes which accompanied the same notes two centuries ago; but the stamen and essence of each is interwoven and transfused through the whole texture and complexion of the other — for sentiment is the soul of song, and sentiment is one imprescriptible property of the common blood of all Irishmen.

What we mean by Irish sentiment, we hope to show in the progress of our notices; and we can execute our purpose only by adhering to the strict severity of literal translation. We have exemplified Irish adulation, Irish whimsicality, and Irish fun and jollity in the songs of Carolan, with a fidelity painful to ourselves, as it was derogatory from the character so long reflected on Carolan's poetic, from his musical talent. If we have done that wonderful musician poetic injustice, we will give his poetic defenders their revenge in kind; for it is our purpose, sometime about the Lammas floods, to give an appendix to this series, containing, along with some communications of considerable interest and from rather distinguished persons, as many versions as we think ourselves and our aids sufficiently happy in, to warrant the assurance which we now beg to give our readers — that whatever versions of Irish song may find their way into our pages shall be as faithful as the best talents of ourselves and our assistants can secure — therefore should any Irish scholar, conscious of a good talent for translation conceive that he can set Carolan right with the English reader, (which we confess we ourselves almost despair of being able to do,) we will be happy to give his versions our best consideration for insertion with those alluded to.

Meanwhile, whatever beauties may remain concealed in the songs of Carolan, we will proceed with those which furnish less suspicious and equally, if not more, available material for a judgment on the subject proposed. Heaven help us! what a key to the whole melancholy mystery is here. It is the first part of the Song of Sorrow, and mournfully true to its name it is.

> If you would go with me to the County Leitrim,
>   Uilecan dubh O!
> I would give the honey of bees and mead as food for you;
>   Uilecan dubh O!
> I shall give you the prospect of ships, and sails, and boats,
> Under the tops of the trees, and we returning from the strand,
> And I would never let any sorrow come upon you.
>   Oh! you are my Uilecan dubh O!

> I shall not go with you, and it is in vain you ask me;
>   Uilecan dubh O!
> For your words will not keep me alive without food:
>   Uilecan dubh O!
> A hundred thousand times better for me to be always a maid,
> Than to be walking the dew and the wilderness with you:
> My heart has not given to you love nor affection,
>   And you are not my Uilecan dubh O!

Desire, despair, and the horrible reality of actual famine — these are three dread prompters of song. Whoever first sung the Song of Sorrow had felt them all; but desire was his paramount inspirer, and the concluding stanzas rise into such a fervid frenzy of undisguised desire that we shrink from exhibiting them in their

39

literal English. Yet there is nothing impure, nothing licentious in their languishing but savage sincerity. This is the one great characteristic of all the amatory poetry of the country; and in its association with the despondency of conscious degradation, and the recklessness of desperate content, is partly to be found the origin of that wild, mournful, incondite, yet not uncouth, sentiment which distinguishes the national songs of Ireland from those of perhaps any other nation in the world. We say in this is 'partly' to be found the source of that peculiarity which marks Irish sentiments; for we believe that great proportion of the characteristics of a people are inherent, not fictitious; and that there are as essential differences between the genius's as between the physical appearances of nations. We believe that no dissipating continuance of defeat, danger, famine, or misgovernment could ever, without the absolute infusion of Milesian blood, Hibernicize the English peasant; and that no stultifying operation of mere security, plenty, or laborious regularity could ever, without actual physical transubstantiation, reduce the native Irishman to the stolid standard of the sober Saxon. Holding these opinions, our object must be rather to ascertain what Irish sentiment is, than why or whence it may be so or so. The great ingredient in the sentiment of the song we have just translated is desire; yet that song is called the Song of Sorrow — not, as we conceive, on account of those misfortunes, however miserable, which rendered that an unattainable desire; but rather because the hopelessness of passion rises to such a paramount excess of anguish as overbears and obliterates all other griefs, and would make the lamentation of the hopeless lover pining among all that wealth and peace could give to comfort him, as bitterly woeful as that of the wan outlaw himself; were it not that the comparatively artificial state of feeling induced by the influences of wealth and refinement, renders such passionate excess in civilized life too rare to justify the general application of such a supposition. No doubt, the poignancy of the fugitive's disappointment must have been greatly exasperated by the recollection that it had been his own rebellion (for the Song of Sorrow was composed by a fugitive rebel,) which had plunged him into this bitter abyss where desire turned to languishment, and hope to despair: still the great strength of the song's concentrated pathos lies in deploring the effect, not in deprecating the cause. He does not blame the illfortune that struck him down before his enemy in battle, or that drove him bleeding and bare from his burned homestead to lead the life of a wild animal among the woods and mountains: there is no reproach against the treachery or cowardice of his people, no complaint of the misery and insecurity of his country — and yet, had it not been for these, black Uilecan had surely been his own — no; he has but one wish, the enjoyment of his love; one grief, the hopelessness of having his desire; and there is nothing for him but to blaspheme heaven and fly — and he does blaspheme heaven —

> Great God! why am I thus denied
> My Uilecan dubh O?

is the last exclamation of his agony, as, diving into the deepest forest of the Black Valley, he bursts away for the Lakes of Leitrim wild as the red deer in September.

Let us no longer imagine that humour is the characteristic of the Irish. Their sentiment is pathetic. Desire is the essence of that pathos — desire, either for the possession of love unenjoyed, or for the continuance of love being enjoyed, or for the restoration of enjoyed love lost. We know no Irish song addressed to the judgment: if an Irish song fail to go to the heart at once, it fails outright. Even in the most whimsical there is some touch of sentiment, some appeal to the pathetic principle. So also in their music, as admirably exemplified by Mr Moore in his dedication of the first number of the Melodies, where, alluding to the characteristic introduction of a flat third, he draws the same inference from its effect in harmony, which we would deduce from the presence when least expected of some pathetic allusion in the lyric composition of some of their most extravagantly humorous rhymes...

III

What constitutes a state? Neither power-loom nor steam-coach. Cover the surface of a country with factories thick as the cabins of its peasantry — reticulate it with railroads, numerous as its lanes and by-paths — lock up every rivulet, till it becomes a navigable canal — convert each promontory of its coast into a pier, and each reef of its sunken rocks into a breakwater; yet if the men be cowards, and the women wantons, it were better a desert. On the other hand, people the desert with bold men and chaste women, and you have the elements of a nation, though its metropolis be a kraal, and its *via regia* a sheep track.

Our capital city is no circle of log huts, our royal road is no green forest pass, no ragged mountain pathway. Dublin with her palaces, deserted though they are, were no unworthy residence for kings or legislators; our great northern line, unfrequent though the travelling carriage of native absentee or foreign proprietor may be upon its level causeway, were no unmeet avenue for the returning march of victorious armies, or the peaceful pomp of regal or viceregal progresses. Our people, we believe, before Heaven, to be as brave and as virtuous a people as the world ever saw. Female purity is ever the concomitant, the crown and halo of true love; and the sentiment of legitimate desire, as we have illustrated it in our preceding paper, is not more nationally characteristic of our courageous countrymen than is this its purer, though twin sister, attribute, of the virgins, wives, and matrons, whom we rejoice to recall our fair and merry countrywomen. No — whatever calamitous degradation the violence of an oppressive conquest, or the lingering tyranny of a debasing priestcraft may have exercised in other regards upon the moral condition of the Irish, however self-respect and manly charity may have been thrust down by the iron heel of an unavoidable civil domination; however reason and free intellect may have been prostrated by the hoofs of a more brutal spiritual ascendancy, virtue, evading alike the spurns of power and the trampling march of superstition, has risen, is rising, and will rise, immaculate as the love it fosters, indomitable as the nation it redeems. Let violence and discord do their worst; while virtue is our people's heritage we will not despair for Ireland. Eight millions of people cannot for ever remain in obscurity; sooner or later Ireland must rise into importance, perhaps as an emulator, perhaps as an equal, perhaps as a superior to the other members of our imperial confederacy. Let politicians quarrel as to the means, all Irishmen must be unanimous in common aspiration for that noble end; but, if our country were to attain to power and distinction only by forfeiting these virtues which have hallowed her adversity, we would rather see her chained for ever to the level of her present civil degradation, than emulating France in military renown, while she imitated her in heartless sensuality, or rivalling England herself in political and commercial influence, while a like indifference to humble honor made the churchwarden's liability her peasant girl's best portion. As this never has been, so, we trust, it never can be in Ireland: the Irish heart must first be stripped of all those characteristics which most ennoble its peculiar constitution; and to effect that revolution, which neither ignorance, nor superstition, nor brutalizing exclusion from humane society has been able to bring about through seven hundred years of outrage and outlawry, will, with God's help, be equally impracticable, by whatever knowledge, or power, or lawful luxury may come in the train of those long centuries of improvement that are yet in store for her.

So far, then, from yielding to despair, we rejoice in all auspicious hopes for our country. The arts of civilized life have already half-forestalled the national civilization. Great works, which in common progress of society must have been preceded by a development of local intelligence and enterprize adequate to their conception and execution are, by a generous anomaly, extended through our most remote and savage districts; high roads, canals, embankments, piers, and harbours, await prospective use and reproductive operation; and dormant facilities for the development of unimagined applications of advancing art are prepared by nature over and under the whole face of the high-destined country. But are our people such as could make a nation of the desert, much more of such a rich and well-conditioned island? Education based upon the only true basis — scriptural education alone is wanted to make our men as bold as our women are chaste — to make us a nation of enlightened, liberal, and prosperous people — assertors of our own rights, respecters of the rights of others — a truly integral and influential portion of the empire, repudiating alike the insolent violence of civil degradation and the hideous impiety of spiritual thraldom — in the fullest sense of the words, bold men, honoured by others and respected by ourselves...

2
Thomas Davis, from *Literary and Historical Essays*, 1846

Thomas Osborne Davis (1814-45) founded the Nation *with C. G. Duffy and J. B. Dillon in 1842. He was for a time closely associated with Daniel O'Connell (1775-1847), especially in his attempts to repeal the Act of Union; but after the fiasco at Clontarf in 1843, when O'Connell backed down in the face of Peel's ban on a huge public meeting, Davis distanced himself from him. Davis contributed numerous political ballads to the* Nation, *as well as the kind of rhetorical prose represented here.*

2(a) from 'The History of Ireland'

Something has been done to rescue Ireland from the reproach that she was a wailing and ignorant slave.

Brag as we like, the reproach was not undeserved, nor is it quite removed.

She is still a serf-nation, but she is struggling wisely and patiently, and is ready to struggle with all the energy her advisers think politic, for liberty. She has ceased to wail — she is beginning to make up a record of English crime and Irish suffering, in order to explain the past, to justify the present and caution the future. She begins to study the past — not to acquire a beggar's eloquence in petition, but a hero's wrath in strife. She no longer tears and parades her wounds, to win her smiter's mercy; and now she should look upon her breast and say — 'That wound makes me distrust, and this makes me guard, and they all will make me steadier to resist, or, if all else fails, fiercer to avenge.'

Thus will Ireland do naturally and honourably.

Our spirit has increased — our liberty is not far off.

But to make our spirit lasting and wise as it is bold — to make

44

our liberty an inheritance for our children, and a charter for our prosperity, we must study as well as strive, and learn as well as feel.

If we attempt to govern ourselves without statesmanship — to be a nation without a knowledge of the country's history, and of the propensities to good and ill of the people — or to fight without generalship, we will fail in policy, society, and war. These — all these things — we, people of Ireland, must know if we would be a free, strong nation. A mockery of Irish independence is not what we want. The bauble of a powerless parliament does not lure us. We are not children. The office of supplying England with recruits, artizans, and corn, under the benign interpositions of an Irish Grand Jury, *shall* not be our destiny. By our deep conviction — by the power of mind over the people, we say, No!

We are true to our colour, 'the green,' and true to our watchword, 'Ireland for the Irish.' We want to win Ireland and keep it. If we win it, we will not lose it, nor give it away to a bribing, a bullying, or a flattering minister. But, to be able to keep it, and use it, and govern it, the men of Ireland must know what it is, what it was, and what it can be made. They must study her history, perfectly know her present state, physical and moral — and train themselves up by science, poetry, music, industry, skill, and by all the studies and accomplishments of peace and war.

If Ireland were in national health, her history would be familiar by books, pictures, statuary, and music to every cabin and shop in the land — her resources as an agricultural, manufacturing, and trading people, would be equally known — and every young man would be trained, and every grown man able to defend her coast, her plains, her towns, and her hills — not with his right arm merely, but by his disciplined habits and military accomplishments. These are the pillars of independence...

2(b) 'Our National Language'

Men are ever valued most for peculiar and original qualities. A man who can only talk common-place, and act according to routine, has little weight. To speak, look, and do what your own soul from its depths orders you, are credentials of greatness which all men understand and acknowledge. Such a man's dictum has more influence than the reasoning of an imitative or common-place man. He fills his circle with confidence. He is self-possessed, firm, accurate, and daring. Such men are the pioneers of civilization, and the rulers of the human heart.

Why should not nations be judged thus? Is not a full indulgence of its natural tendencies essential to a *people's* greatness? Force the manners, dress, language, and constitution of Russia, or Italy, or Norway, or America, and you instantly stunt and distort the whole mind of either people.

The language, which grows up with a people, is conformed to their organs, descriptive of their climate, constitution, and manners, mingled inseparably with their history and their soil, fitted beyond any other language to express their prevalent thoughts in the most natural and efficient way.

To impose another language on such a people is to send their history adrift among the accidents of translation — 'tis to tear their identity from all places — 'tis to substitute arbitrary signs for picturesque and suggestive names — 'tis to cut off the entail of feeling, and separate the people from their forefathers by a deep gulf — 'tis to corrupt their very organs, and abridge their power of expression.

The language of a nation's youth is the only easy and full speech for its manhood and for its age. And when the language of its cradle goes, itself craves a tomb.

What business has a Russian for the rippling language of Italy or India? How could a Greek distort his organs and his soul to speak Dutch upon the sides of Hymetus, or the beach of Salamis, or on the waste where once was Sparta? And is it befitting the fiery, delicate-organed Celt to abandon his beautiful tongue, docile and spirited as an Arab, 'sweet as music, strong as the wave' — is it befitting in him to abandon this wild liquid speech for the mongrel of a hundred breeds called English, which powerful though it be, creaks and bangs about the Celt who tries to use it?

We lately met a glorious thought in the 'Triads of Mochmed,' printed in one of the Welsh codes by the Record Commission: 'There are three things without which there is no country — common language, common judicature, and co-tillage land — for without these a country cannot support itself in peace and social union.'

A people without a language of its own is only half a nation. A nation should guard its language more than its territories — 'tis a surer barrier, and more important frontier, than fortress or river.

And in good times it has ever been thought so. Who had dared to propose the adoption of Persian or Egyptian in Greece — how had Pericles thundered at the barbarian? How had Cato scourged from the forum him who would have given the Attic or Gallic speech to men of Rome? How proudly and how nobly Germany stopped 'the incipient creeping' progress of French! And no sooner had she succeeded, than her genius, which had tossed in a hot trance, sprung up fresh and triumphant.

Had Pyrrhus quelled Italy, or Xerxes subdued Greece for a time long enough to impose new languages, where had been the literature which gives a pedigree to human genius? Even liberty recovered had been sickly and insecure without the language with which it had hunted in the woods, worshipped at the fruit-strewn altar, debated on the council-hill, and shouted in the battle-charge.

There is a fine song of the Fusians, which describes —

> Language linked to liberty.

To lose your native tongue, and learn that of an alien, is the worst badge of conquest — it is the chain on the soul. To have lost entirely the national language is death; the fetter has worn through. So long as the Saxon held to his German speech, he could hope to resume his land from the Norman; now, if he is to be free and locally governed, he must build himself a new home. There is hope for Scotland — strong hope for Wales — sure hope for Hungary. The speech of the alien is not universal in the one; is gallantly held at bay in the other; is nearly expelled from the third.

How unnatural — how corrupting 'tis for us, three-fourths of whom are of Celtic blood, to speak a medley of Teutonic dialects. If we add the Celtic Scots, who came back here from the thirteenth to the seventeenth centuries, and the Celtic Welsh, who colonised many parts of Wexford and other Leinster counties, to the Celts who never left Ireland, probably five-sixths, or more, of us are Celts. What business have we with the Norman-Sassenagh?

Nor let any doubt these proportions because of the number of English *names* in Ireland. With a politic cruelty, the English of the Pale passed an act (3 Edw. IV., chap.3), compelling every Irishman within English jurisdiction,

> to go like to one Englishman in apparel, and shaving off his beard above the mouth,...and shall take to him an English sirname of one town, as Sutton, Chester, Trym, Skryne,

Corke, Kinsale; or colour, as White, Blacke, Browne; or art
or science, as Smith or Carpenter; or office, as Cook, Butler;
and that he and his issue shall use this name, under pain
of forfeiting his goods yearly.

And just as this parliament before the Reformation, so did
another after the Reformation. By the 28th Henry VIII., c. 15,
the dress and language of the Irish were insolently described as
barbarous by the minions of that ruffian king, and were utterly
forbidden and abolished under many penalties and incapacities.
These laws are still in force; but whether the Archaeological
Society, including Peel and O'Connell, will be prosecuted, seems
doubtful.

There was also, 'tis to be feared, an adoption of English names,
during some periods, from fashion, fear, or meanness. Some of
our best Irish names, too, have been so mangled as to require
some scholarship to identify them. For these and many more
reasons, the members of the Celtic race here are immensely greater
than at first appears.

But this is not all; for even the Saxon and Norman colonists,
notwithstanding these laws, melted down into the Irish, and
adopted all their ways and language. For centuries upon centuries
Irish was spoken by men of all bloods in Ireland, and English
was unknown, save to a few citizens and nobles of the Pale. 'Tis
only within a very late period that the majority of the people
learned English.

But, it will be asked, how can the language be restored now?

We shall answer this partly by saying that, through the labours
of the Archaeological and many lesser societies, it *is* being revived
rapidly.

We shall consider this question of the possibility of reviving it
more at length some other day.

Nothing can make us believe that it is natural or honourable
for the Irish to speak the speech of the alien, the invader, the
Sassenagh tyrant, and to abandon the language of our kings and
heroes. What! give up the tongue of Ollamh Fodhla and Brian
Boru, the tongue of McCarty, and the O'Nials, the tongue of
Sarsfield's, Curran's, Mathew's, and O'Connell's boyhood, for
that of Strafford and Poynings, Sussex, Kirk, and Cromwell!

No, oh! no! the 'the brighter days shall surely come,' and the
green flag shall wave on our towers, and the sweet old language
be heard once more in college, mart, and senate.

But, even should the effort to save it as the national language fail, by the attempt we will rescue its old literature, and hand down to our descendants proofs that we had a language as fit for love, and war, and business, and pleasure, as the world ever knew, and that we had not the spirit and nationality to preserve it!

Had Swift known Irish, he would have sowed its seed by the side of that nationality which he planted, and the close of the last century would have seen the one as flourishing as the other. Had Ireland used Irish in 1782,[1] would it not have impeded England's re-conquest of us? But 'tis not yet too late.

For *you*, if the mixed speech called English was laid with sweetmeats on your child's tongue, English is the best speech of manhood. And yet, reader, in that case you are unfortunate. The hills, and lakes, and rivers, the forts and castles, the churches and parishes, the baronies and counties around you, have all Irish names — names which describe the nature of the scenery or ground, the name of founder, or chief, or priest, or the leading fact in the history of the place. To you these are names hard to pronounce, and without meaning.

And yet it were well for you to know them. The knowledge would be a topography, and a history, and romance, walking by your side, and helping your discourse. Meath tells its flatness, Clonmel the abundant riches of its valley, Fermanagh is the land of the Lakes, Tyrone the country of Owen, Kilkenny the Church of St. Canice, Dunmore the great fort, Athenry the Ford of the Kings, Dunleary the Fort of O'Leary; and the Phoenix Park, instead of taking its name from a fable, recognises as christener, the 'sweet water' which yet springs near the East-gate.

All the names of our airs and songs are Irish, and we every day are as puzzled and ingeniously wrong about them as the man who, when asked for the air 'I am asleep, and don't waken me,' called it 'Tommy McCullagh made boots for me.'

The bulk of our history and poetry are written in Irish, and shall we, who learn Italian, and Latin, and Greek, to read Dante, Livy, and Homer in the original — shall we be content with ignorance or a translation of Irish?

The want of modern scientific words in Irish is undeniable, and doubtless we should adopt the existing names into our language. The Germans have done the same thing, and no one calls German mongrel on that account. Most of these names are clumsy and extravagant; they are almost all derived from Greek or Latin, and cut as foreign a figure in French and English as they would in Irish. Once Irish was recognised as a language to be learned as much as French or Italian, our dictionaries would fill up, and our vocabularies ramify, to suit all the wants of life and conversation.

These objections are ingenious refinements, however, rarely thought of till after the other and great objection has been answered.

The usual objection to attempting the revival of Irish is, that it could not succeed.

If an attempt were made to introduce Irish, either through the national schools or the courts of law, into the eastern side of the island, it would certainly fail, and the re-action might extinguish it altogether. But no one contemplates this save as a dream of what may happen a hundred years hence. It is quite another thing to say, as we do, that the Irish language should be cherished, taught, and esteemed, and that it can be preserved and gradually extended.

What we seek is, that the people of the upper classes should have their children taught the language which explains our names of persons or places, our older history, and our music, and which is spoken in the majority of our counties, rather than Italian, German, or French. It would be more useful in life, more serviceable to the taste and genius of young people, and a more flexible accomplishment for an Irish man or woman to speak, sing, and write Irish than French.

At present the middle classes think it a sign of vulgarity to speak Irish — the children are everywhere taught English and English alone in schools — and, what is worse, they are urged by rewards and punishments to speak it at home, for English is the language of their masters. Now, we think the example and exertions of the upper classes would be sufficient to set the opposite and better fashion of preferring Irish; and, even as a matter of taste, we think them bound to do so. And we ask it of the pride, the patriotism, and the hearts of our farmers and shopkeepers, will they try to drive out of their children's minds the native language of almost every great man we had, from Brian Boru to O'Connell — will they meanly sacrifice the language which names their hills, and towns, and music, to the tongue of the stranger?

About half the people west of a line drawn from Derry to Waterford speak Irish habitually, and in some of the mountain tracts east of that line it is still common. Simply requiring the teachers of the National Schools in these Irish-speaking districts to know Irish, and supplying them with Irish translations of the school books, would guard the language where it now exists, and prevent it from being swept away by the English tongue, as the red Americans have been by the English race from New York to New Orleans.

The example of the upper classes would extend and develop a modern Irish literature, and the hearty support they have given to the Archaeological Society makes us hope that they will have sense and spirit to do so.

But the establishment of a newspaper partly or wholly Irish would be the most rapid and sure way of serving the language. The Irish-speaking man would find, in his native tongue, the political news and general information he has now to seek in English; and the English-speaking man, having Irish frequently before him in so attractive a form, would be tempted to learn its characters, and by-and-by its meaning.

These newspapers in many languages are now to be found everywhere but here. In South America many of these papers are Spanish and English, or French; in North America, French and English; in Northern Italy, German and Italian; in Denmark and Holland, German is used in addition to the native tongue; in Alsace and Switzerland, French and German; in Poland, German, French, and Sclavonic; in Turkey, French and Turkish; in Hungary, Maggar, Sclavonic, and German; and the little Canton of Grison uses three languages in its press. With the exception of Hungary, the secondary language is, in all cases, spoken by fewer persons than the Irish-speaking people of Ireland, and while they everywhere tolerate and use one language as a medium of commerce, they cherish the other as the vehicle of history, the wings of song, the soil of their genius, and a mark and guard of nationality.

2(c) from 'Ballad Poetry of Ireland'

How slow we have all been in coming to understand the meaning of Irish Nationality!

Some, dazzled by visions of Pagan splendour, and the pretensions of pedigree, and won by the passions and romance of the olden races, continued to speak in the nineteenth century of an Irish nation as they might have done in the tenth. They forgot the English Pale, the Ulster Settlement, and the filtered colonization of men and ideas. A Celtic kingdom with the old names and the old language without the old quarrels, was their hope; and, though they would not repeat O'Neill's comment, as he passed Barrett's castle on his march to Kinsale, and heard it belonged to a Strongbownian, that 'he hated the Norman churl as if he came yesterday', yet they quietly assumed that the Norman and Saxon elements would disappear under the Gaelic genius, like the tracks of cavalry under a fresh crop.

The Nationality of Swift and Grattan was equally partial. They saw that the Government and laws of the settlers had extended to the island — that Donegal and Kerry were in the Pale; they heard the English tongue in Dublin, and London opinions in Dublin — they mistook Ireland for a colony wronged, and great enough to be a nation.

A lower form of nationhood was before the minds of those who saw in it nothing but a parliament in College Green. They had not erred in judging, for they had not tried to estimate the moral elements and tendencies of the country. They were as narrow bigots to the omnipotency of an institution as any Cockney Radical. Could they, by any accumulation of English stupidity and Irish laziness, have got possession of an Irish government, they would soon have distressed every one by their laws, whom they had not provoked by their administration or disgusted by their dulness.

Far healthier with all its defects, was the idea of those who saw in Scotland a perfect model — who longed for a literary and artistic nationality — who prized the oratory of Grattan and Curran, the novels of Griffin and Carleton, the pictures of Maclise and Burton, the ancient music, as much as any, and far more than most of the political nationalists, but who regarded political independence as a dangerous dream. Unknowingly they fostered it. Their writings, their patronage, their talk was of Ireland; yet it hardly occurred to them that the ideal would flow into the practical, or that they, with their dread of agitation, were forwarding a revolution.

At last we are beginning to see what we are, and what is our destiny. Our duty arises where our knowledge begins. The elements of Irish nationality are not only combining — in fact, they are growing confluent in our minds. Such nationality as merits a good man's help, and wakens a true man's ambition — such nationality as could stand against internal faction and foreign intrigue, such nationality, as would make the Irish hearth happy and the Irish name illustrious, is becoming understood. It must contain and represent the races of Ireland. It must not be Celtic, it must not be Saxon — it must be Irish. The Brehon law, and the maxims of Westminster, the cloudy and lightning genius of the Gael, the placid strength of the Sasanach, the marshalling insight of the Norman — a literature which shall exhibit in combination the passions and idioms of all, and which shall equally express our mind in its romantic, its religious, its forensic, and its practical tendencies — finally, a native government, which shall know and rule by the might and right of all; yet yield to the arrogance of none — these are components of *such* a nationality.

But what have these things to do with the 'Ballad Poetry of Ireland?'[2] Much every way. It is the result of the elements we have named — it is compounded of all; and never was there a book fitter to advance that perfect nationality to which Ireland begins to aspire. That a country is without national poetry proves its hopeless dulness or its utter provincialism. National poetry is the very flowering of the soul — the greatest evidence of its health, the greatest excellence of its beauty. Its melody is balsam to the senses. It is the playfellow of childhood, ripens into the companion of manhood, consoles his age. It presents the most dramatic events, the largest characters, the most impressive scenes, and the deepest passions in the language most familiar to us. It shows us magnified, and ennobles our hearts, our intellects, our country, and our countrymen — binds us to the land by its condensed and gem-like history, to the future by examples and by aspirations. It solaces us in travel, fires us in action, prompts our invention, sheds a grace beyond the power of luxury round our homes, is the recognised envoy of our minds among all mankind and to all time.

In possessing the powers and elements of a glorious nationality, we owned the sources of a national poetry. In the combination and joint development of the latter, we find a pledge and a help to that of the former...

Notes

1. This was the year when Ireland gained its Parliamentary Independence under Grattan.
2. Davis was reviewing a collection of ballads edited by Charles Gavan Duffy.

3

Ernest Renan, from
'The Poetry of the Celtic Races', 1859

*Ernest Renan (1823-92) was one of many European scholars who attended
to the Celtic phenomenon. His essay provided a springboard for Yeats, in
'The Celtic Element in Literature' (see no.10). The text is from William
S. Hutchison's translation of 1896.*

Every one who travels through the Armorican peninsula
experiences a change of the most abrupt description, as soon as
he leaves behind the district most closely bordering upon the
continent, in which the cheerful but commonplace type of face of
Normandy and Maine is continually in evidence, and passes into
the true Brittany, that which merits its name by language and
race. A cold wind arises full of a vague sadness, and carries the
soul to other thoughts; the tree-tops are bare and twisted; the
heath with its monotony of tint stretches away into the distance;
at every step the granite protrudes from a soil too scanty to cover
it; a sea that is almost always sombre girdles the horizon with
eternal moaning. The same contrast is manifest in the people: to
Norman vulgarity, to a plump and prosperous population, happy
to live, full of its own interests, egoistical as are all those who
make a habit of enjoyment, succeeds a timid and reserved race
living altogether within itself, heavy in appearance but capable
of profound feeling, and of an adorable delicacy in its religious
instincts. A like change is apparent, I am told, in passing from
England into Wales, from the Lowlands of Scotland, English by
language and manners, into the Gaelic Highlands; and too, though
with a perceptible difference, when one buries oneself in the
districts of Ireland where the race has remained pure from all
admixture of alien blood. It seems like entering on the

54

subterranean strata of another world, and one experiences in some measure the impression given us by Dante, when he leads us from one circle of his Inferno to another.

Sufficient attention is not given to the peculiarity of this fact of an ancient race living, until our days and almost under our eyes, its own life in some obscure islands and peninsulas in the West, more and more affected, it is true, by external influences, but still faithful to its own tongue, to its own memories, to its own customs, and to its own genius. Especially is it forgotten that this little people, now concentrated on the very confines of the world, in the midst of rocks and mountains whence its enemies have been powerless to force it, is in possession of a literature which, in the Middle Ages, exercised an immense influence, changed the current of European civilisation, and imposed its poetical motives on nearly the whole of Christendom. Yet it is only necessary to open the authentic monuments of the Gaelic genius to be convinced that the race which created them has had its own original manner of feeling and thinking, that nowhere has the eternal illusion clad itself in more seductive hues, and that in the great chorus of humanity no race equals this for penetrative notes that go to the very heart. Alas! it too is doomed to disappear, this emerald set in the Western seas. Arthur will return no more from his isle of faery, and St Patrick was right when he said to Ossian, 'The heroes that thou weepest are dead; can they be born again?' It is high time to note, before they shall have passed away, the divine tones thus expiring on the horizon before the growing tumult of uniform civilisation. Were criticism to set itself the task of calling back these distant echoes, and of giving a voice to races that are no more, would not that suffice to absolve it from the reproach, unreasonably and too frequently brought against it, of being only negative?...

If the excellence of races is to be appreciated by the purity of their blood and the inviolability of their national character, it must needs be admitted that none can vie in nobility with the still surviving remains of the Celtic race.[1] Never has a human family lived more apart from the world, and been purer from all alien admixture. Confined by conquest within forgotten islands and peninsulas, it has reared an impassable barrier against external influences; it has drawn all from itself; it has lived solely on its own capital. From this ensues that powerful individuality, that hatred of the foreigner, which even in our own days has formed the essential feature of the Celtic peoples. Roman civilisation scarcely reached them, and left among them but few traces. The Teutonic invasion drove them back, but did not penetrate them. At the present hour they are still constant in resistance to an invasion dangerous in an altogether different way, — that of modern civilisation, destructive as it is of local variations and national types. Ireland in particular (and herein we perhaps have the secret of her irremediable weakness) is the only country in Europe where the native can produce the titles of his descent, and designate with certainty, even in the darkness of prehistoric ages, the race from which he has sprung.

It is in this secluded life, in this defiance of all that comes from without, that we must search for the explanation of the chief features of the Celtic character. It has all the failings, and all the good qualities, of the solitary man; at once proud and timid, strong in feeling and feeble in action, at home free and unreserved, to the outside world awkward and embarrassed. It distrusts the foreigner, because it sees in him a being more refined than itself, who abuses its simplicity. Indifferent to the admiration of others, it asks only one thing, that it should be left to itself. It is before all else a domestic race, fitted for family life and fireside joys. In no other race has the bond of blood been stronger, or has it created more duties, or attached man to his fellow with so much breadth and depth. Every social institution of the Celtic peoples was in the beginning only an extension of the family. A common tradition attests, to this very day, that nowhere has the trace of this great institution of relationship been better preserved than in Brittany. There is a widely-spread belief in that country, that blood speaks, and that two relatives, unknown one to the other, in any part of the world wheresoever it may be, recognise each other by the secret and mysterious emotion which they feel in each other's presence. Respect for the dead rests on the same principle. Nowhere has reverence for the dead been greater than among the Breton peoples; nowhere have so many memories and prayers clustered about the tomb. This is because life is not for these people a personal adventure, undertaken by each man on his own account, and at his own risks and perils; it is a link in a long chain, a gift received and handed on, a debt paid and a duty done.

It is easily discernible how little fitted were natures so strongly concentrated to furnish one of those brilliant developments, which imposes the momentary ascendency of a people on the world; and that, no doubt, is why the part played externally by the Cymric race has always been a secondary one. Destitute of the means of expansion, alien to all idea of aggression and conquest, little desirous of making its thought prevail outside itself, it has only known how to retire so far as space has permitted, and then, at bay in its last place of retreat, to make an invincible resistance to its enemies. Its very fidelity has been a useless devotion. Stubborn of submission and ever behind the age, it is faithful to its conquerors when its conquerors are no longer faithful to themselves. It was the last to defend its religious independence against Rome — and it has become the staunchest stronghold of Catholicism; it was the last in France to defend its political independence against the king — and it has given to the world the last royalists.

Thus the Celtic race has worn itself out in resistance to its time, and in the defence of desperate causes. It does not seem as though in any epoch it had any aptitude for political life. The spirit of family stifled within it all attempts at more extended organisation. Moreover, it does not appear that the peoples which form it are by themselves susceptible of progress. To them life appears as a fixed condition, which man has no power to alter. Endowed with little initiative, too much inclined to look upon themselves as minors and in tutelage, they are quick to believe in destiny and resign themselves to it. Seeing how little audacious they are against God, one would scarcely believe this race to be the daughter of Japhet.

Thence ensues its sadness. Take the songs of its bards of the sixth century; they weep more defeats than they sing victories. Its history is itself only one long lament; it still recalls its exiles, its flights across the seas. If at times it seems to be cheerful, a tear is not slow to glisten behind its smile; it does not know that strange forgetfulness of human conditions and destinies which is called gaiety. Its songs of joy end as elegies; there is nothing to equal the delicious sadness of its national melodies. One might call them emanations from on high which, falling drop by drop upon the soul, pass through it like memories of another world. Never have men feasted so long upon these solitary delights of the spirit, these poetic memories which simultaneously intercross all the sensations of life, so vague, so deep, so penetrative, that one might die from them, without being able to say whether it was from bitterness or sweetness.

The infinite delicacy of feeling which characterises the Celtic race is closely allied to its need of concentration. Natures that are little capable of expansion are nearly always those that feel most

deeply, for the deeper the feeling, the less it tends to express itself.
Thence we have that charming shamefastness, that veiled and
exquisite sobriety, equally far removed from the sentimental
rhetoric too familiar to the Latin races, and the reflective simplicity
of Germany, which are so admirably displayed in the ballads
published by M. de la Villemarqué.[2] The apparent reserve of the
Celtic peoples, often taken for coldness, is due to this inward
timidity which makes them believe that a feeling loses half its
value if it be expressed; and that the heart ought to have no other
spectator than itself.

If it be permitted us to assign sex to nations as to individuals,
we should have to say without hesitance that the Celtic race,
especially with regard to its Cymric or Breton branch, is an
essentially feminine race. No human family, I believe, has carried
so much mystery into love. No other has conceived with more
delicacy the ideal of woman, or been more fully dominated by it.
It is a sort of intoxication, a madness, a vertigo. Read the strange
Mabinogi of Peredur, or its French imitation *Parceval le Gallois*; its
pages are, as it were, dewy with feminine sentiment. Woman
appears therein as a kind of vague vision, an intermediary between
man and the supernatural world. I am acquainted with no
literature that offers anything analogous to this. Compare
Guinevere or Iseult with those Scandinavian furies Gudrun and
Chrimhilde, and you will avow that woman such as chivalry
conceived her, an ideal of sweetness and loveliness set up as the
supreme end of life, is a creation neither classical, nor Christian,
nor Teutonic, but in reality Celtic.

Imaginative power is nearly always proportionate to
concentration of feeling, and lack of the external development of
life. The limited nature of Greek and Italian imagination is due
to the easy expansiveness of the peoples of the South, with whom
the soul, wholly spread abroad, reflects but little within itself.
Compared with the classical imagination, the Celtic imagination
is indeed the infinite contrasted with the finite. In the fine *Mabinogi*
of the *Dream of Maxen Wledig*, the Emperor Maximus beholds in
a dream a young maiden so beautiful, that on waking he declares
he cannot live without her. For several years his envoys scour the
world in search of her; at last she is discovered in Brittany. So is
it with the Celtic race; it has worn itself out in taking dreams for
realities, and in pursuing its splendid visions. The essential
element in the Celt's poetic life is the *adventure* — that is to say,
the pursuit of the unknown, an endless quest after an object ever

flying from desire. It was of this that St Brandan dreamed, that Peredur sought with his mystic chivalry, that Knight Owen asked of his subterranean journeyings. This race desires the infinite, it thirsts for it, and pursues it at all costs, beyond the tomb, beyond hell itself. The characteristic failing of the Breton peoples, the tendency to drunkenness — a failing which, according to the traditions of the sixth century, was the cause of their disasters — is due to this invincible need of illusion. Do not say that it is an appetite for gross enjoyment; never has there been a people more sober and more alien to all sensuality. No, the Bretons sought in mead what Owen, St Brandan, and Peredur sought in their own way, — the vision of the invisible world. To this day in Ireland drunkenness forms a part of all Saint's Day festivals — that is to say, the festivals which best have retained their national and popular aspect.

Thence arises the profound sense of the future and of the eternal destinies of his race, which has ever borne up the Cymry, and kept him young still beside his conquerors who have grown old. Thence that dogma of the resurrection of the heroes, which appears to have been one of those that Christianity found most difficulty in rooting out. Thence *Celtic Messianism*, that belief in a future avenger who shall restore Cambria, and deliver her out of the hands of her oppressors, like the mysterious Leminok promised by Merlin, the Lez-Breiz of the Armoricans, the Arthur of the Welsh. The hand that arose from the mere, when the sword of Arthur fell therein, that seized it, and brandished it thrice, is the hope of the Celtic races. It is thus that little peoples dowered with imagination revenge themselves on their conquerors. Feeling themselves to be strong inwardly and weak outwardly, they protest, they exult; and such a strife unloosing their might, renders them capable of miracles. Nearly all great appeals to the supernatural are due to peoples hoping against all hope. Who shall say what in our own times has fermented in the bosom of the most stubborn, the most powerless of nationalities, — Poland? Israel in humiliation dreamed of the spiritual conquest of the world, and the dream has come to pass...

Notes

1. To avoid all misunderstanding, I ought to point out that by the

word *Celtic* I designate here, not the whole of the great race which, at a remote epoch, formed the population of nearly the whole of Western Europe, but simply the four groups which, in our days, still merit this name, as opposed to the Teutons and to the Neo-Latin peoples. These four groups are: (1) The inhabitants of Wales or Cambria, and the peninsula of Cornwall, bearing even now the ancient name of *Cymry*; (2) the *Breton bretonnants*, or dwellers in French Brittany speaking Bas-Breton, who represent an emigration of the Cymry from Wales; (3) the Gaels of the North of Scotland speaking Gaelic; (4) the Irish, although a very profound line of demarcation separates Ireland from the rest of the Celtic family. [Renan's notes.] [It is also necessary to point out that Renan in this essay applies the name *Breton* both to the Bretons proper, *i.e.* the inhabitants of Brittany, and to the British members of the Celtic races. — *Translator's Note.*]

2. Theophile Hersart de la Villemarqué (1815-95) produced a famous collection of songs of Brittany, *Barzas-Breiz* (1839).

4

Matthew Arnold, from *On the Study of Celtic Literature*, 1867

Matthew Arnold (1822-88) followed his long lecture of 1867 with several other pieces devoted to Irish matters, 'Thomas Davis rewritten for the Murdstones', in Seamus Deane's memorable phrase. See no.10 for Yeats's reply to Renan and Arnold.

...'For dulness, the creeping Saxons', — says an old Irish poem, assigning the characteristics for which different nations are celebrated:

> For acuteness and valour, the Greeks,
> For excessive pride, the Romans,
> For dulness, the creeping Saxons;
> For beauty and amorousness, the Gaedhils.

We have seen in what sense, and with what explanation, this characterisation of the German may be allowed to stand; now let us come to the beautiful and amorous Gaedhil. Or rather, let us find a definition which may suit both branches of the Celtic family, the Cymri as well as the Gael. It is clear that special circumstances may have developed some one side in the national character of Cymri or Gael, Welshman or Irishman, so that the observer's notice shall be readily caught by this side, and yet it may be impossible to adopt it as characteristic of the Celtic nature generally. For instance, in his beautiful essay on the poetry of the Celtic races, M. Renan, with his eyes fixed on the Bretons and the Welsh, is struck with the timidity, the shyness, the delicacy of the Celtic nature, its preference for a retired life, its embarrassment at having to deal with the great world. He talks of his 'douce petite race naturellement chrétienne,' his 'race fière et timide, à l'extérieur gauche et embarrassée.' But it is evident that this description, however well it may do for the Cymri, will never do for the Gael, never do for the typical Irishman of Donnybrook fair. Again, M. Renan's 'infinie délicatesse de sentiment qui caractérise la race Celtique', how little that accords with the popular conception of an Irishman who wants to borrow money! *Sentiment* is, however, the word which marks where the Celtic races really touch and are one; sentimental, if the Celtic nature is to be characterised by a single term, is the best term to take. An organisation quick to feel impressions, and feeling them very strongly; a lively personality therefore, keenly sensitive to joy and to sorrow; this is the main point. If the downs of life too much outnumber the ups, this temperament, just because it is so quickly and nearly conscious of all impressions, may no doubt be seen shy and wounded; it may be seen in wistful regret, it may be seen in passionate, penetrating melancholy; but its essence is to aspire ardently after life, light, and emotion, to be expansive, adventurous, and gay. Our word *gay*, it is said, is itself Celtic. It is not from *gaudium*, but from the Celtic *gair*, to laugh; and the impressionable Celt, soon up and soon down, is the more down because it is so his nature to be up — to be sociable, hospitable, eloquent, admired, figuring away brilliantly. He loves bright colours, he easily becomes audacious, overcrowing, full of fanfaronade. The German, say the physiologists, has the larger volume of intestines (and who that has ever seen a German at a table-d'hôte will not readily believe this?), the Frenchman has the more developed organs of respiration. That is just the expansive, eager Celtic nature; the head in the air, snuffing and snorting; 'a proud look and a high stomach', as the Psalmist says, but without any such settled savage temper as the Psalmist seems to impute by those words. For good and for bad, the Celtic genius is more airy and unsubstantial, goes less near the ground, than the German. The Celt is often called sensual; but it is not so much the vulgar satisfactions of sense that attract him as emotion and excitement; he is truly, as I began by saying, sentimental.

Sentimental, — 'always ready to react against the despotism of fact'; that is the description a great friend[1] of the Celt gives of him; and it is not a bad description of the sentimental temperament; it lets us into the secret of its dangers and of its habitual want of success. Balance, measure, and patience, these are the eternal conditions, even supposing the happiest temperament to start with, of high success; and balance, measure, and patience are just what the Celt has never had. Even in the world of spiritual creation, he has never, in spite of his admirable gifts of quick perception and warm emotion, succeeded perfectly, because he never has had steadiness, patience, sanity enough to comply with the conditions under which alone can expression be perfectly given to the finest perceptions and emotions. The Greek has the same perceptive, emotional temperament as the Celt, but he adds to this temperament the sense of *measure*; hence his admirable success in the plastic arts, in which the Celtic genius, with its chafing against the despotism of fact, its perpetual straining after mere emotion, has accomplished nothing. In the comparatively petty art of ornamentation, in rings, brooches, crosiers, relic-cases, and so on, he has done just enough to show his delicacy of taste, his happy temperament; but the grand difficulties of painting and sculpture, the prolonged dealings of spirit with matter, he has never had patience for. Take the more spiritual arts of music and poetry. All that emotion alone can do in music the Celt has done; the very soul of emotion breathes in the Scotch and Irish airs; but with all this power of musical feeling, what has the Celt, so eager for emotion that he has not patience for science, effected in music to be compared with what the less emotional German, steadily developing his musical feeling with the science of a Sebastian Bach or a Beethoven, has effected? In poetry, again, — poetry which the Celt has so passionately, so nobly loved; poetry where emotion counts for so much, but where reason, too, reason, measure, sanity, also count for so much, — the Celt has shown genius, indeed, splendid genius; but even here his faults have clung to him, and hindered him from producing great works, such as other nations with a genius for poetry, — the Greeks say, or the Italians, — have produced. The Celt has not produced great poetical works, he has only produced poetry with an air of greatness investing it all, and sometimes giving, moreover, to short pieces, or to passages, lines, and snatches of long pieces, singular beauty and power. And yet he loved poetry so much that he grudged no pains to it; but the true art, the *architectonicé* which shapes great works, such as the *Agamemnon* or the *Divine Comedy*, comes only after a steady, deep-searching survey, a firm conception of the facts of human life, which the Celt has not patience for. So he runs off into technic, where he employs the utmost elaboration, and attains astonishing skill; but in the contents of his poetry you have only so much interpretation of the world as the first dash of a quick, strong perception, and then sentiment, infinite sentiment, can bring you. Here, too, his want of sanity and steadfastness has kept the Celt back from the highest success.

If his rebellion against fact has thus lamed the Celt even in spiritual work, how much more must it have lamed him in the world of business and politics! The skilful and resolute appliance of means to ends which is needed both to make progress in material civilisation, and also to form powerful states, is just what the Celt has least turn for. He is sensual, as I have said, or at least sensuous; loves bright colours, company, and pleasure; and here he is like the Greek and Latin races; but compare the talent the Greek and Latin (or Latinised) races have shown for gratifying their senses, for procuring an outward life, rich, luxurious, splendid, with the Celt's failure to reach any material civilisation sound and satisfying, and not out at elbows, poor, slovenly, and half-barbarous. The sensuousness of the Greek made Sybaris and Corinth, the sensuousness of the Latin made Rome and Baiæ, the sensuousness of the Latinised Frenchman makes Paris; the sensuousness of the Celt proper has made Ireland. Even in his ideal heroic times, his gay and sensuous nature cannot carry him, in the appliances of his favourite life of sociability and pleasure, beyond the gross and creeping Saxon whom he despises; the regent Breas, we are told in the *Battle of Moytura of the Fomorians*, became unpopular because 'the knives of his people were not greased at his table, nor did their breath smell of ale at the banquet'. In its grossness and barbarousness is not that Saxon, as Saxon as it can be? just what the Latinised Norman, sensuous and sociable like the Celt, but with the talent to make this bent of his serve to a practical embellishment of his mode of living, found so disgusting in the Saxon.

And as in material civilisation he has been ineffectual, so has the Celt been ineffectual in politics. This colossal, impetuous, adventurous wanderer, the Titan of the early world, who in primitive times fills so large a place on earth's scene, dwindles and dwindles as history goes on, and at last is shrunk to what we now see him. For ages and ages the world has been constantly slipping, ever more and more, out of the Celt's grasp. 'They went forth to the war,' Ossian says most truly, '*but they always fell.*'

And yet, if one sets about constituting an ideal genius, what a great deal of the Celt does one find oneself drawn to put into it! Of an ideal genius one does not want the elements, any of them, to be in a state of weakness; on the contrary, one wants all of them to be in the highest state of power; but with a law of measure, of harmony, presiding over the whole. So the sensibility of the Celt, if everything else were not sacrificed to it, is a beautiful and admirable force. For sensibility, the power of quick and strong perception and emotion, is one of the very prime constituents of genius, perhaps its most positive constituent; it is to the soul what good senses are to the body, the grand natural condition of successful activity. Sensibility gives genius its materials; one cannot have too much of it, if one can but keep its master and not be its slave. Do not let us wish that the Celt had had less sensibility, but that he had been more master of it. Even as it is, if his sensibility has been a source of weakness to him, it has been a source of power too, and a source of happiness. Some people have found in the Celtic nature and its sensibility the main root out of which chivalry and romance and the glorification of a feminine ideal spring; this is a great question, with which I cannot deal here. Let me notice in passing, however, that there is, in truth, a Celtic air about the extravagance of chivalry, its reaction against the despotism of fact, its straining human nature further than it will stand. But putting all this question of chivalry and its origin on one side, no doubt the sensibility of the Celtic nature, its nervous exaltation, have something feminine in them, and the Celt is thus peculiarly disposed to feel the spell of the feminine idiosyncrasy; he has an affinity to it; he is not far from its secret. Again, his sensibility gives him a peculiarly near and intimate feeling of nature and the life of nature; here, too, he seems in a special way attracted by the secret before him, the secret of natural beauty and natural magic, and to be close to it, to half-divine it. In the productions of the Celtic genius, nothing, perhaps, is so interesting as the evidences of this power: I shall have occasion to give specimens of them by and by. The same sensibility made the Celts full of reverence and enthusiasm for genius, learning, and the things of the mind; *to be a bard, freed a man,* — that is a characteristic stroke of this generous and ennobling ardour of theirs, which no race has ever shown more strongly. Even the extravagance and exaggeration of the sentimental Celtic nature has often something romantic and attractive about it, something which has a sort of smack of misdirected good. The Celt, undisciplinable, anarchical, and turbulent by nature, but out of affection and admiration giving himself body and soul to some leader, that is not a promising political temperament, it is just the opposite of the Anglo-Saxon temperament, disciplinable and steadily obedient within certain limits, but retaining an inalienable part of freedom and self-dependence; but it is a temperament for which one has a kind of sympathy notwithstanding. And very often, for the gay defiant reaction against fact of the lively Celtic nature one has more than sympathy; one feels, in spite of the extravagance, in spite of good sense disapproving, magnetised and exhilarated by it. The Gauls had a rule inflicting a fine on every warrior who, when he appeared on parade, was found to stick out too much in front, — to be corpulent, in short. Such a rule is surely the maddest article of war ever framed, and to people to whom nature has assigned a large volume of intestines, must appear, no doubt, horrible; but yet has it not an audacious, sparkling, immaterial manner with it, which lifts one out of routine, and sets one's spirits in a glow?

...but the Norse poetry seems to have something which from Teutonic sources alone it could not have derived; which the Germans have not, and which the Celts have.

This something is *style*, and the Celts certainly have it in a wonderful measure. Style is the most striking quality of their poetry. Celtic poetry seems to make up to itself for being unable to master the world and give an adequate interpretation of it, by throwing all its force into style, by bending language at any rate to its will, and expressing the ideas it has with unsurpassable intensity, elevation, and effect. It has all through it a sort of intoxication of style, — a *Pindarism*, to use a word formed from the name of the poet, on whom, above all other poets, the power of style seems to have exercised an inspiring and intoxicating effect; and not in its great poets only, in Taliesin, or Llywarch Hen, or Ossian, does the Celtic genius show this Pindarism, but in all its productions:

> The grave of March is this, and this the grave of Gwythyr;
> Here is the grave of Gwgawn Gleddyfrudd;
> But unknown is the grave of Arthur.

That comes from the Welsh *Memorials of the Graves of the Warriors*, and if we compare it with the familiar memorial inscriptions of an English churchyard (for we English have so much Germanism in us that our productions offer abundant examples of German want of style as well as of its opposite):

Afflictions sore long time I bore,
Physicians were in vain,
Till God did please Death should me seize
And ease me of my pain —

if, I say, we compare the Welsh memorial lines with the English, which in their *Gemeinheit* of style are truly Germanic, we shall get a clear sense of what that Celtic talent for style I have been speaking of is.

Or take this epitaph of an Irish Celt, Angus the Culdee, whose *Félire*, or festology, I have already mentioned; — a festology in which, at the end of the eighth or beginning of the ninth century, he collected from 'the countless hosts of the illuminated books of Erin' (to use his own words) the festivals of the Irish saints, his poem having a stanza for every day in the year. The epitaph on Angus, who died at Cluain Eidhnech, in Queen's County, runs thus:

Angus in the assembly of Heaven,
Here are his tomb and his bed;
It is from hence he went to death,
In the Friday, to holy Heaven.

It was in Cluain Eidhnech he was rear'd;
It was in Cluain Eidhnech he was buried;
In Cluain Eidhnech, of many crosses,
He first read his psalms.

That is by no eminent hand; and yet a Greek epitaph could not show a finer perception of what constitutes propriety and felicity of style in compositions of this nature. Take the well-known Welsh prophecy about the fate of the Britons:

Their Lord they will praise,
Their speech they will keep,
Their land they will lose,
Except wild Wales.

To however late an epoch that prophecy belongs, what a feeling for style, at any rate, it manifests! And the same thing may be said of the famous Welsh triads. We may put aside all the vexed questions as to their greater or less antiquity, and still what important witness they bear to the genius for literary style of the people who produced them!...

Note

1. Monsieur Henri Martin, whose chapters on the Celts, in his *Histoire de France*, are full of information and interest. [Arnold's note.]

5

Charles Gavan Duffy, from 'The Revival of Irish Literature', 1892

A book was published in 1894 with the title The Revival of Irish Literature. *It consisted of four addresses: two by Duffy, under this general heading, given respectively before the Irish Literary Society in London, in July 1892 and June 1893; one by George Sigerson, delivered at the opening of the Irish National Literary Society in Dublin, entitled 'Irish Literature: Its Origin, Environment, and Influence'; and Douglas Hyde's 'The Necessity for De-Anglicising Ireland', delivered before the Irish National Literary Society in Dublin, 25 November 1892 (see no.7).*

Sir Charles Gavan Duffy (1816-1903) had helped to found the Nation *in 1842; he emigrated to Australia in 1855, but returned in the 1890s to lock horns with Yeats in a famous if futile debate about a New Irish Library. Sir George Sigerson (1836-1925) edited* The Poets and Poetry of Munster *(1860), and then, in 1897,* Bards of the Gael and Gall. *Douglas Hyde (1860-1949) made an impact with his* Love Songs of Connaught *(1893), became President in 1915 of the Gaelic League he had been instrumental in founding, and from 1939 to 1944 was the first President of Ireland.*

Liberty will do much for a nation, but it will not do everything. Among a people who do not know and reverence their own ancestors, who do not submit cheerfully to lawful authority, and do not love the eternal principles of justice, it will do little. But moral sentiments, generous impulses, religious feelings still survive in the Irish race, and they give assurance that in that mystic clime on the verge of the Western Ocean, where the more debasing currents of European civilisation only reach it at high tide, there is place for a great experiment for humanity. There within our circling seas we may rear a race in which the fine qualities of the Celtic family, fortified by the sterner strength of the North, and disciplined by the Norman genius of Munster may at last have fair play; where, at lowest a pious and gallant race may after long struggles and nameless sufferings possess their own soil and their own souls in peace...

When I say we do not understand Ireland, I do not mean merely that we are imperfectly acquainted with its history, its literature, its art, and its memorable men; but which of us studies Irish statistics till he understands them as he does a current account with a tradesman or a banker? Which of us studies the topography, the political and commercial geography, the botany, the geology, the resources and deficiencies of the country so as to qualify him to handle its interests, in a parish or a parliament, if that task should present itself?

The prosperous wiseacre whom the Germans call a Philistine, and the French an *épicier*, will tell you that study does not pay. But that respectable citizen may be assured that whatever he values most in his narrow life, whatever adds to its comfort and convenience, whatever simplifies and facilitates his beloved trade (of which steam and electricity are the nerves and sinews) is nothing else than the remote result of some student's midnight toil. The garments he wears, the furniture of his trim home, not less than the laws which protect his life and the customs which render it easy and pleasant, even the ideas grown commonplace by time which he daily thinks he is thinking, were discovered, invented, or brought from regions more civilised, by men whose toil he undervalues; and if all he owes to study and the intellectual enterprise it begets were snatched away, his home would be almost as naked as the Redman's wigwam. But if the man of business be moreover a man of meditation and culture, he and his class are among the most indispensable forces of a nation, for it is such men who turn the student's airy speculation into accomplished fact.

Of all studies that one which a nation can least safely dispense with is a study of its own history. Some one has invented the audacious axiom that history never repeats itself, but it would be truer to affirm that history is always repeating itself; assuredly in our own history identical weaknesses and identical virtues recur from generation to generation, and to know them may teach us where weak places in national and individual character need to be fortified and strong ones developed.

Of politics, if it were only the politics of a parish, what can we know worth knowing unless the lamp of history lights the misty way? And the great problem of all — for what special career do the gifts and deficiencies of our race, their position on the globe, their past and their present career best fit them? — only a familiarity with their annals will enable any one to say...

For my part I would rather see our people developed according to their special gifts than see them masters of limitless territory or inexhaustible gold reefs. A Celtic people trained to become all that their nature fits them to be — humane, joyous, and generous, living diligent, tranquil lives in their own land, and sending out from time to time, as of old, men whose gifts and faculties fitted them to become benefactors of mankind — that is the destiny I desire for my country. None of us can be ignorant of the fact that a change has come over the national character in latter times which is not altogether a change for the better. The people are more alert and resolute than of old, and that is well; but they are more gloomy and resentful, and something of the piety and simplicity of old seems to have disappeared. Nature made them blithe, frank, and hospitable; pleasant comrades and trusty friends; but hard laws and hard taskmasters have sometimes perverted their native disposition. To my thinking that patient, long-suffering, bitterly wronged people still preserve fresh and perennial many of the spiritual endowments which are among the greatest possessions of a nation. But, like soldiers returning from a long campaign, who bring back something of the manners and *morale* of the camp, twenty years of agitation, which however just and necessary was inevitably demoralising, has blunted their moral sensibility. Blessed be those who will warn them that to be just and considerate towards friends and opponents, to refrain from cruelty or wrong under any temptation, and to speak and act and applaud only the rigid truth, are the practices which make nations honoured and happy...

I have spoken only of the revival of literature for the people, for happily there has never been altogether wanting a literature for the studious and thoughtful, maintained by the spontaneous zeal of a few gifted men and women. It slept at times, but only for an interval. O'Conor and Curry, Miss Edgeworth and Lady Morgan, Banim and Griffin,[1] have had successors down to our own day when we are still at times delighted with glowing historic or legendary stories, or charming idylls of the people, bright and natural as a bunch of shamrocks with the dew of Munster fresh upon them. One secluded scholar has spent his manhood

71

collecting our national records with a care and zeal which in any other country would compel the recognition and reward of the State; a group of scholars not connected, I think, except by the *camaraderie* of a kindred pursuit, have created a great revival in Gaelic literature; and the Irish press has not for a generation devoted so much thought to native literature and art, national customs and manners, as it does just now. There are still local periodicals full of the enthusiasm of old for our national antiquities, and it is pleasant to know that they are often sustained by men who differ from the majority in race, creed, and political opinions. I rarely see without a strong sentiment of affection and sympathy a little sixpenny magazine conducted for twenty years by the zeal of one solitary priest who watches like a father over whatever concerns the Irish intellect. It is good, therefore, to know that we are not sailing against wind and tide. The spirit of the era, the state of men's minds as well as the manifest need of such an enterprise are favourable to our experiment, and I trust it shall not fail by any indolence or apathy of those who have taken the responsibility of initiating it.

If I were to express in one phrase the aim of this Society, and of kindred societies, and of the literary revival of which I have been speaking, it is to begin another deliberate attempt to make of our Celtic people all they are fit to become — to increase knowledge among them, and lay its foundations deep and sure; to strengthen their convictions and enlarge their horizon; and to tend the flame of national pride, which, with sincerity of purpose and fervour of soul, constitute the motive power of great enterprises. Intellectual experiments have not in our own day been unfruitful of results. Early in this century the philosopher Arago organised a literary propaganda in Paris, before which Louis Philippe in the end vanished like a spectre. Dr Newman and a few of his friends in Oxford attacked the Puritanism of the English Church with results with which we are all familiar. One or two Westminster reviewers, and two or three Manchester manufacturers, reversed the commercial policy of England in less than a dozen years. Do not be deterred by the manifest difficulties of the task. The task is difficult but noble, for it is better to have the teaching of a people than the governing of them. Nor shall such labour lack its fitting reward, for toil and sacrifice in a generous cause are among the keenest enjoyments given to man.

Note

1. Charles O'Conor (1710-91) produced in 1788 an edition of John Curry's *Historical and critical review of the civil wars in Ireland...*; Maria Edgeworth (1767-1849) made her name with *Castle Rackrent* (1800); Lady Morgan (Sydney Owenson, ?1776-1859), wrote several novels, including *The Wild Irish Girl* (1806); of the Banim brothers, Michael (1796-1874) was more prolific than John (1798-1842); Gerald Griffin (1803-40) had his first novel, *The Collegians*, published in 1829.

6

W. B. Yeats, 'Hopes and Fears for Irish Literature', 1892

This was first published in United Ireland, *15 October 1892. The text here is taken from* Uncollected Prose, *ed. John Frayne (London, 1970).*

When I come over here from London or cross over to London I am always struck afresh by the difference between the cultivated people in England and the cultivated people — alas! too few — here in Ireland. They could not differ more if they were divided from each other by a half score of centuries. I am thinking especially of the men of my own age, though not entirely of them. In England amongst the best minds art and poetry are becoming every day more entirely ends in themselves, and all life is made more and more but so much fuel to feed their fire. It is partly the influence of France that is bringing this about. In France a man may do anything he pleases, he may spend years in prison even, like Verlaine, and the more advanced of the young men will speak well of him if he have but loved his art sincerely, and they will worship his name as they worship Verlaine's if he have but made beautiful things and added a little to the world's store of memorable experiences. The influence of France is every year pervading more completely English literary life. The influence of that school which calls itself, in the words of its leader, Verlaine, a school of the sunset, or by the term which was flung at it 'as a reproach, and caught up as a battle cry', Decadants [*sic*] is now the dominating thing in many lives. Poetry is an end in itself; it has nothing to do with thought, nothing to do with philosophy, nothing to do with life, nothing to do with anything but the music of cadence, and beauty of phrase. This is the new doctrine of letters. I well remember the irritated silence that fell upon a noted gathering of the younger English imaginative writers once, when I tried to explain a philosophy of poetry in which I was profoundly interested, and to show the dependence, as I conceived it, of all great art and literature upon conviction and upon heroic life. To them literature had ceased to be the handmaid of humanity, and become instead a terrible queen, in whose services the stars rose and set, and for whose pleasure life stumbles along in the darkness. There is a good deal to be said in favour of all this. Never before, perhaps, were men so anxious to write their best — as they conceive that best — and so entirely loth to bow to the prejudices of the multitude. There is much to be said even for Verlaine, for he who writes well and lives badly is usually of more service to the world at large than he who writes badly and lives well, and he is always better than the crowd who do both indifferently. But one thing cannot be said. It is not possible to call a literature produced in this way the literature of energy and youth. The age which has produced it is getting old and feeble, and sits in the chimney-corner carving all manner of curious and even beautiful things upon the staff that can no longer guide its steps. Here in Ireland we are living in a young age, full of hope and promise — a young age which has only just begun to make its literature. It was only yesterday that it cut from the green hillside the staff which is to help its steps upon the long road. There is no carving upon the staff, the rough bark is still there, and the knots are many upon its side.

When I talk to people of literary ambition here in Ireland, I find them holding that literature must be the expression of conviction, and be the garment of noble emotion and not an end in itself. I found them most interested in the literary forms that give most opportunity for the display of great characters and great passions. Turning to our literature I find that such forms are plenty, often absolutely crude and uninteresting, as in the case of MᶜCarthy's 'Fardiah', and Joyce's 'Blanid'; occasionally crude and interesting, like Joyce's 'Deirdre', and Ferguson's 'Congal';[1] and once or twice beyond all praise and all imitation like Ferguson's 'Conary', and his better known 'Vengeance of the Welshmen of Tirawley'. But side by side with this robustness and rough energy of ours there goes most utter indifference to art, the most dire carelessness, the most dreadful intermixture of the commonplace. I have before me a letter from a young man in a remote part of Ireland asking an opinion about some verses and telling me, as if it was a special merit, that he did them at great speed, two columns in an hour, I think. I have not yet read his poems; but it is obvious that good poetry cannot be done in this fashion. There is a printed letter of John Francis O'Donnell's,[2] in which he claims to have written I know not how many columns of verse and prose in two or three days. Yet, he who would write a memorable song must be ready to give often days to a few lines, and be ready, perhaps, to pay for it afterwards with certain other days of dire exhaustion and depression, and, if he would be remembered when he is in his grave, he must give to his art the devotion the Crusaders of old gave to their cause and be content to be alone among men, apart alike from their joys and their sorrows, having for companions the multitude of his dreams and for reward the kingdom of his pride. He who would belong to things eternal must for the most part renounce his allotted place amid the things of time. Here in Ireland the art of living interests us greatly, and the art of writing but little. We seek effectiveness rather than depth. We produce good correspondence, good journalists, and good talkers, and few profound and solitary students. 'You Irish people', said a witty woman to me once, 'will never have a future because you have a present'. 'We are', said a famous Irishman[3] to me, 'too political to be poets, we are the greatest talkers since the Greeks, we are a nation of brilliant failures.' I no more complain of this absorption in mere living than I complain of the narrow devotion to mere verbal beauty of the newest generation of literary men in France and England. We have the limitations of dawn. They have the limitations of sunset. We also in the coming centuries will grow into the broad noon and pass on at last into twilight and darkness.

Can we but learn a little of their skill, and a little of their devotion to form, a little of their hatred of the commonplace and the banal, we may make all these restless energies of ours alike the inspiration and the theme of a new and wonderful literature. We have behind us in the past the most moving legends and a history full of lofty passions. If we can but take that history and those legends and turn them into dramas, poems, and stories full of the living soul of the present, and make them massive with conviction and profound with reverie, we may deliver that new great utterance for which the world is waiting. Men are growing tired of mere subtleties of form, self-conscious art and no less self-conscious simplicity. But if we are to do this we must study all things Irish, until we know the peculiar glamour that belongs to this nation, and how to distinguish it from the glamour of other countries and other races. 'Know thyself' is a true advice for nations as well as for individuals. We must know and feel our national faults and limitations no less than our national virtues, and care for things Gaelic and Irish, not because we hold them

76

better than things Saxon and English, but because they belong
to us, and because our lives are to be spent among them, whether
they be good or evil. Whether the power that lies latent in this
nation is but the seed of some meagre shrub or the seed from
which shall rise the vast and spreading tree is not for us to consider.
It is our duty to care for that seed and tend it until it has grown
to perfection after its kind.

Notes

1. The references are to Denis Florence MacCarthy's poem 'Ferdiah',
two epics by P. W. Joyce, and Sir Samuel Ferguson's epic *Congal*.
2. John Francis O'Donnell (1837-74), an Irish poet whose collected
poems Yeats reviewed unfavourably in the *Boston Pilot* in April 1891 (see
Letters to the New Island (New York, 1934)).
3. Oscar Wilde.

7

Douglas Hyde, from 'The Necessity for De-Anglicising Ireland', 1892

This was an address delivered before the Irish National Literary Society in Dublin, 25 November 1892 (see no.5).

When we speak of 'The Necessity for De-Anglicising the Irish Nation', we mean it, not as a protest against imitating what is *best* in the English people, for that would be absurd, but rather to show the folly of neglecting what is Irish, and hastening to adopt, pell-mell, and indiscriminately, everything that is English, simply because it *is* English.

This is a question which most Irishmen will naturally look at from a National point of view, but it is one which ought also to claim the sympathies of every intelligent Unionist, and which, as I know, does claim the sympathy of many.

If we take a bird's eye view of our island today, and compare it with what it used to be, we must be struck by the extraordinary fact that the nation which was once, as every one admits, one of the most classically learned and cultured nations in Europe, is now one of the least so; how one of the most reading and literary peoples has become one of the *least* studious and most *un*-literary, and how the present art products of one of the quickest, most sensitive, and most artistic races on earth are now only distinguished for their hideousness.

I shall endeavour to show that this failure of the Irish people in recent times has been largely brought about by the race diverging during this century from the right path, and ceasing to be Irish without becoming English. I shall attempt to show that with the bulk of the people this change took place quite recently, much more recently than most people imagine, and is, in fact, still going on. I should also like to call attention to the illogical position of men who drop their own language to speak English, of men who translate their euphonious Irish names into English monosyllables, of men who read English books, and know nothing about Gaelic literature, nevertheless protesting as a matter of sentiment that they hate the country which at every hand's turn they rush to imitate.

I wish to show you that in Anglicising ourselves wholesale we have thrown away with a light heart the best claim which we have upon the world's recognition of us as a separate nationality. What did Mazzini say?[1] What is Goldwin Smith[2] never tired of declaiming? What do the *Spectator* and *Saturday Review* harp on? That we ought to be content as an integral part of the United Kingdom because we have lost the notes of nationality, our language and customs.

It has always been very curious to me how Irish sentiment sticks in this half-way house — how it continues to apparently hate the English, and at the same time continues to imitate them; how it continues to clamour for recognition as a distinct nationality, and at the same time throws away with both hands what would make it so. If Irishmen only went a little farther they would become good Englishmen in sentiment also. But — illogical as it appears — there seems not the slightest sign or probability of their taking that step. It is the curious certainty that come what may Irishmen will continue to resist English rule, even though it should be for their good, which prevents many of our nation from becoming Unionists upon the spot. It is a fact, and we must face it as a fact, that although they adopt English habits and copy England in every way, the great bulk of Irishmen and Irishwomen over the whole world are known to be filled with a dull, ever-abiding animosity against her, and — right or wrong — to grieve when she prospers, and joy when she is hurt. Such movements as Young Irelandism, Fenianism, Land Leagueism, and Parliamentary obstruction seem always to gain their sympathy and support. It is just because there appears no earthly chance of their becoming good members of the Empire that I urge that they should not remain in the anomalous position they are in, but since they absolutely refuse to become the one thing, that they become the other; cultivate what they have rejected, and build up an Irish nation on Irish lines.

But you ask, why should we wish to make Ireland more Celtic than it is — why should we de-Anglicise it at all?

I answer because the Irish race is at present in a most anomalous position, imitating England and yet apparently hating it. How can it produce anything good in literature, art, or institutions as long as it is actuated by motives so contradictory? Besides, I believe it is our Gaelic past which, though the Irish race does not recognise it just at present, is really at the bottom of the Irish heart, and prevents us becoming citizens of the Empire, as, I think, can be easily proved.

To say that Ireland has not prospered under English rule is simply a truism; all the world admits it, England does not deny it. But the English retort is ready. You have not prospered, they say, because you would not settle down contentedly, like the Scotch, and form part of the Empire. 'Twenty years of good, resolute, grandfatherly government', said a well-known Englishman, will solve the Irish question. He possibly made the period too short, but let us suppose this. Let us suppose for a moment — which is impossible — that there were to arise a series of Cromwells in England for the space of one hundred years, able administrators of the Empire, careful rulers of Ireland, developing to the utmost our national resources, whilst they unremittingly stamped out every spark of national feeling, making Ireland a land of wealth and factories, whilst they extinguished every thought and every idea that was Irish, and left us, at last, after a hundred years of good government, fat, wealthy, and populous, but with all our characteristics gone, with every external that at present differentiates us from the English lost or dropped; all our Irish names of places and people turned into English names; the Irish language completely extinct; the O's and the Macs dropped; our Irish intonation changed, as far as possible by English schoolmasters into something English; our history no longer remembered or taught; the names of our rebels and martyrs blotted out; our battlefields and traditions forgotten; the fact that we were not of Saxon origin dropped out of sight and memory, and let me now put the question — How many Irishmen are there who would purchase material prosperity at such a price? It is exactly such a question as this and the answer to it that shows the difference between the English and Irish race. Nine Englishmen out of ten would jump to make the exchange, and I as firmly believe that nine Irishmen out of ten would indignantly refuse it.

And yet this awful idea of complete Anglicisation, which I have here put before you in all its crudity is, and has been, making silent inroads upon us for nearly a century.

Its inroads have been silent, because, had the Gaelic race perceived what was being done, or had they been once warned of what was taking place in their own midst, they would, I think, never have allowed it. When the picture of complete Anglicisation is drawn for them in all its nakedness Irish sentimentality becomes suddenly a power and refuses to surrender its birthright...

So much for the greatest stroke of all in our Anglicisation, the loss of our language. I have often heard people thank God that if the English gave us nothing else they gave us at least their language. In this way they put a bold face upon the matter, and pretend that the Irish language is not worth knowing, and has no literature. But the Irish language *is* worth knowing, or why would the greatest philologists of Germany, France, and Italy be emulously studying it, and it *does* possess a literature, or why would a German savant have made the calculation that the books written in Irish between the eleventh and seventeenth centuries, and still extant, would fill a thousand octavo volumes.

I have no hesitation at all in saying that every Irish-feeling Irishman, who hates the reproach of West-Britonism,[3] should set himself to encourage the efforts, which are being made to keep alive our once great national tongue. The losing of it is our greatest blow, and the sorest stroke that the rapid Anglicisation of Ireland has inflicted upon us. In order to de-Anglicise ourselves we must at once arrest the decay of the language. We must bring pressure upon our politicians not to snuff it out by their tacit discouragement merely because they do not happen themselves to understand it. We must arouse some spark of patriotic inspiration among the peasantry who still use the language, and put an end to the shameful state of feeling — a thousand-tongued reproach to our leaders and statesmen — which makes young men and women blush and hang their heads when overheard speaking their own language.[4] Maynooth has at last come splendidly to the front, and it is now incumbent upon every clerical student to attend lectures in the Irish language and history during the first three years of his course. But in order to keep the Irish language alive where it is still spoken — which is the utmost we can at present aspire to — nothing less than a house-to-house visitation and exhortation of the people themselves will do, something — though with a very different purpose — analogous to the procedure that James Stephens adopted throughout Ireland when he found her like a corpse on the dissecting table. This and some system of giving medals or badges of honour to every family who will guarantee that they have always spoken Irish amongst themselves during the year. But unfortunately, distracted as we are and torn by contending factions, it is impossible to find either men or money to carry out this simple remedy, although to a dispassionate foreigner — to a Zeuss, Jubainville, Zimmer, Kuno Meyer, Windisch, or Ascoli, and the rest[5] — this is of greater importance than whether Mr. Redmond[6] or Mr. MacCarthy[7] lead the largest wing of the Irish party for the moment, or Mr. So-and-So succeed with his election petition. To a person taking a bird's-eye view of the situation a hundred or five hundred years hence, believe me, it will also appear of greater importance than any mere temporary wrangle, but, unhappily, our countrymen cannot be brought to see this.

We can, however, insist, and we *shall* insist if Home Rule be carried, that the Irish language, which so many foreign scholars of the first calibre find so worthy of study, shall be placed on a par with — or even above — Greek, Latin, and modern languages, in all examinations held under the Irish Government. We can also insist, and we *shall* insist, that in those baronies where the children speak Irish, Irish shall be taught, and that Irish-speaking schoolmasters, petty sessions clerks, and even magistrates be appointed in Irish-speaking districts. If all this were done, it should not be very difficult, with the aid of the foremost foreign scholars, to bring about a tone of thought which would make it disgraceful for an educated Irishman — especially of the old Celtic race, MacDermotts, O'Conors, O'Sullivans, MacCarthys, O'Neills — to be ignorant of his own language — would make it at least as disgraceful as for an educated Jew to be quite ignorant of Hebrew...

I have now mentioned a few of the principal points on which it would be desirable for us to move, with a view to de-Anglicising ourselves; but perhaps the principal point of all I have taken for granted. That is the necessity for encouraging the use of Anglo-Irish literature instead of English books, especially instead of English periodicals. We must set our face sternly against penny dreadfuls, shilling shockers, and still more, the garbage of vulgar English weeklies like *Bow Bells* and the *Police Intelligence*. Every house should have a copy of Moore and Davis. In a word, we must strive to cultivate everything that is most racial, most smacking of the soil, most Gaelic, most Irish, because in spite of the little admixture of Saxon blood in the north-east corner, this island *is* and will *ever* remain Celtic at the core, far more Celtic than most people imagine, because, as I have shown you, the names of our people are no criterion of their race. On racial lines, then, we shall best develop, following the bent of our own natures; and, in order to do this, we must create a strong feeling against West-Britonism, for it — if we give it the least chance, or show it the smallest quarter — will overwhelm us like a flood, and we shall find ourselves toiling painfully behind the English at each step following the same fashions, only six months behind the English ones; reading the same books, only months behind them; taking up the same fads, after they have become stale *there*, following *them* in our dress, literature, music, games, and ideas, only a long time after them and a vast way behind. We will become, what, I fear, we are largely at present, a nation of imitators, the Japanese of Western Europe, lost to the power of native initiative and alive only to second-hand assimilation. I do not think I am overrating this danger. We are probably at once the most assimilative and the most sensitive nation in Europe. A lady in Boston said to me that the Irish immigrants had become Americanised on the journey out before ever they landed at Castle Gardens. And when I ventured to regret it, she said, shrewdly, 'If they did not at once become Americanised they would not be Irish.' I knew fifteen Irish workmen who were working in a haggard in England give up talking Irish amongst themselves because the English farmer laughed at them. And yet O'Connell used to call us the 'finest peasantry in Europe'. Unfortunately, he took little care that we should remain so. We must teach ourselves to be less sensitive, we must teach ourselves not to be ashamed of ourselves, because the Gaelic people can never produce its best before the world as long as it remains tied to the apron-strings of another race and another island, waiting for *it* to move before it will venture to take any step itself.

In conclusion, I would earnestly appeal to every one, whether Unionist or Nationalist, who wishes to see the Irish nation produce its best — surely whatever our politics are we all wish that — to set his face against this constant running to England for our books, literature, music, games, fashions, and ideas. I appeal to every one whatever his politics — for this is no political matter — to do his best to help the Irish race to develop in future upon Irish lines, even at the risk of encouraging national aspirations, because upon Irish lines alone can the Irish race once more become what it was of yore — one of the most original, artistic, literary, and charming peoples of Europe.

Notes

1. Guiseppe Mazzini (1805-72), the Italian patriot often invoked by the Irish.
2. Goldwin Smith (1823-1910) was an historical writer, author of *Irish History and Irish Character* (1861).
3. Thomas Spring-Rice (1790-1866), first Baron Monteagle of Brandon in Kerry, is said by the OED to be the first Irishman to have nicknamed himself a 'West Briton'. It soon became a term of abuse amongst Irish nationalists, and crops up frequently in the debate, and in fictional representations of that debate (such as Joyce's *Dubliners*).
4. As an instance of this, I mention the case of a young man I met on the road coming from the fair of Tuam, some ten miles away. I saluted him in Irish, and he answered me in English. 'Don't you speak Irish', said I. 'Well, I declare to God, sir', he said, 'my father and mother hasn't a word of English, but still, I don't speak Irish.' This was absolutely true for him. There are thousands upon thousands of houses all over Ireland today where the old people invariably use Irish in addressing the children, and the children as invariably answer in English, the children understanding Irish but not speaking it, the parents understanding their children's English but unable to use it themselves. In a great many cases, I should almost say most, the children are not conscious of the existence of two languages. I remember asking a gossoon a couple of miles west of Ballaghaderreen in the Co. Mayo, some questions in Irish and he answered them in English. At last I said to him, 'Nach labhrann tu Gaedheilg?' (i.e., 'Don't you speak Irish?') and his answer was, 'And isn't it Irish I'm spaking?' 'No *a-chuisle*,' said I, 'it's not Irish you're speaking, but English.' 'Well then', said he, 'that's how I spoke it ever'! He was quite unconscious that I was addressing him in one language and he answering in another. On a different occasion I spoke Irish to a little girl in a house near Kilfree Junction, Co. Sligo, into which I went while waiting for a train. The girl answered me in Irish until her brother came in. 'Arrah now, Mary', said he, with what was intended to be a most bitter sneer; 'and isn't that a credit to you!' And poor Mary — whom I had with difficulty persuaded to begin — immediately hung her head and changed to English. This is going on from Malin Head to Galway, and from Galway to Waterford, with the exception possibly of a few spots in Donegal and Kerry, where the people are wiser and more national. [Hyde's note.]
5. These were all distinguished European Celtic scholars.
6. John Redmond (1856-1918) stepped into Parnell's shoes after the latter's death in 1891.
7. Justin MacCarthy (1830-1912) was an anti-Parnellite politician and novelist.

8
W. B. Yeats,
'Nationality and Literature', 1893

This was first published in United Ireland, *27 May 1893. The text here is taken from* Uncollected Prose, *ed. John Frayne (London, 1970).*

I am going to talk a little philosophy. If I were addressing an English audience I would not venture to even use the word philosophy, for it is only the Celt who cares much for ideas which have no immediate practical bearing. At least Matthew Arnold has said so, and I think he is right, for the flood-gates of materialism are only half-open among us as yet here in Ireland; perhaps the new age may close them before the tide is quite upon us. Remembering those but half-open gates, I venture into criticism of the fundamentals of literature, and into the discussion of things which, I am proud to say, have never made two blades of grass grow where one did before, or in any other fashion served the material needs of the race. Criticism has been defined as the separation and isolation of some literary tendency, mood, or impression, until we can look at it separated from all other tendencies, moods, or impressions. I wish to separate the general course of literary development and set it apart from mere historical accident and circumstance, and having so done, to examine the stages it passes through, and then to try and point out in what stage the literature of England is, and in what stage the literature of Ireland is. I will have to go far a-field before I come to the case of Ireland, for it is necessary, in the first instance, to find this general law of development. But first let us see if there is an analogy in external nature for this development. Is there any object which we can isolate and watch going through its growth and decay, and thereby perhaps discover a law of development which is common alike to it and to literature. Any tree or plant is just such an object. It grows from a simple seed, and having sent up a little green sprout of no great complexity, though much more complex than its seed, it develops a complex trunk at last and all innumerable and intricate leaves, and flowers, and fruits. Its growth is from unity to multiplicity, from simplicity to complexity, and if we examine the method of this growth, we find that it takes place through a constant sub-division of the constituent cells. I hope to show you that a literature develops in an analogous way, and that this development takes place by a constant sub-division of moods and emotions, corresponding to the sub-division of the cells in the tree. In its youth it is simple, and in its mid-period it grows in complexity, as does the tree when it puts forth many branches, and in its mature age it is covered by an innumerable variety of fruits and flowers and leaves of thought and experience. I will show you, too, that it must go through these periods no matter how greatly we long for finality, no matter how much we desire to make this or that stage permanent. I wish to show you, too, that all these stages are beautiful in their various fashions, and that our desire should be to make each perfect after its kind, and not to try and make one imitate another quite different one, or even a corresponding one to itself in some quite different literature. For all such endeavours will fail, and perhaps, stunt the tree. If I succeed I will show that not only is this literature of England different in character from the literature of Ireland, as different as the beech tree from the oak, but that the two literatures are in quite different stages of their development. I wish to show you also what it is that we can learn from English and other literatures without loss of national individuality; how, we can learn from their complex mature literature to carry to perfection our own simple and immature one. We are gardeners, trying to grow various kinds of trees and flowers that are peculiar to our soil and climate; but we have to go for the art of gardening to men who grow very different flowers and trees in very different soils and climates. But now to apply in detail the analogy of the tree or plant and of its growth by sub-division from simplicity to complexity.

Let us take for our examples the literatures we all know something of, the literatures of Greece and England, though the literature of any other country would, I believe, serve as well. In both you find three clearly-marked periods: first, the period of narrative poetry, the epic or ballad period; next the dramatic period; and after that the period of lyric poetry. In Greece the first period is represented by Homer, who describes great racial or national movements and events, and sings of the Greek race rather than of any particular member of it. After him come Aeschulus [*sic*] and Sophocles, who subdivide these great movements and events into the characters who lived and wrought in them. The Siege of Troy is now no longer the theme, for Agamemnon and Clytemnestra and Oedipus dominate the stage. After the dramatists come the lyric poets, who are known to us through the Greek anthology. And now not only have the racial events disappeared but the great personages themselves, for literature has begun to centre itself about this or that emotion or mood, about the Love or Hatred, the Hope or Fear which were to Aeschulus and Sophocles merely parts of Oedipus or Agamemnon or Clytemnestra, or of some other great tragic man or woman. The poets had at the beginning for their material the national character, and the nationistory, and the national circumstances, and having found an expression of the first in the second, they divided and sub-divided the national imagination, for there was nought else for them to do. They could not suddenly become Turks, or Englishmen, or Frenchmen, and so start with a new character and a new history. They could but investigate and express ever more minutely and subtly the character, and history, and circumstance of climate and scenery, that they had got. When they could subdivide no more, or when the barbarian had defeated them into silence there came a long blank until the next great creative period, when the literature of England arose and went through the same stages, and set to music its very different national character, national history, and national circumstance of climate and of scenery.

In England the first period was represented by the poems of Chaucer, by Mallory's 'King Arthur', [*sic*] and by the ballad writers. England was not to carry this period to the same perfection as did Greece, for her genius inclined her rather to dramatic and lyric expression. In the writings I have named there is no lack of characterization, but every character exists rather as a part of some story, or for the sake of some action, than for its own sake. England had no great epic tales, and so we find this early literature dealing, not with some tale of Troy, or the like, but with innumerable stories and incidents, expressing the general bustle of the national life. As time passed on, men became more and more interested in character for its own sake, until at last they were ripe for the great dramatic movement of Queen Elizabeth's reign. Poetry now no longer reflected the general life, but gave us Lear, Hamlet, and Macbeth, isolated colossal characters, dominating the whole life about them, and deafening into silence the general bustle of the world. But this dramatic period could not last, for literature can never repeat itself and the human spirit must ever go on analyzing itself further and further, and expressing more and more minutely and subtly its own profound activity. The dramatic gave way to the lyrical, and the poets took for their themes the passions and moods that were once but parts of those great characters, and again the part drove out the whole. The great personages fell like immense globes of glass, and scattered into a thousand iridescent fragments, flashing and flickering in the sun. Men ceased to write of Romeo and sang of Love. They though no more of Iago but sang of Hatred. When the time was ripe the English spirit cast up that lyrical outburst of which Byron, Shelley, and Keats were the most characteristic writers. Character, no longer loved for its own sake, or as an expression of the general bustle of life, became merely the mask for some mood or passion, as in Byron's 'Manfred' and in his 'Don Juan'. In other words, the poets began to write but little of individual men and women, but rather of great types, great symbols of passion and of mood, like Alastor, Don Juan, Manfred, Ahasuerus, Prometheus, and Isabella of the Basil Pot. When they tried, as in Byron's plays, to display character for its own sake they failed.

In the age of lyric poetry every kind of subtlety, obscurity, and intricate utterance prevails, for the human spirit has begun to look in upon itself with microscopic eyes and to judge of ideas and feelings apart from their effects upon action. The vast bulk of our moods and feelings are too fine, too subjective, too impalpable to find any clear expression in action or in speech tending towards action, and epic and dramatic poetry must deal with one or other of these. In a lyric age the poets no longer can take their inspiration mainly from external activities and from what are called matters of fact, for they must express every phase of human consciousness no matter how subtle, how vague, how impalpable. With this advancing subtlety poetry steps out of the market-place, out of the general tide of life and becomes a mysterious cult, as it were, an almost secret religion made by the few for the few. To express its fine shades of meaning, an ever more elaborate language, an ever more subtle rhythm has to be invented. The dramatic form, and the ballad and epic forms exist still, of course, but they do so, as the lyric form existed in the age of drama and of epic, and their whole burden is lyrical. The old simplicity has gone out of them, and an often great obscurity has come in its stead. The form of Browning is more commonly than not dramatic or epic, but the substance is lyrical. Another reason why the poetry of the lyric steps aside further and further from the general life is, that in order to express the intricate meaning and subtle changes of mood, it is compelled to combine external objects in ways never or seldom seen in nature. In other words, it is compelled more and more to idealize nature. But the most obvious distinction between the old and the new is the growing complexity of language and thought. Compare, for instance, the description of nature in almost any old ballad, description in which the sea is simply blue and the grass simply green and the flowers simply sweet-smelling, with such a description as that contained in Tennyson's famous line, 'A roaring moon of daffodils', or compare the simple thought of Chaucer or of the ballad writers, or the writers of the miracle plays with the elaborate thought of modern poems like 'In Memoriam', the 'Paracelsus' and 'Sordello' of Browning; the sonnets of Rossetti, 'The Atalanta in Caledon', [*sic*] or the 'Tristan and Iseult' of Swinburne, or with any of the poetry of George Meredith. The very names of these writers and of these poems are enough to prove my case. The tree has come to its greatest complexity of leaf and fruit and flower. And what is true of England is true also of all the older literatures of Europe. I need but mention to you the name of Goethe, having in my mind more particularly his 'Faust', and of Hugo, having in my mind more particularly his later and more oracular song. Everywhere the elaborate luxuriance of leaf and bud and flower.

Now, I want to notice especially one peculiarity of all these poets. They more often than not go to foreign countries for their subjects; they are, in fact, citizens of the world, cosmopolitans. It is obvious that a story like that of the Siege of Troy or stories like those in Chaucer cannot be separated from the countries they happened in, and that characters like Macbeth and Lear, like Oedipus and Agamemnon, cannot be separated either from the world about them. But tell me to what nations do Hatred, Fear, Hope, and Love belong? The epic and the dramatic periods tend to be national because people understand character and incident best when embodied in life they understand and set amid the scenery they know of, and every man knows and understands his own country the best. They may now and then permit their poets to fare far afield even unto the seacoast of Bohemia, but they soon call them home again. But the lyric age, upon the other hand, becomes as it advances towards an ever complete lyricism, more and more cosmopolitan; for the great passions know nothing of boundaries. As do the great beasts in the forest, they wander without let or hindrance through the universe of God.

Granted fit time and fit occasion, I could apply the same law of division and sub-division and of ever increasing complexity to human society — to human life itself — and show you how in the old civilizations an endless subdivision of society to trades and professions, and of human life to habits and rules, is making men every day more subtle and complex, less forcible and adaptable. The old nations are like old men and women sitting over the fire gossipping [*sic*] of stars and planets, talking of all things in heaven and earth and in the waters under the earth, and forgetting in a trance of subtlety the flaming heart of man.

If time and fit occasion offered, I could take you upon that path, beaten by the feet of the seers, and show you behind human society and human life the causal universe itself, 'falling', in the words of my master, William Blake, 'into division', and foretell with him 'its resurrection into unity'. But this is not fit time or fit occasion. And already the fascination of that beaten path has taken me further than I would. I wished merely to show you that the older literatures of Europe are in their golden sunset, their wise old age, that I might the better prove to you, in the closing parts of my lecture, that we here in Ireland who, like the Scandinavian people, are at the outset [of] a literary epoch, must learn from them but not imitate them, and by so doing we will bring new life and fresh impulse not only to ourselves but to those old literatures themselves. But are we really at the outset of a literary epoch? or are we not, perhaps, merely a little eddy cast up by the advancing tide of English literature and are we not doomed, perhaps, to its old age and coming decline? On the contrary, I affirm that we are a young nation with unexhausted material lying within us in our still unexpressed national character, about us in our scenery, and in the clearly marked outlines of our life, and behind us in our multitude of legends. Look at our literature and you will see that we are still in our epic or ballad period. All that is greatest in that literature is based upon legend — upon those tales which are made by no one man, but by the nation itself through a slow process of modification and adaption, to express its loves and its hates, its likes and its dislikes. Our best writers, De Vere, Ferguson, Allingham, Mangan, Davis, O'Grady, are all either ballad or epic writers, and all base their greatest work, if I except a song or two of Mangan's and Allingham's, upon legends and upon the fortunes of the nation. Alone, perhaps, among the nations of Europe we are in our ballad or epic age. The future will put some of our ballads with 'Percy's Reliques' and with the 'border' ballads, and at least one of our epic songs, the 'Conary' of Ferguson, among the simple, primitive poems of the world. Even the 'Spirit of the Nation' belongs to the epic age, for it deals with great National events. Our poetry is still a poetry of the people in the main, for it still deals with the tales and thoughts of the people. The little foreign criticism of Irish literature which I have seen speaks of it as simple and primitive. They are right. There is a distinct school of Irish literature, which we must foster and protect, and its foundation is sunk in the legend lore of the people and in the National history. The literature of Greece and India had just such a foundation, and as we, like the Greeks and the Indians, are an idealistic people, this foundation is fixed in legend rather than in history. But, we must not imitate the writers of any other country, we must study them constantly and learn from them the secret of their greatness. Only by study of the great models can we acquire style, and this, St Beuf[1] says, is the only thing in literature which is immortal. We must learn, too, from the old nations to make literature almost the most serious thing in our lives if we would understand it properly, and quite the most serious thing if we could write it well. How often do I hear it said that such and such a poet is obscure and therefore bad, as if obscurity had anything to do with greatness, as if obscurity was not inevitable unless much that is most profound in thought and feeling is to be left out of poetry. All poetries in their lyrical age get into obscurity. We in this country go to literature to be rested after our day's work, we must go to it on the other hand that we may be made the stronger for that work. How often do I not hear in this country that literature is to be achieved by some kind of mysterious visitation of God, which makes it needless for us to labor at the literary art, and hearing this long for one hour among my books with the great Flaubert, who talked of art, art and again art, or with Blake, who held that life itself became an art when wisely lived. When I hear this kind of talk I am inclined to say that being inspired by God is a profession that is full, so many

91

men have I met who have held themselves to be thus visited. Alas, the inspiration of God, which is, indeed, the source of all which is greatest in the world, comes only to him who labours at rhythm and cadence, at form and style, until they have no secret hidden from him. This art we must learn from the old literatures of the world. We have hitherto been slovens, and even our best writers, if I except Allingham, have put their best thoughts side by side with the most contemptible commonplaces, and their most musical lines into the midst of the tritest rhythms, and our best prose writers have mingled their own gold dust with every kind of ignoble clay. We have shrunk from the labour that art demands, and have made thereby our best moments of no account. We must learn from the literatures of France and England to be supreme artists and then God will send to us supreme inspiration. There is still much to say, but I have already passed the time I allotted to myself, and in conclusion I must apologise to you for not having spoken from a more familiar and therefore more generally interesting point of view, by repeating the words of the crow who was asked why he went to a wedding in a black suit, 'I had no other.'

Note

1. I.e. Charles-Augustin Sainte-Beuve (1804-69), the French critic with a strong influence on Arnold.

9
Lionel Johnson, from 'Poetry and Patriotism', 1894

This comes from the second of two essays published in book form in 1908 by the Cuala Press, Poetry and Ireland: Essays by W. B. Yeats and Lionel Johnson. *The first essay, by Yeats, dates from August 1907 (see below, no.14, where it appears under the title 'Poetry and Tradition'); Johnson's piece had originally been given as lectures both to the Irish Literary Society in London, and to the National Literary Society in Dublin, in 1894. Yeats had met Johnson (1867-1902) at the Rhymers' Club in London, and the two became good friends. This essay was published posthumously in* Post Liminium: Essays and Critical Papers by Lionel Johnson, *ed. Thomas Whittemore (London, 1911).*

It appears to be the creed of some critics, that in the Irish poetry of some sixty, fifty, and forty years ago, in the poetry of *The Nation* and of 'Young Ireland', with their immediate predecessors and followers, we have a fixed and unalterable standard whereby to judge all Irish poetry, past and present and to come. In the poetry of that great generation lies beauty, all beauty, and nothing but beauty! Against any living Irish poet who writes in any style uncultivated then, is brought the dreadful charge of being artistic: and sometimes, if it be a very flagrant case, the unspeakable accusation of being English. Now I heartily hate the cant of 'Art for art's sake': I have spent years in trying to understand what is meant by that imbecile phrase. Also, I have a healthy hatred of the West Briton heresy. Further, no Irishman living has a greater love, and a greater admiration, for the splendid poetry of Davis, Mangan, and their fellows. But I dislike coercion in literature: and it seems to me an uncritical dictation of the critics, when they tell a writer that he or she is no true Irish poet, because he or she does not write rousing ballads, or half-humorous love-songs, or rhetorical laments, or a mixture of historical and political verse; and because he or she takes exceeding pains with his or her workmanship and art. An attention to form and style is apparently an English vice: well! certainly it is an English thing, just as it was Greek and Roman, yes! and Irish also, once. The intricacy and delicacy, the artfulness and elaboration, of Gaelic and Cymric verse, are unparalleled in European literature: so minute, so detailed, so difficult was the attention paid to the technical side of poetry, that Irish and Welsh scholars of unblemished patriotism have deplored it as fatal to the free poetical spirit. There is not a critic in Europe who has written upon Celtic literature without noting the singular charm, the *curiosa felicitas*, of Celtic style: we all know the admiration of Renan in France, of Arnold in England, for its grace and beauty. Music and poetry were held by our forefathers in an almost religious veneration: the poet passed through a long discipline of the strictest severity before he reached the high dignities of his profession. There is no modern cultivator of arduous poetical forms, the ballade, rondeau, Villanelle, triolet, sonnet, who endures half the labour that was demanded by the ancient laws of Irish and Welsh metre. An Irish poet of today may lack a thousand Irish virtues: but if he give a devoted care to the perfecting of his art, he will have at least one Celtic note, one characteristic Irish virtue. While he is intent upon the artful turns and cadences of his music and the delicate choice of his words, striving to achieve the last graces and perfections possible to his work, he is at one in spirit with the poets of old Ireland. The old Irish forms are barely possible in English: but their spirit is attainable. And if he choose to take the more subtle and ingenious of English forms, he may do so without the crime of borrowing from the enemy: for scarce one of them is native to England. Considering to what magnificent uses Rome turned the forms and metres of Greece, and England those of France and Italy, without ceasing to be Roman and English, we need not fear lest an Irish poet should cease to be Irish, if he study and borrow and adapt the best achievements of foreign art to the service of the Irish Muses. But Irish poetry today, I may be told, should be a national weapon: we want to reach and touch the hearts of our listeners, to fan the sacred fire, to be passionate and burning and impetuous. Why trouble about minute proprieties or delicate graces of art, so long as our verse go with a ring and a swing, celebrating the glories of Ireland, or with a sigh and a cry, lamenting her griefs? Is there not something cold-blooded and slow-pulsed in writing without vehemence and a rush of sentiment? Leave metre-mongering to the young decadents and aesthetes of Paris and London: and let Irish verse sweep unfettered as the Irish winds, and surge free as the Irish seas, and satisfy the Irish people. Well! like most stump oratory, that is very high and mighty and impressive: but it is not argument. Passionate impulse and patient pains are not incompatible. On the other side, there is sometimes an equally unreasoning depreciation of anything rhetorical, anything spontaneous: and the whole battle, the whole confusion, comes of ignoring the fact that there are many legitimate kinds of poetry, that each and every kind has a right to live, and that we can only insist upon a poem's being good of its own kind. One most legitimate kind of poetry is the political and social poetry that is directly practical in its appeal: propagandist poetry. At a time of national excitement, verse may be a tremendous ally of the national cause: verse that is a trumpet-call to action; verse full of great memories and of great prophecies; verse that denounces, inspirits, triumphs, wails in melodies memorable and moving. It may laugh, or weep, or shout the war-cry: use the keenest satire in the homeliest language, or thunder in the accents of a Hebrew prophet; it will be thrown off at a white heat, it must be ready at every turn, and never flag. It passes from singing of a thousand years ago, to singing of yesterday and to-morrow; from the champions of romance, to the champions of to-day. It must be vehement and clear, emphatic and direct: it must employ all the resource of bold rhetoric, large phrases and great words. It must fall irresistibly into music, and be sung by the crowds in the street: it must stir the blood, and thrill the pulses, and set the heart on fire. Such verse was the best verse of Young Ireland: and I do not know, in any language, a body of political and social verse at once so large and so good. Much of it rises far above the level of occasional verse, and is superb national poetry; some of it was written by men who would have been poets under any circumstances, by the compulsion of nature and the gift of fate. There is no lack of reasons for the immense influence of this verse upon subsequent literature: for one thing, it was the first great general outburst of Irish verse in English; Moore had sung by himself, and not only in English, but in England. Now, for the first time, a mass of national literature came into existence, written in English by politicians, scholars, men of the learned professions, as well as by men of the people, all living and working for Ireland and in Ireland. No such literary glory had accompanied the rise of the United Irishman, or any other national movement: it showed the world that if the ancient speech of Ireland were doomed and dying, yet the Irish genius could express the Irish spirit in the language of their conquerors, with no loss of national enthusiasm and national passion. Headed, as the movement was, by at least two or three men of literary genius, and a score or so of exceptional literary talents, its writings, and especially its verse, became as it were, the sacred scriptures of the national cause. And for Ireland, they are indeed κτήματα ἐς ἀεὶ, possessions for all time, justly venerated and loved. But this very splendour of achievement blinded, in some ways, the critical faculties: we have been tempted to forget that the work, done in the rapture and heat of a great enterprise, must have the defects of its qualities. In many cases the penalty paid for immediate success, won on an instant, was a lack of perfection, the abiding marks of haste. And much of the work, admirable alike in intention and in execution, had no pretensions to being work of the highest order: it belongs, definitely and decidedly, to the class of popular political verse. Now, whilst the peasant poetry, the folk-songs of most countries, (and Ireland is no exception), are beautiful, and artistically excellent, the more purely political verse, the verse expressing national sentiments of hope and fear, defiance or doubt, are always inferior to the folk-songs, and are often abominable. If there be a worse poem than 'God save the Queen', I do not know it:

> Confound their politics,
> Frustrate their knavish tricks!

I ask you, is that poetry? Is it even decent verse? Does it show any fine and beautiful use of language? Or, take the 'Marseillaise', and 'Wacht am Rhein'; are they distinguished and superior examples of French and German poetry? Yet to hear a vast multitude of French or Germans singing those songs, swayed with one storm of emotion, brings all the blood to one's heart, and the tears to one's eyes: the air seems charged with electricity. A regimental march may be very far from good music: but the first roll of the drums and thrilling of the fifes make many a man 'burn to be a soldier'. It is simply and solely association that has this magical effect: association can turn downright ugliness into a thing of beauty, or, at the least, into something lovable. Think of some house which you have known all your life: it may be ugly, uncomfortable, and all that is distressing; but what a world of memories centre there, and make it the dearest place on earth to you! It is the same with everything: remember Scott in Italy, blind to its beauty and its charm, hungering for the heather and the wild hills of his home, and murmuring old Jacobite songs in places golden with classic memories: or the Brontës, sick at heart in glittering Brussels, with longing for their lonely Yorkshire moors. Think with what regret we consent to the necessary destruction of some church or public building no longer serviceable, but thronged with old recollections! I need not speak here of the Irish exile's hunger for his old home in the old land, however prosperous he be elsewhere, and however hard may have been the old life. It is this way that things, in themselves undesirable, receive a consecration from memory and habit and association. The most magnificent lyric in the world could not replace 'God save the Queen' in the heart of the loyal Englishman. But associations do not alter facts: the house, the landscape, the poem endeared to us, have no attraction for the stranger, the dispassionate critic, who does not feel their glamour. And so the verse of Young Ireland, good, bad, and indifferent, has been accepted altogether, as a memory to the older men, as a tradition to the younger: this not wholly to the advantage of Irish literature, though much to the credit of Irish nature.

Perhaps the most irritating mode of criticism is to complain of the thing criticized for not being something else. A poet writes a little book of light songs, and he is told that this is all very well in its way, but why does he not try his hand at an epic? He writes, let us say, dreams and all manner of imaginative things, in plaintive, lovely cadences, about the faeries, or about the mysteries of the world, birth and life and death, writing out of the depths of his own nature; and lo! instead of being grateful, we abuse him for not writing historical ballads, valiant and national, upon Patrick Sarsfield or Owen Roe.[1] But what if he be wholly incapable of writing historical ballads? Shelley said of himself, that to go to him for human nature was like going to a ginshop for a leg of mutton. Not every poet can be, or is bound to be, a Tyrtaeus. I know no greater patriotic poems than certain sonnets of Milton or Wordsworth; certain passages of Shakespeare and Spenser, Virgil and Dante; certain plays of Æschylus, and odes of Pindar; but not one of them could send the soldier on to death or victory with such a heroism as many a simple soldier's song could rouse: yet the simple song is not, therefore, the greater poetry. Except, it may be, in some primitive societies, such as was possibly the Homeric, the greater poetry is not the most popular. Perhaps it should be: but that is another question. And when, as in our own country, there is a native instinct that prompts the mass of the people to love music and poetry, and any ancient tradition of reverence towards them, we are not unnaturally disposed to estimate all music and poetry by the popular standards, and not always by the best popular standards. Surely, we say, poetry that touches the hearts of all, learned and unlearned, rich and poor, is the true poetry; let us be simple, unsophisticated, natural in our tastes. Let others write for cliques and coteries, and live upon academic applause or mutual admiration: we are content with a poetry popular and patriotic. It sounds very manly and independent, a refreshing contrast to the affected æstheticism of certain schools: but it cuts us off for ever from the company of the great classics. It is equally fatal to be for ever clamouring for a great classic, and demanding him of all the fates. It is useless to be perpetually longing for a man who shall do for Ireland what Scott did for Scotland: it is ungenerous and unjust, when a writer does his best in his own way, to say that this is not the immortal work which Ireland wants. We do not reproach a buttercup for not being a rose. I am inclined to think that a nation does not produce its greatest art in times of storm and stress, but at and after the period of triumph: when the nation is exulting in its strength and glory, with a sense of new youth and health and joy. Melancholy, and sorrow, and the cry of pain, it has been said by some, are more poetical than serenity and ardour: for my own part, I do not believe it. Rather, I believe that the Irish poetry of free and triumphant Ireland will have the wonderful joyousness and happy splendour of the old heroic and romantic Ireland, chastened and tempered by the seriousness inseparable from Christianity. Meanwhile, let us accept and encourage all excellence: there is room for all. Let us have our ringing rhetoric, strong verse with the clash of swords in it; our sorrowful dirges for the dear and dead of to-day, and of long ages past; our homely songs of laughter and of tears; but let us welcome all who write for the love of Ireland, even if they write in fashions less familiar. It is absurd, and insulting to Ireland, to think that Irish genius cannot make the Irish spirit felt in any form that is good and fine of itself. Think of Farquhar and Steele, Goldsmith and Sheridan: they spent nearly their whole lives in England among Englishmen, under the strongest English influences, and they wrote in English forms for English readers: yet we feel the grace, the gentle humour, the delicacy and charm, which stamp their work as Irish. After all, who is to decide what is, absolutely and definitely, the Celtic and Irish note? Many a time I have shown my English friends Irish poems, which Irish critics have declared to be un-Irish; and the English verdict has constantly been: 'How un-English! how Celtic! what a strange, remote, far-away beauty in the music and in the colour!' These poems, then, can find no resting-place in either country; are they to wait becalmed in mid-channel? The most singular criticisms are sometimes made upon these hapless poets. My friend Mr Yeats has been informed that he is a disciple of Rossetti and of Tennyson; now, no two poets could be less alike than Rossetti and Tennyson; and no one could be less like either of them than Mr Yeats. But he dares to write in his own style, upon his own themes; and because they are not the style and the themes familiar to us from old associations, we rush to the conclusion that he is treading in the footsteps of some English poet, despising Irish art. Another instance: I have heard it said that the four volumes of Mrs Hinkson[2] show a steady increase in artistic power, but a noticeable decrease in the true Irish spirit of poetry: an extremely doubtful compliment to the true Irish spirit. Cardinal Newman tells us of the village schools in his youth, where the charge for teaching good manners was an 'extra twopence'. Is artistic workmanship in our poetry worth but an 'extra twopence'? What the critic meant was that in Mrs Hinkson's earlier work there were a greater fluency and flow of sentiment, less restraint and careful finish, more obvious rhetoric and impulsiveness. The dainty delicacy of the later work, its mastery of rhythm and curbing of haste, were lost upon him: the idea that all art implies discipline and austerity of taste, a constant progress towards an ideal perfection, though his earliest ancestors knew it well, seemed strange to him. Perhaps the most familiar of English poems is Gray's 'Elegy': the two loveliest stanzas Gray ever wrote he deliberately rejected from the poem, because they seemed to him redundant, disproportionate, a dwelling too long upon one thought. Dante speaks of his long labour at his art as the work which had made him lean and gaunt and worn. This passion for perfection seems to me as truly Celtic a thing as the ready indulgence of sentiment; our illuminations, our penmanship, our work in stone and metal, all our arts of design, show an infinite love of taking pains. The very heretics among the Celts, as Pelagius and Erigena, exemplify the Celtic subtlety. But this 'battle of the books' is not confined to the Celts of Ireland: the same question, in very much the same form, rages in Wales. Go to an Eisteddfod, or to any Welsh gathering of literary patriots: you will probably hear discussions upon the true Welsh spirit, upon English influence, upon the characteristics of the ancient literature and the new, upon the possibility of a Welshman's writing English in a way patriotically and unmistakably Welsh. This patriotic anxiety for a national literature is an unimpeachable virtue, but it should be displayed with dignity and confidence. Many of us, at present, are somewhat agitated and nervous; we ask hasty and suspicious questions: 'Is that quite Celtic? Is this book typically Irish? Yes! they are certainly fine poems, but are they not English in quality; have they the geniune national note: is it the work that a patriot should be doing?' All this is put forward with a certain querulousness and captiousness: it seems to imply a certain distrust of the Irish genius, and of one another. And the tumult of our political passions is apt to disturb our judgments. I would rather read a fine poem upon Sarsfield and the 'Defence of Limerick,' than upon Walker and the 'Defence of Derry'; but if Colonel Saunderson,[3] or Dr Kane,[4] were to give us a stirring poem upon the courage and endurance of Walker and the 'prentices of Derry, without ill-feeling and bad blood, I should reckon it a gain to our literature. Yet our Irish critic who spoke his mind to that effect, may be thought a bit of an Orangeman at heart. It would be a case of *Timeo Danaos et dona ferentes*:[5] we should look with suspicion upon the poetical gifts of our political opponents. And there seems to be no place for a poet who, though he be intensely national in temperament and sympathy, may be unfitted by nature to write poetry with an obvious and immediate bearing upon the national cause. Imagine a poet with no strong taste for history, no fierce rhetorical note in his music, no power of stirring a popular enthusiasm; yet, from the crown of his head to the sole of his foot, Irish and nothing but Irish. Upon occasions of great emotion, a leader's death, a national victory, what you will, odes and songs may be forthcoming by the score from others: he will feel as deep a sorrow, or as wild a joy, but his Muse will be silent. He will talk of these things as much as others, or write as much about them in prose; but in poetry he has not the necessary gift. He is not proud of lacking it: he may be sorry that he has not that string to his lyre. But at any rate he has not got it, and so he cannot play upon it. And forthwith we have our doubts: we begin to think that such a poet is of no service to the cause. Or, perhaps we ask him for an historical novel upon Ireland in Tudor or Stuart times; or for an epic of the Red Branch Knights, or the Irish Saints; or for a tragedy upon Emmet or Lord Edward: whilst his whole faculty and disposition may be lyrical, and meditative, and personal. Or, perhaps, we fall foul of his lyrics for not having certain simplicities and beauties dear to us in the folk-songs of our country: but who said that they had, or tried to have, them? There may be charms in the new verse, not less Irish than the old. A wider, deeper, higher vision would recognise that Irish nationality and Irish patriotism can make themselves powerful in a thousand forms and themes of literature. Consider the many English echoes, or reproductions, or imitations of Greek forms and themes: from Milton's 'Samson Agonistes' up to Mr Swinburne's 'Atalanta in Calydon'; they are intensely English, not really Greek. A living literature cannot help being national: it may feed upon the literature of the past, and of other nations; but, if it be good literature, it must bear the sign and seal of its own nationality, and of its own age. Indeed, nationality lives in literature and art, when it is almost dead in other things: they are the expressions of the soul of a country; they are racy of the soil; they refuse to serve their country's conquerors. On the contrary, they take their captors captive, as history has told us a hundred times. A cosmopolitan artist, a citizen of the world, with no local patriotism in his heart, has never yet done anything memorable in poetry, or in anything else. Could all his wild philosophy, his vast pondering upon universal problems, his devotion to the poets and thinkers of Germany, make Carlyle anything but a Scotch Calvinist, a son of John Knox, a child of the Covenanters? Or could the wild romance, the brilliant levity, the mocking gaiety and cynicism of his Parisian life, make the German and Jewish Heine anything but a son of the German Fatherland, and a child of the house of Israel? It is among the strongest of earthly instincts, this clinging to our nationality and race: this, far more than diplomacy, has changed the face of Europe in our country, and may change it still more. Poetry and patriotism are each other's guardian angels, and therefore inseparable. Virgil's master was Homer, Dante's master was Virgil, Milton's masters were Dante, Virgil, and Homer: yet could four poems be less like each other, could four poems be more intensely national than the *Iliad*, the *Æneid*, the *Divine Comedy*, and *Paradise Lost*? Unquestionably, we would rather have our poets choose Irish themes, and sing of Tara sooner than of Troy; of Ossian sooner than of Orpheus: but if they went to China or to Peru for their inspiration, the result would be neither Chinese nor Peruvian, but 'kindly Irish of the Irish' still. Our race is not lost by spreading itself over the world, and our literature would not lose its Irish accent by expeditions into all lands and times. Let Irish literature be de-Anglicized by all means: away with all feeble copies of the fashionable stuff that happens to amuse London Society for a season, and even with mere copies of distinctly good English work! It is neither national, nor patriotic, to wait eagerly and humbly upon the tastes and the verdicts of the English public and of the English press. But if we are to foster, encourage, and develop Irish literature, and not least of all, Irish poetry, it must be with a wise generosity; in a finely national, not in a pettily provincial, spirit. Take the revival of German literature and its emancipation from French influence: that great movement which the Germans call *Aufklärung* and the French the *éclairecissement* of Germany. Beginning, practically, with Lessing and Winckelmann and Herder, continued by Goethe and Schiller, and later by Heine, it created the first splendid period of national German literature. It perpetrated endless absurdities, but it succeeded; and that because of its free and liberal spirit. The pioneers and chiefs of the movement pressed everything into its service: Greek art and literature, all the arts of Italy, the Elizabethan drama, Macpherson's *Ossian*, the folk-songs and ancient lays of many lands, the romance of the Middle Ages; all that an ardent curiosity, or a profound scholarship, could reach, was sought out and studied and brought to bear upon the revival of German literature. And the result was magnificently German: there was no vague, cosmopolitan, unnational spirit in the results of that immense enthusiasm. One cannot read the memoirs, biographies, histories of that time, still less the poetry, without feeling oneself in the presence of an irresistible patriotism. And everything helped, every study and pursuit: if German prose, of all ugly things, came to be written with the lucidity of Plato's Greek; if German poetry rose from the dead, and sang a thousand melodies upon a thousand instruments, it was because a deep desire for knowledge, a passionate ambition for true culture, taught the German poets the way to be German; indeed, showed them how to preserve the ancient German virtues, whilst creating a new literature, which should be the glory of Germany. True,

the social state of Germany then had little in common with the
social state of Ireland now: yet the essential spirit of their
movement is ours also. If we considered the causes and conditions
of all that is greatest, in the Italian Renaissance, or in the
Elizabethan outburst of literary glory, we should find similar facts:
the re-discovery of the ancient classic world; the re-discovery of
the new world; the thirst for knowledge and experience; a sudden
thrill of pride and hope in men's hearts at the thought that Italy,
England, their own countries, were rivalling, in their own national
ways, the great records of the past; all this went to the creation
of those great arts and literatures. France, too, in her romantic
revival of 1830, turned to her own national uses, to uses completely
French, whatever in Italy, Germany, England, Spain, she could
lay her hands upon. Is Ireland to be the only nation which
influences from without are bound to ruin and unnationalize; the
only nation incapable of assimilating to herself, of nationalizing
and naturalizing the heritage of art and learning left by other
nations? It was not so once: not in the early ages of Irish
Christianity. If Saint Sedulius, of whom Dr Sigerson has told us,
were alive to-day, he would certainly find critics to call him
unpatriotic for taking a foreign metre, and ingrafting upon it Irish
graces. As I have pleaded, let us have no coercion in Irish
literature: I would add, let us have no protection. Like the
Norsemen and the Normans, let all that is good in literature and
learning enter Ireland, and become more Irish than the Irish.
Even if, like the Norsemen and the Normans, it enters forcibly
and against opposition, I am sure that the result will be the same:
the Irish genius will captivate the foreign, and grow itself the
stronger and more brilliant. You see, I have faith in the Irish
genius: I do not believe that anything can so take possession of
it, and pervert it, as to drive the nationality out of it. But, perhaps,
some [of those like-minded] are thinking that I am making much
ado about nothing all this time. Well ! of course, no one [who
knows] distrusts the power and indomitable vigour of the Irish
genius. But for some time, both in reading Irish papers from all
parts of the world, and in discussing Irish matters with Irishmen
in England, I have undoubtedly found a certain amiable
narrowness, now and then, here and there: a conservatism rather
obstinate than strong, less resolute than stubborn. Ask these
conservatives to admit some good Irish qualities in this poem or
in that novel written within the last twenty years: the answer is:
'It's not what I call Irish; give me Mangan, give me Carleton.'

Now, it is extremely easy to be less great than Mangan and Carleton; it is not impossible to be greater; but to be Mangan, to be Carleton, is a clear impossibility. It is only possible to aim at it by imitating them. Imitation may be the sincerest flattery, but it usually produces the worst literature. In Mangan's day, perhaps, less fervent nationalists wished that Mangan would write like Moore; and perhaps they exhorted Carleton to study the graces of Miss Edgeworth, and the vivacities of Lady Morgan. The really great and imperishable poets who adorned the middle of this century had no such narrowness. We cannot imagine Mangan jealously and anxiously discouraging new ventures of the Irish Muses. We cannot think of Davis laying down absolute laws upon what is, and is not, verily Celtic and truly Irish. Again, it is not the living scholars, most busy in preserving, elucidating, translating, and transmitting to posterity the Gaelic literature of every age and kind, who impose these fetters upon our modern literature. But I have heard some of my countrymen who have no more Gaelic than I, (and I have none), airily and easily blaming a veteran Irish poet, still among us, Mr de Vere, for having no real Gaelic tone, no insight into the genuine ancient spirit. I should never be surprised to hear Canon O'Hanlon[6] reproached for celebrating the 'Land of Leix' in the Spenserian stanza, one of the few great English forms invented in England, and invented, too, by a very thorough-going enemy of the Irish cause. Again, in projecting some Irish publication, it is surely an open question whether it should be solely and strictly confined to Irish themes, or whether, remembering that

> One in name and in fame
> Are the sea-divided Gaels,

it should sometimes include matters of collateral interest: contrasts and comparisons, in social and literary concerns, with our kinsmen in Wales and Brittany and Scotland. That, surely, is not opening the floodgates, and admitting cosmopolitan culture to overwhelm Ireland! yet such proposals have been denounced as unpatriotic. They may be inexpedient, but they can hardly be called criminal. It is this kind of exclusiveness that has emboldened me to protest: it seems to me a fatal interpretation of patriotism. That true son and servant of Ireland, Berkeley, used to make an execrable pun, and to say that he distinguished between patriotism and pat-riotism; it is the latter quality which produces this feverish alarm lest

Irishmen should forget Ireland, if they try to serve her in ways savouring at all, or seeming to savour, of novelty. It is the truer patriotism which refuses to be panic-stricken, though it is willing to be prudent; a militant faith is one thing, and an irritable fussiness another. I hope there is not an Irishman anywhere, (certainly there cannot be one in the literary societies of Dublin and London), who does not agree with every word of Dr Douglas Hyde's eloquent appeal upon 'the Necessity for de-Anglicizing Ireland'? But I do not see why Irishmen should not make raids upon other countries, and bring home the spoils, and triumphantly Celticize them, and lay them down at the feet of Ireland. It is pleasant to think that Goldsmith, dedicating his first famous poem, not to his great English friends, not to Reynolds or to Johnson, but to his poor Irish brother in his poor Irish home, — pleasant to think of him, all through his sorrows and his triumphs, still remembering the old days in Ireland, and hoping to die in the old country.

> And as a hare, whom hounds and horns pursue,
> Pants to the place from whence at first she flew;
> I still had hopes, my long vexations past,
> Here to return, and die at home at last.

Horace was right, and his old proverbial wisdom has a good sense as well as a bad: 'patriæ quis exul, se quoque fugit: caelum non animum mutant':[7] we may leave Ireland, but we could not if we would, help being Irish. It is so with our poetry, and with all our fine literature; there is an Irish foundation, an Irish origin, for it all. Patriotism, said Dr Johnson, is the last refuge of a scoundrel, and certainly there are many ways of being patriotic, as we have bitter cause to know. But our poetry has been, and is still, patriotic in the best of senses: it has been inspired by our own country in a magnificent variety of ways. It is not now under the discipline of ancient Ireland, the supremacy of bardic colleges; it were a pity, were it to fall under the authority, and to be checked by the iron rod, of an unsympathetic criticism, and by the narrow spirit of a limited outlook. It may be that Irish poetry is in a state of change, losing, perhaps, some virtues, but gaining others; displaying in fresh forms, under new aspects, the glory and the beauty, the deeds and the dreams, the legend and the history, of our country...[8]

Notes

1. Patrick Sarsfield (d.1693) was an Irish Jacobite nobleman, Owen Roe O'Neill (c.1590-1649) a commander of the Ulster forces against Cromwell.

2. Mrs Hinkson (1861-1931) is better known as the novelist and dramatist Katharine Tynan.

3. The Rt Hon. Edward James Saunderson (1831-1906) was MP for Armagh in 1885.

4. His Honour Judge Robert Romney Kane (1842-1902) was a County Court Judge, a Trustee of the National Library of Ireland, and the proud possessor of an LLD.

5. Virgil, *Aeneid*, 2. 49: 'I fear the Greeks, even when they are bringing gifts.'

6. The Very Reverend John Canon O'Hanlon (1821-1905) was a popular writer, sometimes using the pseudonym Lageniensis.

7. Johnson has run together two separate quotations from Horace: *Odes*, 2. 16. 19, 'what exile from his country ever escaped from himself as well?'; and *Epistles*, 1. 11. 27, '[those who cross the sea] change the sky but not their minds'.

8. For the full significance of Johnson's essay, especially its relation to Yeats's thinking in 1908, as well as 1894, see Ian Small's article, 'Yeats and Johnson on the Limitations of Patriotic Art', *Studies*, *63* (Winter 1974), pp. 379-88.

10

W. B. Yeats, 'The Celtic Element in Literature', 1897

This was first published in Cosmopolis, *June 1898, and then in* Ideas of Good and Evil *(1903), and subsequently in* Essays and Introductions.

I

Ernest Renan described what he held to be Celtic characteristics in *The Poetry of the Celtic Races*. I must repeat the well-known sentences: 'No race communed so intimately as the Celtic race with the lower creation, or believed it to have so big a share of moral life.' The Celtic race had 'a realistic naturalism', 'a love of Nature for herself, a vivid feeling for her magic, commingled with the melancholy a man knows when he is face to face with her, and thinks he hears her communing with him about his origin and his destiny'. 'It has worn itself out in mistaking dreams for realities', and 'compared with the classical imagination the Celtic imagination is indeed the infinite contrasted with the finite'. 'Its history is one long lament, it still recalls its exiles, its flights across the seas'. 'If at times it seems to be cheerful, its tear is not slow to glisten behind the smile. Its songs of joy end as elegies; there is nothing to equal the delightful sadness of its national melodies.' Matthew Arnold, in *The Study of Celtic Literature*, has accepted this passion for Nature, this imaginativeness, this melancholy, as Celtic characteristics, but has described them more elaborately. The Celtic passion for Nature comes almost more from a sense of her 'mystery' than of her 'beauty', and it adds 'charm and magic' to Nature, and the Celtic imaginativeness and melancholy are alike 'a passionate, turbulent, indomitable reaction against

107

the despotism of fact'. The Celt is not melancholy, as Faust or Werther are melancholy, from 'a perfectly definite motive', but because of something about him 'unaccountable, defiant and titanic'. How well one knows these sentences, better even than Renan's, and how well one knows the passages of prose and verse which he uses to prove that wherever English literature has the qualities these sentences describe, it has them from a Celtic source. Though I do not think any of us who write about Ireland have built any argument upon them, it is well to consider them a little, and see where they are helpful and where they are hurtful. If we do not, we may go mad some day, and the enemy root up our rose-garden and plant a cabbage-garden instead. Perhaps we must re-state a little Renan's and Arnold's argument.

II

Once every people in the world believed that trees were divine, and could take a human or grotesque shape and dance among the shadows; and that deer, and ravens and foxes, and wolves and bears, and clouds and pools, almost all things under the sun and moon, and the sun and moon, were not less divine and changeable. They saw in the rainbow the still bent bow of a god thrown down in his negligence; they heard in the thunder the sound of his beaten water-jar, or the tumult of his chariot wheels; and when a sudden flight of wild ducks, or of crows, passed over their heads, they thought they were gazing at the dead hastening to their rest; while they dreamed of so great a mystery in little things that they believed the waving of a hand, or of a sacred bough, enough to trouble far-off hearts, or hood the moon with darkness. All old literatures are full of these or of like imaginations, and all the poets of races who have not lost this way of looking at things could have said of themselves, as the poet of the *Kalevala* said of himself, 'I have learned my songs from the music of many birds, and from the music of many waters.' When a mother in the *Kalevala* weeps for a daughter, who was drowned flying from an old suitor, she weeps so greatly that her tears become three rivers, and cast up three rocks, on which grow three birch-trees, where three cuckoos sit and sing, the one 'love, love', the one 'suitor, suitor', the one 'consolation, consolation'. And the makers of the Sagas made the squirrel run up and down the sacred ash-tree carrying words of hatred from the eagle to the worm, and from the worm to the eagle; although they had less of the old way than the makers of the *Kalevala*, for they lived in a more crowded and complicated world, and were learning the abstract meditation which lures men from visible beauty, and were unlearning, it may be, the impassioned meditation which brings men beyond the edge of trance and makes trees, and beasts, and dead things talk with human voices.

The old Irish and the old Welsh, though they had less of the old way than the makers of the *Kalevala*, had more of it than the makers of the Sagas, and it is this that distinguishes the examples Matthew Arnold quotes of their 'natural magic', of their sense of 'the mystery' more than of 'the beauty' of Nature. When Matthew Arnold wrote, it was not easy to know as much as we know now of folk-song and folk-belief, and I do not think he understood that our 'natural magic' is but the ancient religion of the world, the ancient worship of Nature and that troubled ecstasy before her, that certainty of all beautiful places being haunted, which it brought into men's minds. The ancient religion is in that passage of the *Mabinogion* about the making of 'Flower Aspect'. Gwydion and Math made her 'by charms and illusions' 'out of flowers'. 'They took the blossoms of the oak, and the blossoms of the broom, and the blossoms of the meadow-sweet, and produced from them a maiden the fairest and most graceful that man ever saw; and they baptized her, and called her Flower Aspect'; and one finds it in the not less beautiful passage about the burning tree, that has half its beauty from calling up a fancy of leaves so living and beautiful, they can be of no less living and beautiful a thing than flame: 'They saw a tall tree by the side of the river, one half of which was in flames from the root to the top, and the other half was green and in full leaf.' And one finds it very certainly in the quotations Arnold makes from English poets to prove a Celtic influence in English poetry; in Keats's 'magic casements opening on the foam of perilous seas in faery lands forlorn'; in his 'moving waters at their priestlike task of pure ablution round earth's human shores'; in Shakespeare's 'floor of heaven', 'inlaid with patens of bright gold'; and in his Dido standing 'upon the wild sea banks', 'a willow in her hand', and waving it in the ritual of the old worship of Nature and the spirits of Nature, to wave 'her love to come again to Carthage'. And his other examples have the delight and wonder of devout worshippers among the haunts of their divinities. Is there not such delight and wonder in the description of Olwen in the *Mabinogion*: 'More yellow was her hair than the flower of the broom, and her skin was whiter than the foam of the wave, and fairer were her hands and her fingers than the blossoms of the wood-anemone amidst the spray of the meadow fountains'? And is there not such delight and wonder in —

> Meet we on hill, in dale, forest, or mead,
> By paved fountain or by rushy brook,
> Or on the beached margent of the sea?

If men had never dreamed that fair women could be made out of flowers, or rise up out of meadow fountains and paved fountains, neither passage could have been written. Certainly the descriptions of nature made in what Matthew Arnold calls 'the faithful way', or in what he calls 'the Greek way', would have lost nothing if all the meadow fountains or paved fountains were but what they seemed. When Keats wrote, in the Greek way, which adds lightness and brightness to nature —

> What little town by river or sea-shore,
> Or mountain-built with quiet citadel,
> Is emptied of its folk, this pious morn?

when Shakespeare wrote in the Greek way —

> I know a bank where the wild thyme blows,
> Where oxlips and the nodding violet grows;

when Virgil wrote in the Greek way —

> Muscosi fontes et somno mollior herba,[1]

and

> Pallentes violas et summa papavera carpens
> Narcissum et florem jungit bene olentis anethi;[2]

they looked at nature without ecstasy, but with the affection a man feels for the garden where he has walked daily and thought pleasant thoughts. They looked at nature in the modern way, the way of people who are poetical, but are more interested in one another than in a nature which has faded to be but friendly and pleasant, the way of people who have forgotten the ancient religion.

III

Men who lived in a world where anything might flow and change, and become any other thing; and among great gods whose passions were in the flaming sunset, and in the thunder and the thunder-shower, had not our thoughts of weight and measure. They worshipped nature and the abundance of nature, and had always, as it seems, for a supreme ritual that tumultuous dance among the hills or in the depths of the woods, where unearthly ecstasy fell upon the dancers, until they seemed the gods or the godlike beasts, and felt their souls overtopping the moon; and, as some think, imagined for the first time in the world the blessed country of the gods and of the happy dead. They had imaginative passions because they did not live within our own strait limits, and were nearer to ancient chaos, every man's desire, and had immortal models about them. The hare that ran by among the dew might have sat up on his haunches when the first man was made, and the poor bunch of rushes under their feet might have been a goddess laughing among the stars; and with but a little magic, a little waving of the hands, a little murmuring of the lips, they too could become a hare or a bunch of rushes, and know immortal love and immortal hatred.

All folk literature, and all literature that keeps the folk tradition, delights in unbounded and immortal things. The *Kalevala* delights in the seven hundred years that Luonnotar wanders in the depths of the sea with Wäinämöinen in her womb, and the Mahomedan king in the *Song of Roland*, pondering upon the greatness of Charlemagne, repeats over and over, 'He is three hundred years old, when will he be weary of war?' Cuchulain in the Irish folk-tale had the passion of victory, and he overcame all men, and died warring upon the waves, because they alone had the strength to overcome him. The lover in the Irish folk-song bids his beloved come with him into the woods, and see the salmon leap in the rivers, and hear the cuckoo sing, because death will never find them in the heart of the woods. Oisin, new come from his three hundred years of faeryland, and of the love that is in faeryland, bids Saint Patrick cease his prayers a while and listen to the blackbird, because it is the blackbird of Derrycarn that Finn brought from Norway, three hundred years before, and set its nest upon the oak-tree with his own hands. Surely if one goes far enough into the woods, one will find there all that one is seeking? Who knows how many centuries the birds of the woods have been singing?

All folk literature has indeed a passion whose like is not in modern literature and music and art, except where it has come by some straight or crooked way out of ancient times. Love was held to be a fatal sickness in ancient Ireland, and there is a love-poem in the *Love Songs of Connacht* that is like a death-cry:

> My love, O she is my love, the woman who is most for destroying me, dearer is she for making me ill than the woman who would be for making me well. She is my treasure, O she is my treasure, the woman of the grey eyes... a woman who would not lay a hand under my head...She is my love, O she is my love, the woman who left no strength in me; a woman who would not breathe a sigh after me, a woman who would not raise a stone at my tomb...She is my secret love, O she is my secret love. A woman who tells me nothing,...a woman who does not remember me to be out...She is my choice, O she is my choice, the woman who would not look back at me, the woman who would not make peace with me...She is my desire, O she is my desire: a woman dearest to me under the sun, a woman who would not pay me heed, if I were to sit by her side. It is she ruined my heart and left a sigh for ever in me.

There is another song that ends,

> The Erne shall be in strong flood, the hills shall be torn down, and the sea shall have red waves, and blood shall be spilled, and every mountain valley and every moor shall be on high, before you shall perish, my little black rose.

Nor do the old Irish weigh and measure their hatred. The nurse of O'Sullivan Bere in the folksong prays that the bed of his betrayer may be the red hearth-stone of Hell for ever. And an Elizabethan Irish poet cries:

> Three things are waiting for my death. The Devil, who is waiting for my soul and cares nothing for my body or my

wealth; the worms, who are waiting for my body but care nothing for my soul or my wealth; my children, who are waiting for my wealth and care nothing for my body or my soul. O Christ, hang all three in the one noose.

Such love and hatred seek no mortal thing but their own infinity, and such love and hatred soon become love and hatred of the idea. The lover who loves so passionately can soon sing to his beloved like the lover in the poem by A.E., 'A vast desire awakes and grows into forgetfulness of thee.'

When an early Irish poet calls the Irishman famous for much loving, and a proverb a friend[3] has heard in the Highlands of Scotland talks of the lovelessness of the Irishman, they may say but the same thing, for if your passion is but great enough it leads you to a country where there are many cloisters. The hater who hates with too good a heart soon comes also to hate the idea only; and from this idealism in love and hatred comes, as I think, a certain power of saying and forgetting things, especially a power of saying and forgetting things in politics, which others do not say and forget. The ancient farmers and herdsmen were full of love and hatred, and made their friends gods, and their enemies the enemies of gods, and those who keep their tradition are not less mythological. From this 'mistaking dreams', which are perhaps essences, for 'realities', which are perhaps accidents, from this 'passionate, turbulent reaction against the despotism of fact', comes, it may be, that melancholy which made all ancient peoples delight in tales that end in death and parting, as modern peoples delight in tales that end in marriage bells; and made all ancient peoples, who, like the old Irish, had a nature more lyrical than dramatic, delight in wild and beautiful lamentations. Life was so weighed down by the emptiness of the great forests and by the mystery of all things, and by the greatness of its own desires, and, as I think, by the loneliness of much beauty; and seemed so little and so fragile and so brief, that nothing could be more sweet in the memory than a tale that ended in death and parting, and than a wild and beautiful lamentation. Men did not mourn merely because their beloved was married to another, or because learning was bitter in the mouth, for such mourning believes that life might be happy were it different, and is therefore the less mourning, but because they had been born and must die with their great thirst unslaked. And so it is that all the august sorrowful persons of literature, Cassandra and Helen and Deirdre, and Lear and

Tristan, have come out of legends and are indeed but the images of the primitive imagination mirrored in the little looking-glass of the modern and classic imagination. This is that 'melancholy a man knows when he is face to face' with Nature, and thinks 'he hears her communing with him about' the mournfulness of being born and of dying; and how can it do otherwise than call into his mind 'its exiles, its flights across the seas', that it may stir the ever-smouldering ashes? No Gaelic poetry is so popular in Gaelic-speaking places as the lamentations of Oisin, old and miserable, remembering the companions and the loves of his youth, and his three hundred years in faeryland, and his faery love: all dreams withering in the winds of time lament in his lamentations:

> The clouds are long above me this night; last night was a long night to me; although I find this day long, yesterday was still longer. Every day that comes to me is long...No one in this great world is like me — a poor old man dragging stones. The clouds are long above me this night. I am the last man of the Fianna, the great Oisin, the son of Finn, listening to the sound of bells. The clouds are long above me this night.

Matthew Arnold quotes the lamentation of Llywarch Hen as a type of the Celtic melancholy, but I prefer to quote it as a type of the primitive melancholy:

> O my crutch, is it not autumn when the fern is red and the water-flag yellow? Have I not hated that which I love?...Behold, old age, which makes sport of me, from the hair of my head and my teeth, to my eyes which women loved. The four things I have all my life most hated fall upon me together — coughing and old age, sickness and sorrow. I am old, I am alone, shapeliness and warmth are gone from me, the couch of honour shall be no more mine; I am miserable, I am bent on my crutch. How evil was the lot allotted to Llywarch, the night he was brought forth! Sorrows without end and no deliverance from his burden.

An Elizabethan writer describes extravagant sorrow by calling it 'to weep Irish'; and Oisin and Llywarch Hen are, I think, a little nearer even to us modern Irish than they are to most people.

That is why our poetry and much of our thought is melancholy. 'The same man', writes Dr Hyde in the beautiful prose which he first writes in Gaelic, 'who will to-day be dancing, sporting, drinking, and shouting, will be soliloquising by himself to-morrow, heavy and sick and sad in his own lonely little hut, making a croon over departed hopes, lost life, the vanity of this world, and the coming of death.'

IV

Matthew Arnold asks how much of the Celt must one imagine in the ideal man of genius. I prefer to say, how much of the ancient hunters and fishers and of the ecstatic dancers among hills and woods must one imagine in the ideal man of genius? Certainly a thirst for unbounded emotion and a wild melancholy are troublesome things in the world, and do not make its life more easy or orderly, but it may be the arts are founded on the life beyond the world, and that they must cry in the ears of our penury until the world has been consumed and become a vision. Certainly, as Samuel Palmer wrote, excess is the vivifying spirit of the finest art, and we must always seek to make excess more abundantly excessive. Matthew Arnold has said that if he were asked 'where English got its turn for melancholy and its turn for natural magic', he 'would answer with little doubt that it got much of its melancholy from a Celtic source, with no doubt at all that from a Celtic source it got nearly all its natural magic'.

I will put this differently and say that literature dwindles to a mere chronicle of circumstance, or passionless fantasies, and passionless meditations, unless it is constantly flooded with the passions and beliefs of ancient times,[4] and that of all the fountains of the passions and beliefs of ancient times in Europe, the Slavonic, the Finnish, the Scandinavian, and the Celtic, the Celtic alone has been for centuries close to the main river of European literature. It has again and again brought 'the vivifying spirit' 'of excess' into the arts of Europe. Ernest Renan has told how the visions of Purgatory seen by pilgrims to Lough Derg — once visions of the pagan underworld, as the boat made out of a hollow tree that bore the pilgrim to the holy island were alone enough to prove — gave European thought new symbols of a more abundant penitence; and had so great an influence that he has written, 'It cannot be doubted for a moment that to the number of poetical themes Europe owes to the genius of the Celt is to be added the framework of the *Divine Comedy*.'

A little later the legends of Arthur and his Table, and of the Holy Grail, once, it seems, the cauldron of an Irish god, changed the literature of Europe, and, it may be, changed, as it were, the very roots of man's emotions by their influence on the spirit of chivalry and on the spirit of romance; and later still Shakespeare found his Mab, and probably his Puck, and one knows not how much else of his faery kingdom, in Celtic legend; while at the beginning of our own day Sir Walter Scott gave Highland legends and Highland excitability so great a mastery over all romance that they seem romance itself.

In our own time Scandinavian tradition, because of the imagination of Richard Wagner and of William Morris and of the earlier and, as I think, greater Henrik Ibsen, has created a new romance, and, through the imagination of Richard Wagner, become all but the most passionate element in the arts of the modern world. There is indeed but one other element as passionate, the still unfaded legends of Arthur and of the Holy Grail; and now a new fountain of legends, and, as I think, a more abundant fountain than any in Europe, is being opened, the fountain of Gaelic legends: the tale of Deirdre, who alone among women who have set men mad had equal loveliness and wisdom; the tale of the Sons of Tuireann, with its unintelligible mysteries, an old Grail Quest as I think; the tale of the four children changed into four swans, and lamenting over many waters; the tale of the love of Cuchulain for an immortal goddess, and his coming home to a mortal woman in the end; the tale of his many battles at the ford with that dear friend he kissed before the battles, and over whose dead body he wept when he had killed him; the tale of his death and of the lamentations of Emer; the tale of the flight of Grania with Diarmuid, strangest of all tales of the fickleness of woman, and the tale of the coming of Oisin out of faeryland, and of his memories and lamentations. 'The Celtic movement', as I understand it, is principally the opening of this fountain, and none can measure of how great importance it may be to coming times, for every new fountain of legends is a new intoxication for the imagination of the world. It comes at a time when the imagination of the world is as ready as it was at the coming of the tales of Arthur and of the Grail for a new intoxication. The reaction against the rationalism of the eighteenth century has mingled with a reaction against the materialism of the nineteenth

century, and the symbolical movement, which has come to
perfection in Germany in Wagner, in England in the Pre-
Raphaelites, in France in Villiers de l'Isle-Adam, and Mallarmé,
and in Belgium in Maeterlinck, and has stirred the imagination
of Ibsen and D'Annunzio, is certainly the only movement that is
saying new things. The arts by brooding upon their own intensity
have become religious, and are seeking, as I think Verhaeren[5]
has said, to create a sacred book. They must, as religious thought
has always done, utter themselves through legends; and the
Slavonic and Finnish legends tell of strange woods and seas, and
the Scandinavian legends are held by a great master, and tell also
of strange woods and seas, and the Welsh legends are held by
almost as many great masters as the Greek legends, while the
Irish legends move among known woods and seas, and have so
much of a new beauty that they may well give the opening century
its most memorable symbols.

Notes

1. Virgil, *Eclogues*, 7. 45, 'mossy springs and grass softer than sleep'.
2. Virgil, *Eclogues*, 2. 48, '[the shining Naiad] picks pale irises and
poppy heads and mixes them with the narcissus and the sweet smelling
anice'.
3. William Sharp, who probably invented the proverb, but, invented
or not, it remains true. [Yeats's note of 1924.]
4. I should have added as an alternative that the supernatural may
at any moment create new myths, but I was timid. [Yeats's note of 1924.]
5. Emile Verhaeren (1855-1916), Belgian poet and dramatist.

11

John Eglinton (ed.), from *Literary Ideals in Ireland*, 1899

A debate took place in the pages of the Saturday issues of the Daily Express *in 1898, which developed, as Eglinton explained in his Introduction to this volume, 'a certain organic unity'. It started with Eglinton's essay 'What Should be the Subjects of National Drama?', to which Yeats partially replied in a piece on the 'Poems and Stories of Miss Nora Hopper' (a minor writer). Apart from the essays reprinted here, there were pieces by Yeats on 'John Eglinton and Spiritual Art', and 'The Autumn of the Flesh', John Eglinton on 'Mr Yeats and Popular Poetry', and W. Larminie on 'Legends as Material for Literature'. For Yeats, the whole debate was some kind of 'holding operation' before the announcement of the Irish Literary Theatre in December.*

Eglinton (William Kirkpatrick Magee, 1868-1961) published Anglo-Irish Essays *in 1917, and a* Memoir *of his friend AE in 1937. AE (George Russell, 1867-1935) was actively involved in the cultivation of the Celtic Twilight, and produced a large body of poetry, drama and journalism.*

11(a) John Eglinton, 'What Should be the Subjects of National Drama?'

Supposing a writer of dramatic genius were to appear in Ireland, where would he look for the subject of a national drama? This question might serve as a test of what nationality really amounts to in Ireland — a somewhat trying one, perhaps, yet it is scarcely unfair to put the question to those who speak of our national literature with hardly less satisfaction in the present than confidence in the future. Would he look for it in the Irish legends, or in the life of the peasantry and folk-lore, or in Irish history and patriotism, or in life at large as reflected in his own

118

consciousness? There are several reasons for thinking that the growing hopes of something in store for national life in this country are likely to come to something. In the great countries of Europe, although literature is apparently as prosperous as ever and is maintained with a circumstance which would seem to ensure it eternal honour, yet the springs from which the modern literary movements have been fed are probably dried up — the springs of simplicity, hope, belief, and an absolute originality like that of Wordsworth. If also, as seems likely, the approaching ages on the Continent are to be filled with great social and political questions and events which can hardly have immediate expression in literature, it is quite conceivable that literature, as it did once before, would migrate to a quiet country like Ireland, where there is no great tradition to be upset or much social sediment to be stirred up, and where the spectacle of such changes might afford a purely intellectual impulse. More important, of course, and certain than any such chances from without is the positive feeling of encouragement which is now taking the place of the hatreds and despondencies of the past. We may think that the peasantry are outside the reach of culture, that the gentry exhaust their function in contributing able officers to the British army, and that, frankly, there is nothing going on in the political or ecclesiastical or social life of Ireland on which to rest any but the most sober hopes for the future, still no one can say that political feebleness or stagnation might not be actually favourable to some original manifestation in the world of ideas. What Renan says, in speaking of the Jews, that 'a nation whose mission it is to revolve in its bosom spiritual truths is often weak politically', may be used with regard to Ireland as an argument that at least nothing stands in its way in this direction.

The ancient legends of Ireland undoubtedly contain situations and characters as well suited for drama as most of those used in the Greek tragedies which have come down to us. It is, nevertheless, a question whether the mere fact of Ireland having been the scene of these stories is enough to give an Irish writer much advantage over anyone else who is attracted by them, or whether anything but belles lettres, as distinguished from a national literature, is likely to spring from a determined pre-occupation with them. Belles lettres seek a subject outside experience, while a national literature, or any literature of a genuine kind, is simply the outcome and expression of a strong interest in life itself. The truth is, these subjects, much as we may admire them and regret that we have nothing equivalent to them in the modern world, obstinately refuse to be taken up out of their old environment and be transplanted into the world of modern sympathies. The proper mode of treating them is a secret lost with the subjects themselves. It is clear that if Celtic traditions are to be an active influence in future Irish literature they must seem to us worthy of the same compliment as that paid by Europe to the Greeks; we must go to them rather than expect them to come to us, studying them as closely as possible, and allowing them to influence us as they may. The significance of that interest in folk-lore and antiquities, which is so strong in this country, can hardly be different from that of the writings of Herder and others in German literature, and may lie in this, that some hint is caught in such studies of the forgotten mythopœic secret.

As to Irish history and the subjects which it offers — a well-known Scotch Professor once said that Ireland was not a nation because it had never had a Burns nor a Bannockburn. It is, however, as reasonable to think that these glorious memories of Scottish nationality will form a drag on its further evolution as that the want of a peasant poet, or of a recollection of having at least once given the Saxons a drubbing, will be fatal to an attempt to raise people above themselves in this country by giving expression to latent ideals. Ireland must exchange the patriotism which looks back for the patriotism which looks forward. The Jews had this kind of patriotism, and it came to something, and the Celtic peoples have been remarkable for it. The Saxon believes in the present, and, indeed, it belongs to him. The Romance nations, from whose hold the world has been slipping, can hardly be expected just yet to give up the consolations of history.

In short, we need to realise in Ireland that a national drama or literature must spring from a native interest in life and its problems and a strong capacity for life among the people. If these do not, or cannot exist, there cannot exist a national drama or literature. In London and Paris they seem to believe in theories and 'movements', and to regard individuality as a noble but 'impossible' savage; and we are in some danger of being absorbed into their error. Some of our disadvantages are our safeguards. In all ages poets and thinkers have owed far less to their countries than their countries have owed to them.

11(b) John Eglinton, 'National Drama and Contemporary Life'

I am sorry that Mr Yeats, in his recent article on Miss Norah Hopper's poems, should have taken for granted that my intention in raising the question I did was combative, as, in truth, I simply wished to put it as clearly as possible, without suggesting any definite answer. It should hardly have occurred to me to put it at all, but that Mr Yeats' own dramatic poems seemed to open up the possibility of a drama with a distinctive note in this country.

Mr Yeats mentions Ibsen's *Peer Gynt* and Wagner's musical dramas as examples of national literature founded on the ancient legends of the authors' countries. I should say at once that I did not deny the possibility of a poet being inspired by the legends of his country; it would be strange indeed if he did not sometimes look towards them. The extent to which a great poetic intelligence, supremely interested in life, would use these legends for his images and themes would depend a good deal on the kind and degree of interest prevalent concerning them. If they yielded him typical situations and characters, such as Shakespeare looked for in legend and history, I fancy his joy would be great to discover these in stories which were the peculiar heritage of his country, and known to every one in it. But in the hands of such a poet these characters and situations become entirely new creations by virtue of the new spirit and import which he puts into them; the mode of treating them as they exist in tradition is a lost secret, but the power to make them live again in a new way is a secret of which the artist must be possessed. Prospero, in *The Tempest*, lying in Shakespeare's mind, drew the vitality by which he still lives from that source. Brutus and Cassius in *Julius Cæsar* are rather reincarnations of Romans in the Elizabethan age than archæologically Romans. Finn and Cuculain, if they are to appear once more in literature — and I, for one, shall welcome them — must be expected to take up on their broad shoulders something of the weariness and fret of our age, if only to show how lightly they may be carried, and to affright with shadowing masses of truth, such as mortals hurl not now, the uneasy seats of error.

I was not aware, I confess, of the fact which Mr Yeats mentions, that Wagner's dramas are becoming to Germany what the Greek tragedies were to Greece. The crowd of elect persons seated in curiously-devised seats at Bayreuth does not seem very like the whole Athenian democracy thronging into their places for a couple of obols supplied by the State, and witnessing in good faith the deeds of their ancestors. Perhaps the strongest part of Tolstoi's recent manifesto, *What is Art?* was his analysis of Wagner's theory that the two arts of drama and music could supplement each other and coincide, as Wagner supposed. The Greeks were a poetical people, just as the Germans are a musical people, and as the Greek dramas have come down to us without the music, so, one fancies, Wagner's music, or fragments of it, will go down to posterity without the words. His weakness as a dramatist is perhaps proportional to the passionateness of his music and the elaborateness of his stage accessories; and, indeed, I should not care to have to argue seriously against his being to this age what Sophocles and Shakespeare were to theirs. The national poet, and even dramatist, of Germany is still, I think, another man, whose themes were not always German, and whose poetry remains the record of an age awakening to new ideas. As to *Peer Gynt* — if *Faust* is reproached with a lack of coherence, what are we to say of *Peer Gynt*, which is a sort of *Faust* in nubibus? Ibsen appears to have found himself in a drama which is not ideal drama, because neither in its form nor in its dominating ideas is it poetical, but which seems the nearest thing to a distinctive drama reached in this century.

There are two conceptions of poetry, mutually antagonistic so far, and not to be reconciled except in the life-work of another great poet, of which one may be called Wordsworthian, which regards the poetic consciousness as acting from within outward and able to confer on even common things the radiance of the imagination; the other, to which those who are rather in sympathy with art than with philosophy are inclined, regards the poet as passive to elect influences and endowing old material with new form. The first regards the poet as a seer and a spiritual force; the second as an aristocratic craftsman. The first looks to man himself as the source of inspiration; the second to tradition, to the forms and images in which old conceptions have been embodied — old faiths, myths, dreams. The weakness of the first is an inclination to indifference toward the form and comeliness of art, as in Whitman; while the second, if it hold aloof from the first, cuts itself asunder from the source of all regeneration in art. The bias of the first is toward naked statement, hard fact, dogmatism; the bias of the second toward theory, diffuseness, insincerity. The latter appears to me to be the bias of belles lettres at present. The poet looks too much away from himself and from his age, does not feel the facts of life enough, but seeks in art an escape from them. Consequently, the art he achieves cannot be the expression of the age and of himself—cannot be representative or national.

The whole subject of the drama derives an interest from a consideration of the weakness of the present century in this respect. English literature, as a recent writer in the American *Dial* says, has nothing to show but Shelley's 'Cenci'; and the same writer urges that the drama is the 'top achievement of the human intellect'.

11(c) AE, 'Literary Ideals in Ireland'

It is a dangerous thing to intervene between two such masters of dialectic as W. B. Yeats and John Eglinton, but the comparatively simple issue raised at first has been found to need, for its just discussion, a divergence into the elemental principles of art and a consideration of life itself; and now the disputants ask of each other questions as difficult to answer as the question asked of Christ by Pilate. I think that they have only vaguely apprehended each other's position, and that there is little real difference between them. What has caused this misapprehension is, that although they stand on much the same ground they have come to it by different roads; they represent different intellectual traditions. John Eglinton is a disciple of Thoreau, Emerson, Arnold, and Whitman. Mr Yeats is a romanticist of the line of Shelley and Keats; but his is a romanticism exalted so that a spiritual passion breathes through his work, and earthly love and beauty in it become the symbols of divine things. I think also, if I rightly understand John Eglinton's admiration of Wordsworth, it is because Wordsworth, more than any of his contemporaries, divined a spiritual presence in nature — a being veiled by light and clouds and stars and seas. Though both seek as best in literature the traces of an identical essence, there yet seems a division of aim. I would be glad to reconcile these differences, which are bewildering in a country which has hesitated so long before adopting a literary ideal — where a conflict of opinion on such matters, not very clearly argued, may delay the day of better things we hope for.

I am not sure that 'these ancient legends refuse to be taken out of their old environment'. I think that the tales which have been preserved for a hundred generations in the heart of the people must have had such a power, because they had in them a core of eternal truth. Truth is not a thing of today or tomorrow. Beauty, heroism, and spirituality do not change like fashion, being the reflection of an unchanging spirit. The face of faces which looks at us through so many shifting shadows has never altered the form of its perfection since the face of man, made after its image, first looked back on its original:

> For these red lips, with all their mournful pride,
> Troy passed away in one high funeral gleam,
> And Usna's children died.

These dreams, antiquities, traditions, once actual, living, and historical, have passed from the world of sense into the world of memory and thought; and time, it seems to me, has not taken away from their power nor made them more remote from sympathy, but has rather purified them by removing them from earth unto heaven: from things which the eye can see and the ear can hear; they have become what the heart ponders over, and are so much nearer, more familiar, more suitable for literary use, than the day they were begotten. They have now the character of symbol, and, as symbol, are more potent than history. They have crept through veil after veil of the manifold nature of man, and now each dream, heroism, or beauty, has laid itself nigh the divine power it represents, the suggestion of which made it first beloved; and they are ready for the use of the spirit, a speech of which every word has a significance beyond itself, and Deirdre is like Helen, a symbol of eternal beauty, and Cuculain represents as much as Prometheus the heroic spirit, the redeemer in man.

It is for such a treatment, I think, Mr Yeats argues; but I do not believe John Eglinton has so understood him, or he would, I think, have hesitated before entering on this discussion. In so far as these ancient ideals live in the memory of man, they are contemporary to us as much as electrical science; for the shows which time brings now to our senses, before they can be used in literature, have to enter into exactly the same world of human imagination as the Celtic traditions live in. And their fitness for literary use is not there determined by their freshness, but by their power of suggestion. Modern literature, where it is really literature and not bookmaking, grows more subjective year after year, and the mind has a wider range over time than the physical nature has. Many things live in it — empires which have never crumbled, beauty which has never perished, love whose fires have never waned; and, in this formidable competition for use in the artist's mind, today stands only its chance with a thousand days. To question the historical accuracy of the use of such memories is not a matter which can be rightly raised; the question is — do they express lofty things to the soul? If they do they have justified themselves.

Mr Eglinton, here I think rather petulantly, asks what does Mr Yeats mean by saying, 'the poetic passion is not in nature', and that 'art is to be liberated from life'? A little reflection should have suggested the exact sense of the words to so subtle a mind. But, as I said before, the misapprehension may be due to a difference of intellectual tradition: in the various schools, words are used with a different significance; the light of the mystic is not the light of the scientist, nor the light of the educator, nor the light of the common man; he may not be familiar with the transcendental philosophy which Mr Yeats, in common with an ever-increasing number of thoughtful men, has adopted, to which the spirit in man is not a product of nature, but antecedes nature, and is above it as sovereign, being of the very essence of that spirit which breathed on the face of the waters, and whose song, flowing from the silence as an incantation, summoned the stars into being out of chaos. To regain that spiritual consciousness with its untramelled ecstasy, is the hope of every mystic. That ecstasy is the poetic passion; it is not of nature, though it may breathe within it, and use it, and transform its images by a magical power. To liberate art from life is simply to absolve it from the duty laid upon it by academic critics of representing only what is seen, what is heard, what is felt, what is thought by man in his normal — that is, his less exalted, less spiritual moments, when he is least truly himself. Though he has been for a hundred years absorbed in the lust of the flesh, the lust of the eyes, and the pride of life, in the moment he has attained to spiritual vision and ecstasy he has come to his true home, to his true self, to that which shall exist when the light of the sun shall be dark and the flocks of stars withdrawn from the fields of heaven. The art which is inspired by the Holy Breath must needs speak of things which have no sensuous existence, of hopes all unearthly, and fires of which the colours of day are only shadows. The 'quaint rhythmic trick' is a mnemonic by which the poet records, though it be but an errant and faltering tune, the inner music of life. To sum it all up, Mr Yeats, in common with other literary men, is trying to ennoble literature by making it religious rather than secular, by using his art for the revelation of another world rather than to depict this one. John Eglinton would not, I think, dissent greatly from this as a high aim. He has been misled as to Mr Yeats' position by an unfamiliarity with the symbols which the poet employs in his subtle and mystic art.

11(d) AE, 'Nationality and Cosmopolitanism in Literature'

As one of those who believe that the literature of a country is for ever creating a new soul among its people, I do not like to think that literature with us must follow an inexorable law of sequence, and gain a spiritual character only after the bodily passions have grown weary and exhausted themselves. Whether the art of any of the writers of the decadence does really express spiritual things is open to doubt. The mood in which their work is conceived, a sad and distempered emotion through which no new joy quivers, seems too often to tell rather of exhausted vitality than of the ecstasy of a new life. However much, too, their art refines itself, choosing ever rarer and more exquisite forms of expression, underneath it all an intuition seems to disclose only the old wolfish lust hiding itself beneath the golden fleece of the spirit. It is not the spirit breaking through corruption, but the life of the senses longing to shine with the light which makes saintly things beautiful; and it would put on the jewelled raiment of seraphim, retaining still a heart of clay smitten through and through with the unappeasable desire of the flesh: so Rossetti's women, who have around them all the circumstances of poetry and romantic beauty, seem through their sucked-in lips to express a thirst which could be allayed in no spiritual paradise. Art in the decadence in our times might be symbolized as a crimson figure undergoing a dark crucifixion; the hosts of light are overcoming it, and it is dying filled with anguish and despair at a beauty it cannot attain. All these strange emotions have a profound psychological interest. I do not think because a spiritual flaw can be urged against a certain phase of life that it should remain unexpressed. The psychic maladies which attack all races when their civilization grows old must needs be understood to be dealt with; and they cannot be understood without being revealed in literature or art.

But in Ireland we are not yet sick with this sickness. As psychology it concerns only the curious. As expressing a literary ideal, I think a consideration of it was a mere side-issue in the discussion Mr Yeats' article continued. The discussion on the one side was really a plea for nationality in our literature, and on the other a protest on behalf of individualism. It is true that nationality may express itself in many ways; it may not be at all evident in the subject matter, but may be very evident in the sentiment. But a literature loosely held together by some emotional characteristics common to the writers, however great it may be, does not fulfil the purpose of a literature or art created by a number of men who have a common aim in building up an overwhelming ideal — who create, in a sense, a soul for their country, and who have a common pride in the achievement of all. The world has not seen this since the great antique civilizations of Egypt and Greece passed away. We cannot imagine an Egyptian artist daring enough to set aside the majestic attainment of many centuries. An Egyptian boy as he grew up must have been overawed by the national tradition and have felt that it was not to be set aside; it was beyond his individual rivalry. The soul of Egypt incarnated in him, and, using its immemorial language and its mysterious lines, the efforts of the least workman who decorated a tomb seem to have been directed by the same hand that carved the Sphinx. This adherence to a traditional form is true of Greece, though to a less extent. The little Tanagra terra-cottas might have been done by Phidias, and in literature Ulysses and Agamemnon were not the heroes of one epic, but appeared endlessly in epic and drama. Since the Greek civilization no European nation has had an intellectual literature which was genuinely national. In the present century, leaving aside a few things in outward circumstance, there is little to distinguish the work of the best English writers or artists from that of their Continental contemporaries. Millais, Leighton, Rossetti, Turner — how different from each other, and yet they might have painted the same pictures as born Frenchmen and it would not have excited any great surprise as a marked divergence from French art. The cosmopolitan spirit, whether for good or for evil, is hastily obliterating distinctions. What is distinctly national in these countries is less valuable than the immense wealth of universal ideas; and the writers who use this wealth appeal to no narrow circle: the foremost writers, the Tolstois and Ibsens, are conscious of addressing a European audience.

If nationality is to justify itself in the face of all this, it must be because the country which preserves its individuality does so with the profound conviction that its peculiar ideal is nobler than that which the cosmopolitan spirit suggests — that this ideal is so precious to it that its loss would be as the loss of the soul, and that it could not be realised without an aloofness from, if not an actual indifference to, the ideals which are spreading so rapidly over Europe. Is it possible for any nationality to make such a defence of its isolation? If not, let us read Goethe, Balzac, Tolstoi, men so much greater than any we can show, try to absorb their universal wisdom and no longer confine ourselves to local traditions. But nationality was never so strong in Ireland as at the present time. It is beginning to be felt, less as a political movement than as a spiritual force. It seems to be gathering itself together, joining men, who were hostile before, in a new intellectual fellowship; and if all these could unite on fundamentals it would be possible in a generation to create a national ideal in Ireland, or rather to let that spirit incarnate fully which began among the ancient peoples, which has haunted the hearts and whispered a dim revelation of itself through the lips of the bards and peasant story-tellers.

Every Irishman forms some vague ideal of his country, born from his reading of history, or from contemporary politics, or from an imaginative intuition; and this Ireland in the mind it is, not the actual Ireland, which kindles his enthusiasm. For this he works and makes sacrifices; but because it has never had any philosophical definition, or a supremely beautiful statement in literature which gathered all aspirations about it, the ideal remains vague. This passionate love cannot explain itself; it cannot make another understand its devotion. To reveal Ireland in clear and beautiful light, to create the Ireland in the heart, is the province of a national literature. Other arts would add to this ideal hereafter, and social life and politics must in the end be in harmony. We are yet before our dawn, in a period comparable to Egypt before the first of her solemn temples constrained its people to an equal mystery, or to Greece before the first perfect statue had fixed an ideal of beauty which mothers dreamed of to mould their yet unborn children. We can see, however, as the ideal of Ireland grows from mind to mind it tends to assume the character of a sacred land. The Dark Rosaleen of Mangan expresses an almost religious adoration, and to a later writer it seems to be nigher to the Spiritual Beauty than other lands:

> And still the thoughts of Ireland brood
> Upon her holy quietude.

The faculty of abstracting from the land their eyes behold, another Ireland through which they wandered in dream, has always been a characteristic of the Celtic poets. This inner Ireland which the visionary eye saw, was the Tir-na-noge, this country of immortal youth, for they peopled it only with the young and beautiful. It was the Land of the Living Heart, a tender name which showed that it had become dearer than the heart of woman, and overtopped all other hopes as the last dream of the spirit, the bosom where it would rest after it had passed from the fading shelter of the world. And sure a strange and beautiful land this Ireland is, with a mystic beauty which closes the eyes of the body as in sleep, and opens the eyes of the spirit as in dreams; and never a poet has lain on our hillsides but gentle, stately figures, with hearts shining like the sun, move through his dreams, over radiant grasses, in an enchanted world of their own; and it has become alive through every haunted rath and wood and mountain and lake, so that we can hardly think of it otherwise than as the shadow of the thought of God. The last Celtic poet who has appeared shows the spiritual qualities of the first, when he writes of the grey rivers in their 'enraptured' wanderings, and when he sees in the jewelled bow which arches the heavens

> The Lord's seven spirits that shine through
> the rain.

This mystical view of nature, peculiar to but one English poet, Wordsworth, is a national characteristic; and much in the creation of the Ireland in the mind is already done, and only needs retelling by the new writers. More important, however, for the literature we are imagining as an offset to the cosmopolitan ideal, would be the creation of heroic figures, types, whether legendary or taken from history, and enlarged to epic proportions by our writers, who would use them in common, as Cuculain, Fionn, Ossian, and Oscar, were used by the generations of poets who have left us the bardic history of Ireland, wherein one would write of the battle fury of a hero, and another of a moment when his fire would turn to gentleness, and another of his love for some beauty of his time, and yet another tell how the rivalry of a spiritual beauty made him tire of love; and so from iteration and persistent dwelling on a few heroes their imaginative images found echoes in life, and other heroes arose continuing their tradition of chivalry.

That such types are of the highest importance and have the most ennobling influence on a country, cannot be denied. It was this idea led Whitman to 'exploit' himself as the typical American. He felt that what he termed a 'stock personality' was needed to elevate and harmonise the incongruous human elements in the States. English literature has always been more sympathetic with actual beings than with ideal types, and cannot help us much. A man who loves Dickens, for example, may grow to have a great tolerance for the grotesque characters which are the outcome of the social order in England, but he will not be assisted in the conception of a higher humanity; and this is true of very many English writers who lack a fundamental philosophy, and are content to take man, as he seems to be for the moment, rather than as the pilgrim of eternity — as one who is flesh today but who may hereafter grow divine, and who may shine at last like the stars of the morning, triumphant among the sons of God.

Mr Standish O'Grady, in his notable epic of Cuculain, was the first in our time to treat the Celtic traditions worthily. He has contributed one hero who awaits equal comrades, if, indeed, the tales of the Red Branch chivalry do not absorb the thoughts of many imaginative writers, and Cuculain remain the typical hero of the Gael, becoming to every boy who reads the story a revelation of what his own spirit is.

I have written at some length on the two paths which lie before us, for we have arrived at a parting of ways. One path leads, and has already led many Irishmen, of whom Professor Dowden[1] is a type, to obliterate all nationality from their work. The other path winds spirally upwards to a mountain-top of our own, which may be in the future the Meru to which many worshippers will turn. To remain where we are as a people, indifferent to literature, to art, to ideas, wasting the precious gift of public spirit we possess so abundantly in the sordid political rivalries, without practical or ideal ends, is to justify those who have chosen the other path and followed another star than ours. I do not wish anyone to infer from this a contempt for those who, for the last hundred years or so, have guided public opinion in Ireland. If they failed in one respect, it was out of a passionate sympathy for wrongs of which many are memories, thanks to them. And to them is due the creation of a force which may be turned in other directions,

not without a memory of those pale sleepers to whom we may
turn in thought, placing

A kiss of fire on the dim brow of failure,
A crown upon her uncrowned head.

Note

1. Edward Dowden (1843-1913), who was appointed to the Chair of
English at Trinity College, Dublin in 1867, was an opponent of
Nationalism.

12

W. B. Yeats, 'Ireland and the Arts', 1901

This was first published in United Ireland, *August 1901, and then in* Ideas of Good and Evil *(1903), and subsequently in* Essays and Introductions.

The arts have failed; fewer people are interested in them every generation. The mere business of living, of making money, of amusing oneself, occupies people more and more, and makes them less and less capable of the difficult art of appreciation. When they buy a picture it generally shows a long-current idea, or some conventional form that can be admired in that lax mood one admires a fine carriage in or fine horses in; and when they buy a book it is so much in the manner of the picture that it is forgotten, when its moment is over, as a glass of wine is forgotten. We who care deeply about the arts find ourselves the priesthood of an almost forgotten faith, and we must, I think, if we would win the people again, take upon ourselves the method and the fervour of a priesthood. We must be half humble and half proud. We see the perfect more than others, it may be, but we must find the passions among the people. We must baptize as well as preach.

The makers of religions have established their ceremonies, their form of art, upon fear of death, upon the hope of the father in his child, upon the love of man and woman. They have even gathered into their ceremonies the ceremonies of more ancient faiths, for fear a grain of the dust turned into crystal in some past fire, a passion that had mingled with the religious idea, might perish if the ancient ceremony perished. They have re-named wells and images and given new meanings to ceremonies of spring and midsummer and harvest. In very early days the arts were so

possessed by this method that they were almost inseparable from
religion, going side by side with it into all life. But, today, they
have grown, as I think, too proud, too anxious to live alone with
the perfect, and so one sees them, as I think, like charioteers
standing by deserted chariots and holding broken reins in their
hands, or seeking to go upon their way drawn by that sexual
passion which alone remains to them out of the passions of the
world. We should not blame them, but rather a mysterious
tendency in things which will have its end some day. In England,
men like William Morris, seeing about them passions so long
separated from the perfect that it seemed as if they could not be
changed until society had been changed, tried to unite the arts
once more to life by uniting them to use. They advised painters
to paint fewer pictures upon canvas, and to burn more of them
on plates; and they tried to persuade sculptors that a candlestick
might be as beautiful as a statue. But here in Ireland, when the
arts have grown humble, they will find two passions ready to
their hands, love of the Unseen Life and love of country. I would
have a devout writer or painter often content himself with subjects
taken from his religious beliefs; and if his religious beliefs are
those of the majority, he may at last move hearts in every cottage;
while even if his religious beliefs are those of some minority, he
will have a better welcome than if he wrote of the rape of
Persephone, or painted the burning of Shelley's body. He will
have founded his work on a passion which will bring him to many
besides those who have been trained to care for beautiful things
by a special education. If he is a painter or a sculptor he will find
churches awaiting his hand everywhere, and if he follows the
masters of his craft our other passion will come into his work
also, for he will show his Holy Family winding among hills like
those of Ireland, and his Bearer of the Cross among faces copied
from the faces of his own town. Our art teachers should urge their
pupils into this work, for I can remember, when I was myself a
Dublin art student, how I used to despond, when youthful ardour
burned low, at the general indifference of the town.

But I would rather speak to those who, while moved in other
things than the arts by love of country, are beginning to write,
as I was some sixteen years ago, without any decided impulse to
one thing more than another, and especially to those who are
convinced, as I was convinced, that art is tribeless, nationless, a
blossom gathered in No Man's Land. The Greeks looked within
their borders, and we, like them, have a history fuller than any

133

modern history of imaginative events; and legends which surpass, as I think, all legends but theirs in wild beauty, and in our land, as in theirs, there is no river or mountain that is not associated in the memory with some event or legend; while political reasons have made love of country, as I think, even greater among us than among them. I would have our writers and craftsmen of many kinds master this history and these legends, and fix upon their memory the appearance of mountains and rivers and make it all visible again in their arts, so that Irishmen, even though they had gone thousands of miles away, would still be in their own country. Whether they choose for the subject the carrying off of the Brown Bull or the coming of Patrick, or the political struggle of later times, the other world comes so much into it all that their love of it would move in their hands also, and as much, it may be, as in the hands of the Greek craftsmen. In other words, I would have Ireland re-create the ancient arts, the arts as they were understood in Judaea, in India, in Scandinavia, in Greece and Rome, in every ancient land; as they were understood when they moved a whole people and not a few people who have grown up in a leisured class and made this understanding their business.

I think that my reader will have agreed with most that I have said up till now, for we all hope for arts like these. I think indeed I first learned to hope for them myself in Young Ireland Societies, or in reading the essays of Davis. An Englishman, with his belief in progress, with his instinctive preference for the cosmopolitan literature of the last century, may think arts like these parochial, but they are the arts we have begun the making of.

I will not, however, have all my readers with me when I say that no writer, no artist, even though he choose Brian Borúmha or Saint Patrick for his subject, should try to make his work popular. Once he has chosen a subject he must think of nothing but giving it such an expression as will please himself. As Walt Whitman has written:

> The oration is to the orator, the acting is to the actor and
>   actress, not to the audience:
> And no man understands any greatness or goodness, but his
>   own or the indication of his own.

He must make his work a part of his own journey towards beauty and truth. He must picture saint or hero, or hillside, as he sees them, not as he is expected to see them, and he must comfort himself, when others cry out against what he has seen, by remembering that no two men are alike, and that there is no 'excellent beauty without strangeness'. In this matter he must be without humility. He may, indeed, doubt the reality of his vision if men do not quarrel with him as they did with the Apostles, for there is only one perfection and only one search for perfection, and it sometimes has the form of the religious life and sometimes of the artistic life; and I do not think these lives differ in their wages, for 'The end of art is peace', and out of the one as out of the other comes the cry: 'Sero te amavi, Pulchritudo tam antiqua et tam nova! Sero te amavi!'[1]

The Catholic Church is not the less the Church of the people because the Mass is spoken in Latin, and art is not less the art of the people because it does not always speak in the language they are used to. I once heard my friend Mr Ellis[2] say, speaking at a celebration in honour of a writer whose fame had not come till long after his death, 'It is not the business of a poet to make himself understood, but it is the business of the people to understand him. That they are at last compelled to do so is the proof of his authority.' And certainly if you take from art its martyrdom, you will take from it its glory. It might still reflect the passing modes of mankind, but it would cease to reflect the face of God.

If our craftsmen were to choose their subjects under what we may call, if we understand faith to mean that belief in a spiritual life which is not confined to one Church, the persuasion of their faith and their country, they would soon discover that although their choice seemed arbitrary at first, it had obeyed what was deepest in them. I could not now write of any other country but Ireland, for my style has been shaped by the subjects I have worked on, but there was a time when my imagination seemed unwilling, when I found myself writing of some Irish event in words that would have better fitted some Italian or Eastern event, for my style had been shaped in that general stream of European literature which has come from so many watersheds, and it was slowly, very slowly, that I made a new style. It was years before I could rid myself of Shelley's Italian light, but now I think my style is myself. I might have found more of Ireland if I had written in Irish, but I have found a little, and I have found all myself. I am persuaded that if the Irishmen who are painting conventional pictures or writing conventional books on alien subjects, which have been worn away like pebbles on the shore, would do the

135

same, they, too, might find themselves. Even the landscape-painter, who paints a place that he loves, and that no other man has painted, soon discovers that no style learned in the studios is wholly fitted to his purpose. And I cannot but believe that if our painters of Highland cattle and moss-covered barns were to care enough for their country to care for what makes it different from other countries, they would discover, when struggling, it may be, to paint the exact grey of the bare Burren Hills, and of a sudden, it may be, a new style, their very selves. And I admit, though in this I am moved by some touch of fanaticism, that even when I see an old subject written of or painted in a new way, I am yet jealous for Cuchulain, and for Baile and Aillinn, and for those grey mountains that still are lacking their celebration. I sometimes reproach myself because I cannot admire Mr Hughes' beautiful, piteous *Orpheus and Eurydice*[3] with an unquestioning mind. I say with my lips, 'The Spirit made it, for it is beautiful, and the Spirit bloweth where it listeth', but I say in my heart, 'Aengus and Edain would have served his turn'; but one cannot, perhaps, love or believe at all if one does not love or believe a little too much.

And I do not think with unbroken pleasure of our scholars who write about German writers or about periods of Greek history. I always remember that they could give us a number of little books which would tell, each book for some one county, or some one parish, the verses, or the stories, or the events that would make every lake or mountain a man can see from his own door an excitement in his imagination. I would have some of them leave that work of theirs which will never lack hands, and begin to dig in Ireland the garden of the future, understanding that here in Ireland the spirit of man may be about to wed the soil of the world.

Art and scholarship like these I have described would give Ireland more than they received from her, for they would make love of the unseen more unshakable, more ready to plunge deep into the abyss, and they would make love of country more fruitful in the mind, more a part of daily life. One would know an Irishman into whose life they had come — and in a few generations they would come into the life of all, rich and poor — by something that set him apart among men. He himself would understand that more was expected of him than of others because he had greater possessions. The Irish race would have become a chosen race, one of the pillars that uphold the world.

Notes

1. Augustine, *Confessions*, X, ch. 27, 'Too late I came to love thee, O thou Beauty so ancient and so fresh, too late I came to love thee.'
2. Yeats collaborated with Edwin Ellis on an edition of Blake.
3. A famous piece of sculpture by John Hughes (1865-1941).

13

Lady Gregory (ed.), from *Ideals in Ireland*, 1901

These passages are all taken from a volume edited in 1901 by Lady Gregory. Lady Isabella Augusta Gregory (1852-1932), who first met Yeats at Coole Park in 1896, was a formative influence both on him and on the whole of the Irish Literary Revival, especially the dramatic aspects as represented by Yeats, Edward Martyn, Synge and O'Casey. In her Introduction to Ideals in Ireland, *dated December 1900, she explained that she had gathered together articles from various journals, ranging from the* New Ireland Review *to the* Leader: 'My object in collecting them is to show to those who look beyond politics and horses, in what direction thought is moving in Ireland.'*

D. P. Moran (1871-1936) was the editor and proprietor of the Leader, *which started in 1900; his volume of essays,* The Philosophy of Irish Ireland, *appeared in 1905. George Moore (1852-1933) was a prolific novelist, but well known also for his autobiography* Hail and Farewell *(1911-14). Standish O'Grady (1846-1928) was an assiduous historian of Ireland, and another important influence on Yeats.*

13(a) AE, 'Nationality and Imperialism'

The idea of the national being emerged at no recognisable point in our history. It is older than any name we know. It is not earth born, but the synthesis of many heroic and beautiful moments, and these it must be remembered are divine in their origin. Every heroic deed is an act of the spirit, and every perception of beauty is vision with the divine eye, and not with the mortal sense. The spirit was subtly intermingled with the shining of old romance, and it was no mere phantasy which shows Ireland at its dawn in a misty light thronged with divine figures, and beneath and nearer to us, demigods and heroes fading into recognisable men. The bards took cognisance only of the most notable personalities who preceded them; and of these only the acts which had a symbolic or spiritual significance; and these grew thrice refined as generations of poets in enraptured musings along by the mountains or in the woods, brooded upon their heritage of story until, as it passed from age to age, the accumulated beauty grew greater than the beauty of the hour, the dream began to enter into the children of our race, and their thoughts turned from earth to that world in which it had its inception.

It was a common belief among the ancient peoples that each had a national genius or deity who presided over them, in whose all-embracing mind they were enclosed, and by whom their destinies were shaped. We can conceive of the national spirit in Ireland as first manifesting itself through individual heroes or kings; and, as the history of famous warriors laid hold upon the people, extending its influence through the sentiment engendered in the popular mind until it created therein the germs of a kindred nature.

An aristocracy of lordly and chivalrous heroes is bound in time to create a great democracy by the reflection of their character in the mass, and the idea of the divine right of kings is succeeded by the idea of the divine right of the people. If this sequence cannot be traced in any one respect with historical regularity, it is because of the complexity of national life, its varied needs, and its infinite changes of sentiment; but the threads are all taken up in the end, and ideas which were forgotten and absent from the voices of men will be found, when recurred to, to have grown to a rarer and more spiritual beauty in their quiet abode in the heart. The seeds which are sown at the beginning of a race bear their flowers and fruits towards its close; and those antique names which already begin to stir us with their power, Angus, Lu, Deirdre, Finn, Ossian, and the rest, will be found to be each one the symbol of enduring qualities, and their story a trumpet through which will be blown the music of an eternal joy, the sentiment of an inexorable justice, the melting power of beauty in sorrow, the wisdom of age, and the longings of the spirit.

The question arises how this race inheritance can best be preserved and developed. To some it is of no value, but these are voices of dust. To some the natural outcome is coalition with another power, and a frank and full acceptance of the imperial ideal. To some the solution lies in a self-centred national life. I will not touch here upon the material advantages of one or other course, which can best be left to economists to discuss. The literary man, who is, or ought to be, concerned mainly with intellectual interests, should only intervene in politics when principles affecting the spiritual life of his country are involved. To me the imperial ideal seems to threaten the destruction of that national being which has been growing through centuries, and I ask myself, What can it profit my race if it gain the empire of the world and yet lose its own soul — a soul which is only now growing to self-consciousness, and this to be lost simply that we may help to build up a sordid trade federation between England and her Colonies? Was our divine origin for this end? Did the bards drop in song the seed of heroic virtues, and beget the mystic chivalry of the past, and flood our being with spiritual longings, that we might at last sink to clay and seek only to inherit the earth? The mere area of the empire bewitches the commonplace mind, and turns it from its own land; yet the State of Athens was not so large as the Province of Munster, and, though dead, the memory of it is brighter than the living light of any people on earth today. Some, to whom I would be the last to deny nobility of thought and sincere conviction, would lead us from ourselves through the belief that the moral purification of the empire could be accomplished by us. I wish I could believe it. I am afraid our own political and social ethics demand all the attention we can give. There is a reservoir of spiritual life in the land, but it is hardly strong enough to repel English materialism, while we are nominally hostile to English ideas; and shall it be triumphant when we have given over our hopes of a separate national existence, and merged our dreams and longings with a nation which has become a byword for materialism? Under no rule are people so free, — we are told. A little physical freedom more or less matters nothing. Men are as happy and as upright as we, in countries where a passport is necessary to travel from one town to another. No form of government we know is perfect, and none will be permanent. The federation of the world and its typical humanity, exists in germ in the spiritual and intellectual outcasts of our time, who can find no place in the present social order. A nation is sacred as it holds few or many of those to whom spiritual ideals are alone worth having; the mode of life, prosperous or unfortunate, which brings them to birth and enables them to live is the best of any; and the genius of our country has acted wisely in refusing any alliance offering only material prosperity and power. Every race must work out its own destiny. England and the Colonies will, as is fit and right, work out theirs without our moral guidance. They would resent it if offered, just as we resent it from them. It may be affirmed that the English form of government is, on the whole, a good one, but it does not matter. It may be good for Englishmen, but it is not the expression of our national life and ideas. I express my ideals in literature; you, perhaps, in social reform. Both may be good; yours, indeed, may be best, but I would feel it a bitter injustice if I was compelled to order my life in accordance with your aims. I would do poorly what you shine in. We ask the liberty of shaping the social order in Ireland to reflect our own ideals, and to embody that national soul which has been slowly incarnating in our race from its cloudy dawn. The twentieth century may carry us far from Finn and Oscar and the stately chieftains and heroes of their time, far even from the ideals of Tone, Mitchell,[1] and Davis, but I hope it will not carry us into contented acceptance of the deadness, the dulness, the commonplace of English national sentiment, or what idealism remains in us, bequeathed from the past, range itself willingly under a banner which is regarded chiefly as a commercial asset by the most famous exponent of the imperial idea.

I feel that the idea expressed by several writers lately, that with many people in Ireland patriotism and nationality are only other names for race hatred, must be combated. It may be so with a few, but the charge has been levelled not at isolated individuals here and there, but at a much larger class who seriously think about their country.

We are told our attitude towards England and English things is a departure from the divine law of love. Let us look into the circumstances: a number of our rapidly dwindling race have their backs to a wall, they are making an appeal for freedom, for the right to choose their own ideals, to make their own laws, to govern their own lives according to the God-implanted law within them; seeing everywhere, too, the wreck of their hopes, the supremacy of an alien will, — to such people, striving desperately for a principle which is sacred and eternal, these moral platitudes are addressed. Is not freedom as necessary as love to my human soul or to any people? Can there be any real brotherhood without it? If we are debarred from the freedom we would have, how narrow is the range for human effort! We in Ireland would keep in mind our language, teach our children our history, the story of our heroes, and the long traditions of our race which stretch back to

God. But we are everywhere thwarted. A blockhead of a professor drawn from the intellectual obscurity of Trinity, and appointed as commissioner to train the national mind according to British ideas, meets us with an ultimatum: 'I will always discourage the speaking of Gaelic wherever I can.' We feel poignantly it is not merely Gaelic which is being suppressed, but the spiritual life of our race. A few ignoramuses have it in their power, and are trying their utmost, to obliterate the mark of God upon a nation. It is not from Shelley or Keats our peasantry derive their mental nourishment, now that they are being cut off from their own past. We see everywhere a moral leprosy, a vulgarity of mind creeping over them. The Police Gazettes, the penny novels, the hideous comic journals, replace the once familiar poems and the beautiful and moving memoirs of classic Ireland. The music that breathed Tir-nan-og and overcame men's hearts with all gentle and soft emotions is heard more faintly, and the songs of the London music halls may be heard in places where the music of fairy enchanted the elder generations. The shout of the cockney tourist sounds in the cyclopean crypts and mounds once sanctified by druid mysteries, and divine visitations, and passings from the mortal to the immortal. Ireland Limited is being run by English syndicates. It is the descent of a nation into hell, not nobly, not as a sacrifice made for a great end, but ignobly and without hope of resurrection. If we who watch protest bitterly at the racial degradation — for we have none of us attained all the moral perfections — we are assured that we are departing from the law of love. We can have such a noble destiny if we will only accept it. When we have lost everything we hoped for, lost our souls even, we can proceed to spiritualise the English, and improve the moral tone of the empire. Some, even those who are Celts, protest against our movements as forlorn hopes. Yet what does it matter whether every Celt perished in the land, so that our wills, inviolate to the last, make obeisance only to the light which God has set for guidance in our souls? Would not that be spiritual victory and the greatest success? What would be the success we are assured of if we lay aside our hopes? What could we have or what could we give to humanity if our mental integrity is broken? God gives no second gift to a nation if it flings aside its birthright. We cannot put on the ideals of another people as a garment. We cannot, with every higher instinct of our nature shocked and violated, express ourselves as lovers of the law that rules us. We would be slaves if we did. The incarnate love came not with peace but a sword. It does not speak only with the Holy Breath, but has in its armoury death and the strong weapons of the other immortals. It is better to remain unbroken to the last, and I count it as noble to fight God's battles as to keep His peace.

I confess I do not love England. Love is a spirit which will not, with me at least, come at all. It bestows itself, and will not be commanded, having laws and an end of its own. But for that myriad humanity which throngs the cities of England I feel a profound pity; for it seems to me that in factory, in mine, in warehouse, the life they have chosen to live in the past, the lives those born into that country must almost inevitably lead now, is farther off from beauty, more remote from spirit, more alien from deity, than that led by any people hitherto in the memory of the world. I have no hatred for them. I do not think any of my countrymen have, however they may phrase the feeling in their hearts. I think it is a spiritual antagonism they feel which they translate into terms of the more limited conscious mind. I think their struggle is in reality not against flesh and blood, but is a portion of the everlasting battle against principalities and powers and spiritual wickedness in high places, which underlies every other battle which has been or will be fought by men. I do not say that everything English is stupid, invariably and inevitably wrong. But I do say that every act by which England would make our people other than they would be themselves, is stupid, invariably and inevitably wrong. Not invariably wrong, perhaps, when judged from the external point of view, but invariably wrong when judged from the interior spiritual standpoint. How terrible a thing it is to hinder the soul in its freedom, let the wild upheavals and the madness of protest bear witness.

Though we are old, ethnologically considered, yet as a nation, a collective unit, we are young or yet unborn. If the stupefying influence of foreign control were removed, if we had charge of our own national affairs, it would mean the starting up into sudden life of a thousand dormant energies, spiritual, intellectual, artistic, social, economic, and human. The national spirit, like a beautiful woman, cannot or will not reveal itself wholly while a coarse presence is near, an unwelcome stranger in possession of the home. It is shy, hiding itself away in remote valleys, or in haunted mountains, or deep in the quiet of hearts that do not reveal themselves. Only to its own will it come and sing its hopes and dreams; not selfishly for itself alone, but sharing in the universal human hopes, and desirous of solving some of the eternal problems. Being still so young as a nation, and before the true starting of our career, we might say of ourselves as the great American poet of his race, with which so many of our own have mingled —

Have the elder races halted?
Do they droop and end their lesson, wearied, over there
    beyond the seas?
We take up the task eternal, and the burden, and the lesson.
Pioneers! Oh, pioneers!

13(b) D. P. Moran, 'The Battle of Two Civilizations'

I and many others have convinced ourselves, that Ireland during this century has in many vital matters played the fool. If this view in any way soothes the conscience of the English for their own country's cruel injustices to Ireland I cannot help it. Let the truth be stated though the sky should fall. We are sick of 'Irish national' make-believes and frauds, sick of shouting nation when there is no nation; and the much-abused national consciousness of the Irish people cries for truth and light, and death to shams and impostures.

The cry of the friendly Englishman, fully responded to by the 'reasonable' Irishman, is, 'Let us know more about Irishmen, and let Irishmen know more about us; we will learn to like and understand one another.' As against this view it is absolutely clear to me, though the expression may appear to have some of the form of a 'bull', that when two nations understand one another there is from that moment only one nation in it. International misunderstanding is one of the marks of nationhood. Our modern differences have largely arisen, not only because the English persisted in their attempt to bring up the Irish after their own pattern, but because the Irish, though vividly conscious of a separate national identity, did nearly their best to be English and completely failed. Where the English were dull, was in their attempt to throttle Irish civilization instead of allowing it to grow and develop in all its native vigour; and where the Irish were dull — dull beyond comprehension — was that while they with much noisy demonstration made a desperate stand for something which they called the eternal cause of Irish nationality, they did nearly their level best to turn themselves into Saxons.

144

Unfortunately it is difficult to get the Englishman to admit that there is any civilization in the world other than British. (And anglicised Ireland naturally enough has come roughly to that conclusion too.) This is one of his most flagrant examples of dulness. When he talks of morality, he thinks only of the British variety, of liberty, progress, good taste, and so on; he shows somewhat more intelligence on the question of manners, for here he allows himself to be haunted by the suspicion that his may after all be only second rate. He wants to anglicise the world; and everything is tainted with barbarism that is not British. This heroic state of self-conceit is perhaps natural to a vigorous but dull race that has made its mark upon the world; but it is not founded upon truth. There are other worthier things between heaven and earth than English music halls, May meetings, company promoters, and bean feasts. These may represent some of the highest points of English civilization, but there are other struggling civilizations that will have little or none of them; that may, in fact, have the hardihood to look upon most of them with contempt. The world is divided into civilizations: for several reasons I think this word is more expressive than the word nation. And surely, on the principle of liberty, which England prides herself so much upon, each civilization has as much right to look out on the world in its own way, as an individual has of holding his own views. England will not admit this. I do not blame her for attempting to spread by legitimate means, that form of civilization which, as it is her own, she not unnaturally holds to be the best; but her impatience of, and her ill-mannered contempt for, other civilizations, her denial that, if they happen to be any way weak, there is any justification whatever for their existence, makes her hated all over the world; and I fear that when a weak civilization impedes her advance, killing stands in great danger of ceasing to be murder. I think it would be a bad day for the world were one common form of civilization to embrace it all; when the individual and independent growth of separate nations was stopped. However, I cannot stay to develop this point now. I have used the word civilization instead of the word nation: the development of nationality is the natural development of a distinct civilization, and any power that kills the one, is guilty of the death of the other.

In Grattan's time Irish civilization was thrown overboard; but 'Irish nationality' was stuck up on a flag of green — even the colour was new fledged — and the people were exhorted to go forward and cover themselves with glory. If I am right in equating nationality with a distinct civilization, we get now a vivid glimpse of the first great source of the insincerity — all the more insidious because unconscious — the muddled thinking, the confusion of ideas, the contradictory aims which even the most cursory observer discerns in the Ireland of today. Since Grattan's time every popular leader, O'Connell, Butt,[2] Parnell, Dillon,[3] and Redmond, has perpetuated this primary contradiction. They threw over Irish civilization whilst they professed — and professed in perfect good faith — to fight for Irish nationality. What potential genius that contradiction has choked, what dishonesties and tragedies, above all what comedies, it has been responsible for, I will pass over without detailed inquiry. The Irish all this time, as they are at the present day, were absolutely different from the English. The genius of each nation was distinct. To English ideals we did not respond; English literature did not kindle our minds: we continued to be born the brightest, and continued to be reared the most stupid and helpless of peoples. There is something, be it instinct or the living subconscious tradition of an almost dead civilization, that says to nearly every Irish heart — 'Thou shalt be Irish: thou shalt not be English.' This is written plainly even over the history of the last hundred years — in every respect the most decadent century that Ireland has seen.

The propaganda of the Gaelic League has effected a partial revolution in Ireland. The criticism that it has inspired has been largely destructive; the energy it has let loose decidedly constructive. Much of the perpetual flow of wholesale and largely unreasonable denunciation of England was turned from its course and directed back — where it was badly wanted — upon Irishmen themselves; much of the energy that husbanded itself in idleness until certain political reforms were granted, commenced under the new inspiration to move and bestir itself at once. It is moving with increasing velocity as the conviction gains ground, that at last Ireland has gained some kind of footing, and can advance — somewhere.

The League found Ireland wrangling over the corpse of Parnell. When A, who shouted one cry, called himself an Irish Nationalist, and declared with many strong adjectives that B, who shouted a different cry, was a West Briton, it began gradually to dawn upon the average mind that, as there was practically no difference between A and B but a cry, 'Irish nationality' must be made of a very cloudy substance indeed. Under the inspiration of the new gospel of the Gaelic League, the common man, much to his surprise, was driven to the conclusion that A and B were, after all, a pair of ordinary, unmannerly, politicians, and nothing else. And then the light dawned upon him, that politics is not nationality, and that the nineteenth century had been for Ireland mostly a century of humbug. That, in brief, is the revolution that the Gaelic League has worked; and that revolution has fundamentally altered the Irish problem. Until a few years ago, no one challenged the accepted view that politics was the begin-all and end-all of Irish nationality. And as politics in Ireland consisted in booing against the English Government, and as Irish nationality was politics, the English Government became logically the sole destroyer of nationality. Of course it was an utterly false and an almost fatal position for us to have taken up. All the time that we were doing our share in the killing of our nation, everything was put down to England. An infallible way to distract criticism from domestic affairs — and this can be clearly seen by observing the state of the public temper in England at the present time — is to get entangled in a foreign war. When a great struggle is on hand, domestic reformers may sing for an audience. A people who are watching their nation in death-grips with another, are in little humour for attending to the parish pumps, least of all for listening to uncomplimentary criticism. But, supposing this condition of things lasted for a hundred years, what would become of the home economy? And this has practically been the condition under which Ireland has spent the century. We have been fighting England as our only enemy, looking to her as the sole source of all our evils, as the only possible source of all our blessings, inasmuch as until we had settled with her, we could do nothing for ourselves. All the while, like Pendennis, we ourselves were our greatest enemies. As politics was nationality, every patriotic Irishman who watched his decaying nation, felt new drops of hate for England descend into his heart. Until England could be brought to her senses no progress could be made, and as the life was all the time ebbing out of the Irish nation, then ten thousand curses be upon her oppressor. This attitude flows reasonably from the first false position that politics was nationality. When Ireland was great, she sent men of learning and religion to instruct and enlighten Europe; when she was at her lowest ebb, she sent out desperadoes with infernal machines. The commandment, 'Thou shalt be Irish', was written alike upon the hearts of all.

From the great error that nationality is politics, a sea of

corruption has sprung. Ireland was practically left unsubjected to wholesome native criticism, without which any collection of humanity will corrupt. If a lack of industrial energy and initiative were pointed out, the answer naturally was — 'Away, traitor. England robbed us of our industries; we can do nothing until she restores our rights.' If you said that the people drank too much — 'Well, what are the poor people to do; they are only human; wait until our rights are restored, and all that will be altered.' And so on. To find fault with your countrymen was to play into the hands of England, and act the traitor. There were enough abusing us, without Ireland's own joining in the chorus. This was the negative side of the matter: there was a positive side also. It manifestly became the policy of Irishmen to praise and bolster up their own people, and make out the most glowing account of their virtues and importance. The minor political leaders let themselves loose over the country, telling their audiences that they belonged to a great and immortal nation, that they were engaged in a noble struggle for Irish freedom, and that the eyes of the civilized world were upon them. Irish popular oratory was corrupted under these influences into one string of uncomplimentary adjectives applied to England and the English, and another string of an opposite description applied to Ireland. Thought had been squeezed out of the platform and the press, and every vestige of distinctive nationality was fast leaving the country. This was certainly a pretty pass for a quick-witted people to allow themselves to drift into. But once, I submit, that the Irish mind allowed itself to be muddled into considering politics and nationality convertible terms, the condition of things that resulted became, as an eminent Englishman might put it, 'inevitable'.

I will now attempt to trace, in broad outline, the influence which the state of things that I have referred to has had upon literary taste and literary production in Ireland, on social progress and the development of polite society, on the Irish attitude towards England and its powerful bearing upon the economic helplessness and stagnation of the country.

I think I have read somewhere that the great Duke of Marlborough knew no English history except that which he learned from Shakespeare's works. I mention this in order to point out that it takes an Englishman to get the most out of English literature, as it takes a Frenchman to get the most out of French literature. A literature steeped in the history, traditions, and genius of one nation is at the best only an imperfect tutor to the people of another nation; in fact, the common half-educated people of another nation will have none of it. The Irish nation has, this century, been brought up on English literature. Of course it never really kindled their minds or imaginations; they were driven to look at literature as a thing not understandable and above them — a position, I need scarcely say, not making for the development of self-respect or intellectual self-dependence. In most cases, when they left school they ceased to read anything but the newspapers. Of course there are many exceptions to this generalisation. If an Irishman received a higher English education, and lost touch with Irish aspirations, he practically became an Englishman; and many people with less advantages, by force of exceptional ability, got their heads above the entanglements around them and breathed something like free air. But I am talking of the common run of men who make up a nation, and not of the few exceptions. Tell me of any ordinary man in Dublin, Cork, or elsewhere, who professes an appreciation for the best products of English literature, and I will have no hesitation in informing you that he is an intellectual snob, mostly composed of affectation. Literature, to the common Irishman, is an ingenious collection of fine words which no doubt have some meaning, but which he is not going to presume to understand. A good speaker in Ireland is not a man who talks keen sense well, but one with 'the divil's flow of words'; and Irish 'oratory' has developed into the windiest thing on earth. The state of literature, and thought, and original intellectual activity of any kind had indeed dropped to a low level. The 'Irish National' literary output chiefly consisted of a few penny magazines in which the most commonplace rhymes were passed off as 'Irish' poetry, and which contained an unceasing and spirit-wearying flow of romances about '48, '98, and other periods, in all of which, of course, Ireland was painted spotless white. Romances in which Irish heroes of a couple of hundred years ago, who probably never spoke a word of English in their lives, were made to prate heroics in English of the 'Seest thou yon battlements' type, were so manifestly absurd that no one but very young boys could put up with them. Thought was necessarily absent from all this literature, for assuredly the first effort of thought would be to let the light through all this make-believe that passed current as part and parcel of 'Irish national' literature. Criticism had died, and this sort of thing, along with 'oratory', was allowed to swell like soap bubbles all over the land. The Irish people dropped off reading, not from any lack of intellectual desire, but because nowhere was to be found that which would interest them. Then the great rise of cheap periodicals came about in England, and the market in Ireland was flooded with them. Ireland being a poor country, the cheapest class of periodicals only is within the popular resources, and it soon became evident that a grave evil was threatening us, and that Ireland was largely feeding on a questionable type of British reading matter. And the commandment — 'Thou shalt be Irish' — was all the while troubling Irish hearts...

If thought and literature dwindled away in modern Ireland, an inquiry into social life and manners presents even a more muddled and hopeless picture. It was all very well for people to say that everything would come straight when we obtained our rights from England, but in the meantime people had to do something, for what we understand in current language as 'doing nothing' is in reality a form of doing something. Even those who shouted most about Irish Parliaments and Irish Republics were swayed by the general desire, common to all aspiring men, to be gentlemen of some kind, to be socially 'superior', to reach to some point of social vantage. And in this department of Irish life we will observe the deepest muddle of all. What is a gentleman from the point of view of an English-speaking Irishman? Manifestly the same thing as a gentleman is in England. What are good breeding, good taste, etiquette, from the same man's point of view? Manifestly again the same as these things are in England. The English-speaking Irishman and the Englishman were children of one common civilization. Social advance under modern Irish conditions could therefore only lead in one way, and that way was in the direction of the English ideals. But there was still that commandment like a fallen oak across the road, barring the way — 'Thou shalt be Irish and not English.' Here was a serious question which the modern Irishman had to solve. Like many another question, he refused to face it; he merely tried to shelve it. And too often he avoided becoming an English gentleman by becoming an Irish vulgarian. Ireland had either to advance socially along English lines or along Irish lines. She refused to do the former with any thoroughness; she had cut herself completely adrift from the latter. Had Ireland developed her own civilization, the manners and etiquette of Irish society would, I think, be very formal and elegant; but as she had thrown over Irish civilization, there was nothing for her to do but imitate

England with the best grace she could. But the conventions and manners of English society, owing to various local and particular reasons, as well as in consequence of the radical difference in the genius of the two peoples, she found repellant to her. Society without conventions is necessarily vulgar and chaotic, and much of the social life of Ireland was driven to prove itself Irish by kicking against convention altogether. There are various degrees in this long procession of vulgarity, and those who had least convention were perhaps less vulgar than many mean-spirited imitators of every thing they considered English and 'respectable'. You would, I believe, search the world in vain for the equals of the latter class. English conventions were known to them mostly by hearsay, and these hearsay accounts they copied with a dog-like fidelity. They cultivated English accents, they sent their children to English schools, they tucked in their skirts from contact with the 'low Irish', and they played tennis, not because they liked it, but because it was English and 'respectable'. However, if we look charitably upon them, and keep in mind the impossible conditions under which they were compelled to live, we shall find much to say in their extenuation. Fate has revenged herself upon them, for she has decreed that all of them, from those who live in fashionable Dalkey, on through the ranks of the 'gentleman farmers', down to the huxter who is making his son a doctor and his daughter a 'lady', should be known to the world under the comprehensive title of 'shoneens'.

I now pass on to consider briefly the effect which the conditions of modern Ireland had upon our attitude towards England. A professed hatred of England, but not of things English, which is a different matter altogether, not illogically became part and parcel of Irish nationality. This led to more muddle. The Irish people do not hate England or any other country. As a matter of fact, the genius of our nation is far more prone to love than hate. There is no gospel of personal or national hate in our religion; we are told at our mothers' knees to love all men, including our enemies. But as England, in consequence of the situation I have attempted to sketch, became in our view the source of all our ills, was responsible not only for her own sins against us — which heaven knows are many and great — but also responsible for our own blunders and stupidity, she came in for a double dose of resentment. Whenever an Irishman contemplated anything hurtful to his national pride, a curse against England gurgled in his throat. No wonder Englishmen completely misunderstood us, and classed us as a lot of grown-up children, when Ireland swayed and writhed in a helpless entanglement herself. It was certainly difficult to deal satisfactorily with a country that had missed her own path, and had only a very muddled idea of what she wanted herself. All this light has been thrown upon Ireland by the propaganda of the Gaelic League. It has compelled us to ask ourselves the elementary question — What is Irish nationality, and what in reality do we want to see realised in Ireland? Will a few soldiers dressed in green, and a republic, absolutely foreign to the genius of the Irish people, the humiliation of England, a hundred thousand English corpses with Irish bullets or pike wounds through them, satisfy the instinct within us that says: 'Thou shalt be Irish'? These things we probably can never see, though we may try to drown our national conscience by dreaming of them. But were they possible, they were vain; for a distinct nation is a distinct civilization, and if England went down to the bottom of the sea to-morrow, that distinct civilization which we have turned our backs upon, that woof of national tradition which we have cast from us, would not be restored. Our nation cannot be resurrected merely by the weakness of England, but mainly by the strength and effort of Ireland herself. This then is the new situation that has been created — the political disabilities of Ireland remain, and the political fight must go on until they are redressed, but England stands in our mental view no longer as the sole destroyer of Irish nationality; we have learned that we ourselves have been acting like fools, that we, during this century, have been the greatest sinners against that nationality whose death we were only too anxious to lay at the door of England. The Irish nationality that has sprung merely from a misguided hatred, or affected hatred, of England has not been a brilliant success, if we judge it by its fruits. Hate, I suggest, inspires nothing but destruction. And looking over this great century during which the civilized world has made such strides, we find that Ireland, representing one of the oldest and independent civilizations, has attempted nothing and achieved nothing. She has gone back in every department where other nations have advanced. She threw away her initiative and her language, and became a mean and sulky imitator of another people whom she professed to hate. Whilst clamouring and organising insurrections to bring about something which she called 'National Independence', she willingly cast away the main functions of independent existence, which, notwithstanding English misgovernment, she was still in a large measure free to exercise.

The baneful effect of the state of things that I have attempted to describe did not stop at literature, public opinion, and social development; it sapped the very foundations of economic advance. At the first blush it may appear a far-fetched idea that there is a strong connection between the development of a native civilization having its roots in the native language, and the production of economic wealth. English thought was, until comparatively recently, in a rather muddled state over economics; and it passes the understanding of modern man to comprehend by what mental process certain not very old theories were held by the best thinkers of those days. We have come now to see that land, though an indispensable, is by no means the main, source of modern economic wealth. Human skill in all its manifold manifestations has taken the premier place, and conditions precedent to the production of that skill are the existence of initiative and self-dependence. If you have to begin with a self-distrusting people who are afraid to rely on their own judgment, who have learnt by a long and reluctant effort to imitate a rich and highly developed people foreign to their genius, to conceive a mean and cringing opinion of themselves, you will never get much economic initiative out of them. You will find it difficult to raise what economists call their 'standard of comfort'. Creatures may heave bricks and draw water, but it takes men to command, to think, to initiate, to organise, and to will. The first step in the acquirement of skill is a man, and if you have not a man but a sulky, imitating being to begin with, it is a poor look-out for your economic projects. For behind and above the economics of a nation is the heart of a nation. And Anglo-Ireland of to-day has no heart. It is led by a hempen cord and frightened by a shadow. The economic ills of Ireland can be traced to many diverse minor causes, but if you follow them up you arrive at the great common source — the lack of Irish heart. Ireland has not courage to say — I will wear this, or, I will not wear that. So the draper from Ballyduff goes to London, — sometimes he gives out that he has been as far as Paris, — and a hideous poster in three colours announces that the latest novelties and fashions from London and Paris have arrived. This sends a thrill through the households of the village. The greasy draper rubs his hands and dilates on 'the circulation of money'; and the moss on the still wheels of the village mill weeps for the native heart of other days. Ireland, because she has lost her heart, imports today what, on sound economic principles, she could produce for herself. She who once gave ideas to the world, begs the meanest tinsel from that world now. She is out in the cold amongst the nations, standing on a sort of nowhere, looking at a civilization which she does not understand, refuses to be absorbed into, and is unable to copy. She exports cattle, drink, and human beings; and she imports, amongst other things, men with initiative and heart. A dolt from England manages a naturally able man born of the soil, because the dolt uses his head, such as it is, and the native of the soil has lost his heart. The great modern economic tradition of Ireland is simply this — Nothing Irish succeeds! We have not even heart to amuse ourselves, and our 'humour' and our 'drama' — God save us from most of both — are imported, as well as our shoddy. The tinker of thought — and modern Ireland is full of that type — has traced the ills of Ireland to everything in turns and to nothing long. His curses and complainings are ever floating over the seas; and he stands by the side of a native civilization that he has neglected almost unto death, and is never inspired to exclaim: 'It is the cause, it is the cause, my soul!' In fact, he is not aware that he ever had a civilization. He frets and moans and curses as he gropes in the dark recesses between two of them. If I were autocrat of Ireland tomorrow, and someone were to come to me and ask what I wanted most, I should have no hesitation in answering — Men. And if we are to have men, we must make the population of Ireland either thoroughgoing English or thoroughgoing Irish. No one who knows Ireland will entertain for a moment the idea that the people can be made English; the attempt has been made, and a country of sulky, dissatisfied and self-distrusting mongrels is the result. Ireland will be nothing until she is a nation, and as a nation is a civilization, she will never accomplish anything worthy of herself until she falls back upon her own language and traditions, and, recovering there her old pride, self-respect, and initiative, develops and marches forward from thence.

I have attempted to trace the evil effects arising from our efforts to imitate England whilst the commandment 'Thou shalt be Irish' is written upon our hearts. I hope I am no quack. The influences that mould a nation are infinite, and cannot be clearly grasped by the human mind. We can only hope to trace them in the broadest outline. Of what English legislation has done to undo Ireland I have a lively appreciation, but that matter does not come within the scope of this article. I have confined myself to an inquiry into the effects of causes which it is within Ireland's power, and within her power alone, to remove. The only hope that I see for Ireland is that she may set to work to create what does not exist now, what mere political independence, a parliament in College Green, or the humiliation of British arms, will not necessarily bestow — to create a nation. Abroad, during this century, wherever Irishmen have unreservedly thrown themselves in with the particular civilization of their adopted countries, they have done honour alike to themselves and their neighbours. During previous centuries Spain and France and other countries had hundreds of thousands of our bravest and our best, and well, and not without good reason, were they welcomed. The Irishman of modern times has succeeded in every land but his own. For at home is the only place where he cannot make up his mind — he will not be one thing or the other, he will not be English or Irish. Grattan, though not a great statesman, was visited with many vivid flashes of insight. The history of this century gives a new and deeper meaning to one sentence he uttered more than a hundred years ago concerning the relations of Ireland and England. 'As her equal we shall be her sincerest friend; as anything less than her equal we shall be her bitterest enemy.' Unless we are a nation we are nothing, and the growth of a civilization springing from the roots of one of the oldest in Europe, will alone make us a nation, give us scope to grow naturally, give us something to inspire what is best in us, cultivate our national pride and self-respect, and encourage our self-dependence. Marching along that line, the hurt or humiliation of England will cease, must cease, to be our ambition; for our master-passions will be wrapped up in the construction of our own nation, not in the destruction of another. Whether an Ireland of the future, relying upon her own genius, will ever do for mankind what the old Ireland of the early centuries did with such generosity, love, and enthusiasm for Europe, is a matter for faith rather than for speculation. The prospect of such a new Ireland rising up out of the foundations of the old, with love and not hate as its inspiration, has already sent a great thrill through the land. It is a new and unlooked-for situation, full with fate, not only for Ireland, but for the world.

13(c) George Moore, 'Literature and the Irish Language'

Lady Gregory prefaced this with the comment: 'The following was given as a speech at a meeting of the supporters of the Irish Literary Theatre in February 1900, and was afterwards published in the New Ireland Review. *I do not agree with Mr Moore in thinking there will be but few in the theatre who will understand an Irish play. He underrates the success of the Language Movement in Dublin.'*

I feel that I must apologise for appearing before you with a MS. of my speech in my hand. The sight of a MS. in the country where oratory flourishes everywhere, in all ranks of society and in all conditions of intellect, must appear anomalous and absurd. But I am an exception among my gifted countrymen. I have not inherited any gift of improvisation, and the present is certainly no time for experiment, for I believe I have a matter of importance to lay before you, and it will be less labour for you to give the extra attention which the consideration of the written phrase demands than to reduce to order the painful jumble of words and ideas, mixed with painful hesitations, which is the public speech of every one except the born orator.

Of the plays which were performed this week I do not intend to speak, and of the plays which the Irish Literary Theatre hopes to produce next year I only propose to say that Mr Yeats and myself are writing a play entitled *Grania and Darmuid*.[4] A more suitable subject than the most popular of our epic stories could hardly be found for a play for the Irish Literary Theatre, and I may say that it would be difficult to name any poet that Ireland has yet produced more truly elected by his individual and racial genius to interpret the old legend than the distinguished poet whose contemporary and collaborateur I have the honour to be. But even if this play should prove to be that dramatic telling of the great story which Ireland has been waiting for these many years, it will not, in my opinion, be the essential point of next year's festival, for next year we have decided to give a play in our own language — the language which, to our great disgrace, we do not understand. Alas! there will be fewer in the theatre who will understand the Irish text than a Latin or a Greek one; so the play will be performed for the sake of the example it will set. The performance of plays in our language is part and parcel of the Irish Literary Theatre, which was founded to create a new centre of Irish enthusiasm, a new outlet for the national spirit and energy.

Lady Gregory, Mr Martyn, Mr Yeats, and myself were all agreed as to the necessity of producing a play in our original language; but I am responsible for the decision to produce a translation rather than an original play in Irish. In my opinion an original play in Irish would be too hazardous an adventure.[5] The art of writing for the stage is not easily acquired, the number of Irish writers is limited, and to produce a bad play written in Irish would be a misfortune. Moreover, I wish our first Irish play to rest on a solid literary foundation, so that it may be possessed of a life beyond its stage life, which is necessarily transitory. I wish to present those who read our language with a piece of solid literature, and for this end my choice fell on a play at once simple and literary, *The Land of Heart's Desire*, by Mr W. B. Yeats. It will be translated by Dr Douglas Hyde, whose Irish scholarship has passed beyond question...Mr Yeats will make what further explanations he deems advisable regarding his play, and I will hasten to speak on the subject on which I have come to speak to you — the necessity of the revival of the language if Ireland is to preserve her individuality among nations.

It will be conceded to me that the three great distinctions of nations are — Religion, Language, Law. The distinction of religion Ireland holds secure; for this distinction she has suffered robbery, violence, and contumely, but on this point I do not think I need insist. She has struggled no less fiercely for the distinction of law. But for the third distinction, the distinction of language, she has shown less determination and perseverance. Fellow-countrymen, the language is slipping into the grave, and if a great national effort be not made at once to save the language it will be dead in another generation. We must return to the language. It came we know not whence or how; it is a mysterious inheritance, in which resides the soul of the Irish people. It is through language that a tradition of thought is preserved, and so it may be said that the language is the soul of a race. It is through language that the spirit is communicated, and it is through language that a nation becomes aware of itself.

My fellow-countrymen, the language is slipping into the grave, and what you have to remember is, that when the language is dead the soul of Cuchillin, which we all share still a little, will have vanished. The restoration of the language is the nation's need; even if we had a National Government, it would not be a real National Government if the language had perished, for the Celt would have been robbed of his original home.

We want our language; we desire it with our whole heart and soul. Our desire may be foolish, unpractical, unwise, according to the lights of the English nation at the present moment; but our desire is our desire, our folly is our own, and if we wish to start ill equipped in the business race of the world, knowing no language which is understood outside of Ireland, shall we be gainsaid like children? But this is not our desire; our desire is to make Ireland a bi-lingual country — to use English as a universal language, and to save our own as a medium for some future literature.

That a nation should express itself in the language fashioned by the instinct of the race out of its ideas and spiritual aspirations is, I think, certain. On the possibility of reviving a language, of making a dying language the literary and political language of a country, little is known. It is said that when the Welsh began the language movement there were only 10,000 who spoke Welsh, and that today there are nine times the number. It is vain to consider possibilities; we must strive for what is noblest, and I know no more noble ideal to strive for than the re-establishment of our language in our country.

You will be told that these are sentimental reasons, transcendental reasons. Well, I know of no better reasons; all other reason is merely for the moment. You will be told that out of Ireland no one will understand the language, and therefore, for the practical purpose of earning a livelihood, it will be useless. You will be told that for the purposes of art the language is useless, that ancient Irish literature is formless folk-tales, and that in modern Irish there is no literature whatever. You will be told that if a genius such as Burns should arise tomorrow among the Irish peasantry and write his great work in Irish it would remain unread. Ibsen writes a language which is spoken by very few millions, yet his plays are read all over Europe, and the old Irish poems, written in a form no longer spoken, are known to European scholars. There is no such thing as a beautiful unknown page of literature, there is no such thing as a beautiful unknown poem, there is no such thing as a beautiful unknown line of poetry. Were a great work written in Irish tomorrow, in a few years it would have travelled all over Europe. To the objection often urged against the Irish language, that it is not as suitable for literary purposes as English, I answer that a language wears out like a coat. The Latin language, which had said all it was capable of saying at the end of the second century, became from the third to the tenth — I might say to the twelfth century — the common language of Europe: the language of the Court, the Church, and the library. Thousands of volumes of poetry were written in the Latin language between the third and twelfth centuries, but all these books have been forgotten, and to explain this oblivion we must assume that in eight hundred years in no country in Europe a great man of letters was born, or that the Latin language had expressed all that it was capable of expressing. Dante began his poem in Latin; he wrote two cantos in Latin before he discovered the Latin language to be incapable of literary expression, then turning to the vernacular, he made it at once into the medium of his high purpose, and Italy produced a new literature: but Greece, which clung to her ancient language, in which all had been said that the language was capable of saying, has produced no new literature. And as it was with the Latin in the fourth, so it is with English in the nineteenth century. From universal use and journalism, the English language in fifty years will be as corrupt as the Latin of the eighth century, as unfit for literary usage, and will become in my opinion, a sort of volapuk, strictly limited to commercial letters and journalism.

Walter Pater, England's last great writer, said that he wished to write in English as in a learned language. The language, he thought, had reached the same stage of decay as the Latin language had reached in the second century. He knew he was writing in a decaying language, and he treated it as such. Since his death we have seen the English language pass through the patty-pans of Stevenson into the pint-pot of Mr Kipling. If we would write with distinction we must do as Pater did, compile a special vocabulary, and strip ourselves of all ideas and words except those which seem to us to reflect the intimate colour of our minds. It would seem that it is only by narrowing our hearts and limiting our words that we can write at all now. The opposite was the practice of the ancient writers, who opened their hearts to all the ideas of their time, and accepted the idiom of their beautiful streets. Ancient architecture, whether in palace or in cottage, is beautiful; all the coins and weapons and pottery of the ancient world are beautiful. And finding beauty in every corner of ancient life, can we doubt that our ancestors spoke more beautiful English than we do?

It was with the Renaissance that the individual note came into art, for as life declined in beauty the personal selection of the artist became necessary. But Michael Angelo, his predecessors and his contemporaries, worked in co-operation with the spirit of their time; even the art of Reynolds and Gainsborough is conclusive of the taste of the eighteenth century. The art of Manet, Whistler, Degas, Pater, and Ibsen is the art of protest, and every year the protest of the artist against the taste of the multitude will become sterner, more energetic. The art world which was in antiquity, and which the Renaissance revived, and of which some traces linger down to the present day, is passing away, and the commercial world which has begun is the worst form of barbarism which has yet been seen. Those who believe that dreams, beauty, and divine ecstasy are essential must pray that all the empires may perish and the world be given back to the small peasant states, whose seas and forests and mountains shall create national aspirations and new gods. Otherwise the world will fall into gross naturalism, into scientific barbarism more terrible than the torch and the sword of the Hun...The commercial platitude which has risen up in England, which is extending over the whole world, is horrible to contemplate. Its flag, which Mr Rhodes has declared to be 'the most valuable commercial asset in the world', is everywhere. England has imposed her idea upon all nations, and to girdle the world with Brixton seems to be her ultimate destiny. And we, sitting on the last verge, see into the universal suburb, in which a lean man with glasses on his nose and a black bag in his hand is always running after his bus.

My fellow-countrymen, the moment has come to save, or let perish, our language. It is the one sod of Irish earth on which we can all stand united. In this cause every one may help, landlord and peasant alike, nationalist and unionist, and a cause cannot be a lost cause to which every one can contribute: some by learning the language, some with sums of money, some by having their children taught the language. In my youth Irish was still spoken everywhere; but the gentry took pride in not understanding their own language. It was our misfortune that such false fashion should have prevailed and kept us in ignorance of our language, but it will be our fault if our children do not learn their own language. I have no children and am too old to learn the language, but I shall at once arrange that my brother's children shall learn Irish. I have written to my sister-in-law telling her that I will at once undertake this essential part of her children's education. They shall have a nurse straight from Aran; for it profits a man nothing if he knows all the languages in the world and knows not his own.

13(d) W. B. Yeats, from 'The Literary Movement in Ireland'

This was first published in the North American Review, *December 1899, and then, with some textual alterations, in Lady Gregory's volume. See* Uncollected Prose, *ed. Frayne and Johnson (London, 1975), vol. 2, pp. 184-96.*

I have just come to a quiet Connaught house from seeing a little movement, in a great movement of thought which is fashioning the dreams of the next generation in Ireland, grow to a sudden maturity. Certain plays, which are an expression of the most characteristic ideals of what is sometimes called the 'Celtic movement', have been acted in Dublin before audiences drawn from all classes and all political sections, and described at great length in every Nationalist newspaper. Whatever be the merit of these plays, and that must be left to the judgment of time, their success means, as I think, that the 'Celtic movement', which has hitherto interested but a few cultivated people, is about to become a part of the thought of Ireland.

Before 1891, Unionists and Nationalists were too busy keeping one or two simple beliefs at their fullest intensity for any complexity of thought or emotion; and the national imagination uttered itself, with a somewhat broken energy, in a few stories and in many ballads about the need of unity against England, about the martyrs who had died at the hand of England, or about the greatness of Ireland before the coming of England. They built up Ireland's dream of Ireland, of an ideal country weighed down by immemorial sorrows and served by heroes and saints, and they taught generations of young men to love their country with a love that was the deepest emotion they were ever to know; but they built with the virtues and beauties and sorrows and hopes that would move to tears the greatest number of those eyes before whom the modern world is but beginning to unroll itself; and, except when some rare, personal impulse shaped the song according to its will, they built to the formal and conventional rhythm which would give the most immediate pleasure to ears that had forgotten Gaelic poetry and not learned the subtleties of English poetry. The writers who made this literature or who shaped its ideals, in the years before the great famine, lived at the moment when the middle class had brought to perfection its ideal of the good citizen, and of a politics and a philosophy and a literature which would help him upon his way; and they made a literature full of the civic virtues and, in all but its unbounded patriotism, without inconvenient ardours. They took their style from Scott and Campbell and Macaulay, and that 'universally popular' poetry which is really the poetry of the middle class, and from Beranger and that 'peasant poetry' which looks for its models to the Burns of 'Highland Mary' and 'The Cottar's [*sic*] Saturday Night'. Here and there a poet or a story-writer found an older dream among the common people or in his own mind, and made a personality for himself, and was forgotten; for it was the desire of everybody to be moved by the same emotions as everybody else, and certainly one cannot blame a desire which has thrown so great a shadow of self-sacrifice.

The fall of Parnell and the wreck of his party and of the organisations that supported it were the symbols, if not the causes, of a sudden change. They were followed by movements and organisations that brought the ideas and the ideals which are the expression of personalities alike into politics, economics, and literature. Those who looked for the old energies, which were the utterance of the common will and hope, were unable to see that a new kind of Ireland, as full of energy as a boiling pot, was rising up amid the wreck of the old kind, and that the national life was finding a new utterance. This utterance was so necessary that it seems as if the hand that broke the ball of glass, that now lies in fragments full of a new iridescent life, obeyed some impulse from beyond its wild and capricious will. More books about Irish subjects have been published in these last eight years than in the thirty years that went before them, and these books have the care for scholarship and the precision of speech which had been notoriously lacking in books on Irish subjects. An appeal to the will, a habit of thought which measures all beliefs by their intensity, is content with a strenuous rhetoric; but an appeal to the intellect needs an always more perfect knowledge, an always more malleable speech. The new writers and the new organisations they work through — for organisations of various kinds take the place held by the critical press in other countries — have awakened Irish affections among many from whom the old rhetoric could never have got a hearing, but they have been decried for weakening the national faith by lovers of the old rhetoric. I have seen an obscure Irish member of Parliament rise at one of those monthly meetings of the Irish Literary Society, when the members of the society read sometimes their poems to one another, and ask their leave to read a poem. He did not belong to the society, but leave was given him, and he read a poem in the old manner, blaming the new critics and praising the old poems which had made him patriotic and filled his imagination with the images of the martyrs, and, as he numbered over their names, Wolfe Tone, Emmet, Owen Roe, Sarsfield, his voice shook and many were angry with the new critics.

The organisations that are making this change are the Irish Literary Society in London, the National Literary Society in Dublin, which has founded, or rather sheltered with its influence, the Irish Literary Theatre, and the Feis Ceoil Committee in Dublin, at whose annual series of concerts of Irish music, singers and pipers from all parts of Ireland compete; and more important than all, the Gaelic League, which has worked for the revival of the Gaelic language with such success that it has sold fifty thousand of its Gaelic text-books in a year. All these organisations have been founded since the fall of Parnell; and all are busy in preserving, or in moulding anew and without any thought of the politics of the hour, some utterance of the national life, and in opposing the vulgar books and vulgarer songs that come to us from England. We are preparing, as we hope, for a day when Ireland will speak in Gaelic, as much as Wales speaks in Welsh, within her borders, but speak, it may be, in English to other nations of those truths which were committed to her when 'He set the borders of the nations according to His angels'; as Dionysius the Areopagite[6] has written. Already, as I think, a new kind of romance, a new element in thought, is being moulded out of Irish life and traditions, and this element may have an importance for criticism, even should criticism forget the writers who are trying to embody it in their work, while looking each one through his own colour in the dome of many-coloured glass.

Contemporary English literature takes delight in praising England and her Empire, the master-work and dream of the middle class; and, though it may escape from this delight, it must long continue to utter the ideals of the strong and wealthy. Irish intellect has always been preoccupied with the weak and with the poor, and now it has begun to collect and describe their music and stories, and to utter anew the beliefs and hopes which they alone remember. It may never make a literature preoccupied with the circumstance of their lives, like the 'peasant poetry', whose half deliberate triviality, passionless virtue, and passionless vice has helped so many orderly lives; for a writer who wishes to write with his whole mind must knead the beliefs and hopes, which he has made his own, with the circumstance of his own life. Burns had this preoccupation, and nobody will deny that he was a great poet; but even he had the poverty of emotions and ideas of a peasantry that had lost, like the middle class into which it would have its children absorbed, the imagination that is in tradition without finding the imagination that is in books. Irish literature may prolong its first inspiration without renouncing the complexity of ideas and emotions which is the inheritance of cultivated men, for it will have learned from the discoveries of modern learning that the common people, wherever civilization has not driven its plough too deep, keep a watch over the roots of all religion and all romance. Their poetry trembles upon the verge of incoherence with a passion all but unknown among modern poets, and their sense of beauty exhausts itself in countless legends and in metaphors that seem to mirror the energies of nature...Ireland has no great wealth, no preoccupation with successful persons to turn her writers' eyes to any lesser destiny. Even the poetry which had its form and much of its matter from alien thought dwelt, as the Gaelic ballads had done before it, on ideas living in the perfection of hope, on visions of unfulfilled desire, and not on the sordid compromise of success. The popular poetry of England celebrates her victories, but the popular poetry of Ireland remembers only defeats and defeated persons. A ballad that is in every little threepenny and sixpenny ballad book asks if Ireland has no pride in her Lawrences[7] and Wellingtons, and answers that these belong to the Empire and not to Ireland, whose 'heart beats high' for men who died in exile or in prison; and this ballad is a type of all. The popular poetry, too, has made love of the earth of Ireland so much a part of her literature that it should not be a hard thing to fill it with the holiness of places. Politics are, indeed, the forge in which nations are made, and the smith has been so long busy making Ireland according to His will that she may well have some important destiny. But whether this is so or not, whether this destiny is to make her in the arts, as she is in politics, a voice of the idealism of the common people, who still remember the dawn of the world, or to give her an unforeseen history, it can but express the accidents and energies of her past, and criticism does its natural work in trying to prophesy this expression; and, even if it is mistaken, a prophecy is not always made all untrue by being unfulfilled. A few years will decide if the writers of Ireland are to shape themselves in our time for the fulfilment of this prophecy, for need and much discussion will bring a new national agreement, and the political tumult awake again.

13(e) Standish O'Grady, 'The Great Enchantment'

Lady Gregory prefaced this with with a brief comment:

I have taken the following extracts from a series of articles which have appeared during this year in the *All Ireland Review*. It will be remembered that two years ago, on the report of the Childers' Commission that Ireland, through the breaking of a pledge made at the time of the Union, was being enormously overtaxed, all parties and all classes joined in public protest. Lieutenants and magistrates of counties called and spoke at meetings, and twenty-five county committees were formed to deal with the matter. Mr O'Grady draws attention to the fact that of these twenty-five committees, not one has ever met. The 'Enchantment' he attributes this paralysis to has not yet been broken or explained.

In primitive literatures we read much about enchantment; in our own, instances that come readily to the mind are 'The Stupefaction of the Ultonians';[8] and the enchantment of Finn and his Fianna in the weird palace of the Quicken Boughs. I always thought such tales to be mere exercises of imagination, but it is not so. Enchantment is a fact in nature. Through suggestion or self-suggestion a man may be flung into such a condition that his senses will cease to discharge their normal functions; in a stone he will see a flashing diamond, and in a flashing diamond a stone; in discord he will hear music, and in the sweetest music a jarring discord. Nations too, like individuals, may, as the punishment of their crimes and follies, find themselves flung into such an enchanted condition, and suffer that worst loss of all, the loss of reason.

The political understanding of Ireland today is under a spell, and its will paralysed. If proof be demanded for this startling assertion, how can proof to any good result be supplied? It is the same spellbound understanding which will consider the proof...Was or was not the political understanding of at least a great proportion of Ireland under a spell in the year 1853? In that year, while the country was still staggering under the combined effects of the great famine and of Free Trade,...the British statesmen imposed upon this country financial burdens which have resulted in the direct loss to Ireland of from 100 to 150 millions of pounds sterling, and the indirect loss of an amount which is incalculable. The agrarian agitations and their horrors, the flight of our people, the destruction of our aristocracy, the general impoverishment and degradation of our land, are perceived now clearly by all thinking men to be the consequences of that great betrayal of the national interest in 1853; and men can see that, and know it for a truth, who are quite capable today of committing political crimes and follies as great as that of the 'brass band' and of the hierarchy and priesthood and the poor deluded Irish multitudes who sustained them. For the enchantment only changes its mode of action — it does not cease to act. From generation to generation and from year to year, in the night time and in the day time, this horrible obsession knows no abatement of its power; it lies as heavy on the land today as in the decade that witnessed the great betrayal. Nay, it is more potent today, and exerts a mightier sway, as if dimly conscious of the coming of the hour of crisis — the hour when Ireland must either break the spell or sink for ever into the abyss prepared for all the nations who have forgotten the source of their life, who have loved lies and hated the truth, welcomed darkness and shrunk from the light. That fatal hour is drawing nigh...

In 1898 the unknown dealer in his distribution of the cards filled our hands with winning cards, yet we could not table them, so great was the power of the spell. I perceive that our ancestors, from the date of the Battle of the Boyne up to about 1779, were under the control of a political enchantment somewhat similar. Under that control they assisted in the destruction of their own woollen trade and ocean-going commerce. Protestant Ireland starved or expatriated some 300,000 Protestant weavers, for the power of the spell was very heavy on the land. Patriotic historians attribute things like this to the wickedness and greed of a neighbouring people. It is not so; like the collapse of the Financial Reform movement, they spring from ourselves. We worship phantoms; and phantoms powerless *per se*, once worshipped — so they tell me — become endowed with a terrible and malignant vitality and activity. We know that that is so with regard to idols, in themselves only sticks and stones. Did not our own ancestors slay their poor little children in honour of Crom, a shapeless hulk of stone?...

What I work against — for my fighting days, if I ever had any, are I think, over — is this 'Great Enchantment', whose modes of operation are past counting and whose subtlety transcends the human faculties to discern...

Someone has written: 'The passions must be held in reverence; they must not, they cannot, be excited at will.' Now, though some are made differently in this respect, I confess I could not go into politics myself save passionately — that is to say, when excited and inflamed by some matter of transcendent importance and of evident practicability. Though always a steady voter and always forming an opinion, good or bad, about public questions as they arose, I never made but two incursions into politics in all my life. The first was in 1881-82, when I thought our land question might be settled to the satisfaction of the people and without involving the destruction of our landed gentry; the other was at the end of '96, when I thought that an universal movement was on foot for a change of the incidence of imperial taxation as it affects this country.

In 1853 Mr Gladstone extended income-tax to Ireland for a period of seven years, in order to enable us to pay four million pounds worth of 'Consolidated Annuities', a debt due, as alleged, by Ireland to the Treasury, and that Irish income-tax having been made perpetual, we have already paid that debt some eight times over...

I never took an interest in this subject on account of the many millions which a successful prosecution of the controversy would have retained in Ireland or brought back into Ireland, but because it supplied a grand common platform on which, for public purposes, all Ireland might unite.

On the first of these occasions we appointed a committee of five eminent members of the landlord class to look after our interests, which committee never sat and was never brought to an account for not sitting; and on the second, we appointed twenty-five county committees, not one of which ever sat...

Aids and allies were hurrying to join us just at the moment that we elected to make fools of ourselves, when we broke rank and abandoned sure victory in order to chase hares, which was bad enough, and to resume the ancient Irish custom of destroying each other, which was a great deal worse... Alas! I have seen the nobility and gentry and clergy and popular representatives of all the South and West, break their ranks of war and go a-hunting,

167

though to all of them 'the right' was very clear...Silence is preferable to the things I would have to say about this 'Lost Land' and its enchanted inhabitants; its aristocracy, with dull woe-begone eyes fixed on London! and its 'United Irish' coming on for the final destruction of an Irish class and order; and all the pity and the folly and the shame and the ruin of the whole tragical business, in the midst of which I think that silence is better than speech...

Surely we are a great people and deserve to get on! Now, these ludicrous breaks-down — or whatever we must call them — these incredible lapses and aberrations, exhibited by a people not only as intelligent and spirited as the average, but more intelligent than the average, at the time of their occurrence only filled me with amazement and consternation. I had not then traced to its source all that folly, nor quite realised how it was the inevitable outcome and resultant of a cause, operative, in different forms, through all our tragical history; nor did I connect it with a national fault, perhaps a national crime, which has checked our progress from century to century, which has brought about the destruction of aristocracy after aristocracy, and which bids fair, as I write to involve us all in one common ruin, and leave this land free for the exploitation of tourist touts, and commercial syndicates formed for the promotion of sport in waste countries. For if things continue to go on as they are going on today in Ireland, the bullock, which is now superseding the man, will be himself superseded by the wild beast and the wild bird, which the British and American sporting plutocracy will pleasantly shoot and pleasantly pursue, sustained by a little host of Irish uniformed gillies; which certainly would be rather a dismal ending for this ancient and famous nation. And yet things are moving that way steadily, sometimes, I think, inevitably.

The spell does not only affect the minds of our aristocracy. Its power is not so limited. It covers the whole land; every class and order of men in the island are held inescapably in the grip of that dead hand. With such a document in our possession as the Report of the Childers' Commission, with such a preponderating political power as is ours, and with such hosts of good British friends, why can we do nothing? — strengthless, purposeless, and resourceless, as were the Ultonians sunk under the curse of the great mother and queen whom they had outraged, drowned in the avenging tides of that fountain of their life which they had polluted...

Heavy as lead, cold as death, the Great Enchantment obsesses the soul of the land, and not one but all classes lie supine under its sway — supine under the fanning of the gigantic wings...

One thing only we desire, the luxury of lamentation. We prefer spoliation, degradation, extermination, and the British tourist as a half-way house to Hell; and this is the 'Great Enchantment'!...

They (the aristocracy) might have been so much to this afflicted nation; half-ruined as they are, they might be so much tomorrow, but the curse that has fallen on the whole land, seems to have fallen on them with double power — the understanding paralysed, the will gone all to water, and for consequence, a sure destruction...During that six weeks' financial agitation when they seemed to be giving the country a lead,...the war of classes stopped, stopped utterly...The people thought they were about to lead them, and upon a matter upon which all Ireland was in virtual unanimity; a great question — great essentially, and involving gigantic issues. This marvellous opportunity, thrust into their hands by kind destiny, they flung away; and for what? For the Fry Commission! If it be asked what hope I now entertain regarding them, I would answer that I have none; but I do think that, here and there, I may be able to touch individual members of the class, and one man of the right kind, if awake and alive, might do much.

Aristocracies come and go like the waves of the sea; and some fall nobly and others ignobly. As I write, this Protestant Anglo-Irish aristocracy, which once owned all Ireland from the centre to the sea, is rotting from the land in the most dismal farce-tragedy of all time, without one brave deed, without one brave word.

Our last Irish aristocracy was catholic, intensely and fanatically Royalist and Cavalier, and compounded of elements which were Norman-Irish and Milesian-Irish. They worshipped the Crown when the Crown had become a phantom or a ghost, and the god whom they worshipped was not able to save them or himself. They were defeated and exterminated. They lost everything, but they never lost honour; and because they did not lose that, their overthrow was bewailed in songs and music which will not cease to sound for centuries yet.

> Shawn O'Dwyer a Glanna,
> We're worsted in the game.

Worsted they were, for they made a fatal mistake, and they had to go; but they brought their honour with them, and they

169

founded noble or princely families on the Continent.

Who laments the destruction of our present Anglo-Irish aristocracy? Perhaps in broad Ireland not one. They fall from the land while innumerable eyes are dry, and their fall will not be bewailed in one piteous dirge, or one mournful melody.

Notes

1. John Mitchel (1815-75) founded the *United Irishman* in honour of his revolutionary hero, Wolfe Tone (1763-98); he was tried for treason in 1848, and transported for fourteen years; his *Jail Journal* (1854) became a classic.

2. Isaac Butt (1813-79) was a co-founder, in 1833, of the *Dublin University Magazine*.

3. J. B. Dillon (1816-66) was a co-founder, with Duffy and Davis, of the *Nation* in 1842.

4. The collaborative venture of *Diarmuid and Grainne* was something of a disaster in 1901; the same bill contained Hyde's Irish language play, referred to in the next note.

5. Dr Hyde has, since this speech was made, written a play in Irish for our Literary Theatre, *Casad na Sugan*, full of humour and pathos, which will, I think, upset Mr Moore's theories by its success. [Lady Gregory's note.]

6. Yeats was drawn to *The Hierarchies of Dionysius the Areopagite* (*fl.* 500), which were translated into English by J. Parker in 1894.

7. Alexander Lawrence (1764-1835) led the attack on Seringapatam, India, in 1799.

8. Inhabitants of Ulster.

14
W. B. Yeats, from 'Poetry and Tradition', 1907

For the history of this essay, dated August 1907, and published in 1908, see no. 9.

When O'Leary died[1] I could not bring myself to go to his funeral, though I had been once his close fellow-worker, for I shrank from seeing about his grave so many whose Nationalism was different from anything he had taught or that I could share. He belonged, as did his friend John F. Taylor, to the romantic conception of Irish Nationality on which Lionel Johnson and myself founded, so far as it was founded on anything but literature, our art and our Irish criticism. Perhaps his spirit, if it can care for or can see old friends now, will accept this apology for an absence that has troubled me. I learned much from him and much from Taylor, who will always seem to me the greatest orator I have heard; and that ideal Ireland, perhaps from this out an imaginary Ireland, in whose service I labour, will always be in many essentials their Ireland. They were the last to speak an understanding of life and Nationality, built up by the generation of Grattan, which read Homer and Virgil, and by the generation of Davis, which had been pierced through by the idealism of Mazzini, and of the European revolutionists of the mid-century.

O'Leary had joined the Fenian movement with no hope of success, as we know, but because he believed such a movement good for the moral character of the people; and had taken his long imprisonment without complaining. Even to the very end, while often speaking of his prison life, he would have thought it took from his Roman courage to describe its hardship. The worth of a man's acts in the moral memory, a continual height of mind in the doing of them, seemed more to him than their immediate result, if, indeed, the sight of many failures had not taken away the thought of success. A man was not to lie, or even to give up his dignity, on any patriotic plea, and I have heard him say, 'I have but one religion, the old Persian: to bend the bow and tell the truth', and again, 'There are things a man must not do to save a nation', and again, 'A man must not cry in public to save a nation', and that we might not forget justice in the passion of controversy, 'There was never cause so bad that it has not been defended by good men for what seemed to them good reasons.' His friend had a burning and brooding imagination that divided men not according to their achievement but by their degrees of sincerity, and by their mastery over a straight and, to my thought, too obvious logic that seemed to him essential to sincerity. Neither man had an understanding of style or of literature in the right sense of the word, though both were great readers, but because their imagination could come to rest no place short of greatness, they hoped, John O'Leary especially, for an Irish literature of the greatest kind. When Lionel Johnson and Katharine Tynan (as she was then), and I, myself, began to reform Irish poetry, we thought to keep unbroken the thread running up to Grattan which John O'Leary had put into our hands, though it might be our business to explore new paths of the labyrinth. We sought to make a more subtle rhythm, a more organic form, than that of the older Irish poets who wrote in English, but always to remember certain ardent ideas and high attitudes of mind which were the nation itself, to our belief, so far as a nation can be summarised in the intellect. If you had asked an ancient Spartan what made Sparta Sparta, he would have answered, the Laws of Lycurgus, and many Englishmen look back to Bunyan and to Milton as we did to Grattan and to Mitchel. Lionel Johnson was able to take up into his art one portion of this tradition that I could not, for he had a gift of speaking political thought in fine verse that I have always lacked. I, on the other hand, was more preoccupied with Ireland (for he had other interests), and took from Allingham and Walsh their passion for country spiritism, and from Ferguson his pleasure in heroic legend, and while seeing all in the light of European literature found my symbols of expression in Ireland. One thought often possessed me very strongly. New from the influence, mainly the personal influence, of William Morris, I dreamed of enlarging Irish hate, till we had come to hate with a passion of patriotism what Morris and Ruskin hated. Mitchel had already all but poured some of that hate drawn from Carlyle, who had it of an earlier and, as I think, cruder sort, into the blood of Ireland, and were we not a poor nation with ancient courage, unblackened fields and a barbarous gift of self-sacrifice? Ruskin and Morris had spent themselves in vain because they had found no passion to harness to their thought, but here were unwasted passion and precedents in the popular memory for every needed thought and action. Perhaps, too, it would be possible to find in that new philosophy of spiritism coming to a seeming climax in the work of Frederick Myers,[2] and in the investigations of uncounted obscure persons, what could change the country spiritism into a reasoned belief that would put its might into all the rest. A new belief seemed coming that could be so simple and demonstrable, and above all so mixed into the common scenery of the world, that it would set the whole man on fire and liberate him from a thousand obediences and complexities. We were to forge in Ireland a new sword on our old traditional anvil for that great battle that must in the end re-establish the old, confident, joyous world. All the while I worked with this idea, founding societies that became quickly or slowly everything I despised, one part of me looked on, mischievous and mocking, and the other part spoke words which were more and more unreal, as the attitude of mind became more and more strained and difficult. Miss Maud Gonne could still gather great crowds out of the slums by her beauty and sincerity, and speak to them of 'Mother Ireland with the crown of stars about her head'; but gradually the political movement she was associated with, finding it hard to build up any fine lasting thing, became content to attack little persons and little things. All movements are held together more by what they hate than by what they love, for love separates and individualises and quiets, but the nobler movements, the only movements on which literature can found itself, hate great and lasting things. All who have any old traditions have something of aristocracy, but we had opposing us from the first, though not strongly from the first, a type of mind which had been without influence in the generation of Grattan, and almost without it in that of Davis, and which has made a new nation out of Ireland, that was once old and full of memories.

I remember, when I was twenty years old, arguing, on my way home from a Young Ireland Society, that Ireland, with its hieratic Church, its readiness to accept leadership in intellectual things, — and John O'Leary spoke much of this readiness,[3] — its Latin hatred of middle paths and uncompleted arguments, could never create a democratic poet of the type of Burns, although it had tried to do so more than once, but that its genius would in the long run be distinguished and lonely. Whenever I had known some old countryman, I had heard stories and sayings that arose out of an imagination that would have understood Homer better than *The Cotter's Saturday Night* or *Highland Mary*, because it was an ancient imagination, where the sediment had found the time to settle, and I believe that the makers of deliberate literature could still take passion and theme, though but little thought, from such as he. On some such old and broken stem, I thought, have all the most beautiful roses been grafted...

When I saw John O'Leary first, every young Catholic man who had intellectual ambition fed his imagination with the poetry of Young Ireland; and the verses of even the least known of its poets were expounded with a devout ardour at Young Ireland Societies and the like, and their birthdays celebrated. The school of writers I belonged to tried to found itself on much of the subject-matter of this poetry, and, what was almost more in our thoughts, to begin a more imaginative tradition in Irish literature, by a criticism at once remorseless and enthusiastic. It was our criticism, I think, that set Clarence Mangan at the head of the Young Ireland poets in the place of Davis, and put Sir Samuel Ferguson, who had died with but little fame as a poet, next in the succession. Our attacks, mine especially, on verse which owed its position to its moral or political worth, roused a resentment which even I find it hard to imagine today, and our verse was attacked in return, and not for anything peculiar to ourselves, but for all that it had in common with the accepted poetry of the world, and most of all for its lack of rhetoric, its refusal to preach a doctrine or to consider the seeming necessities of a cause. Now, after so many years, I can see how natural, how poetical even, an opposition was, that showed what large numbers could not call up certain high feelings without accustomed verses, or believe we had not wronged the feelings when we did but attack the verses. I have just read in a newspaper that Sir Charles Gavan Duffy recited upon his death-bed his favourite poem, one of the worst of the patriotic poems of Young Ireland, and it has brought all this to mind, for the opposition to our school claimed him as its leader. When I was at Siena, I noticed that the Byzantine style persisted in faces of Madonnas for several generations after it had given way to a more natural style in the less loved faces of saints and martyrs. Passion had grown accustomed to those narrow eyes, which are almost Japanese, and to those gaunt cheeks, and would have thought it sacrilege to change. We would not, it is likely, have found listeners if John O'Leary, the irreproachable patriot, had not supported us. It was as clear to him that a writer must not write badly, or ignore the examples of the great Masters in the fancied or real service of a cause, as it was that he must not lie for it or grow hysterical. I believed in those days that a new intellectual life would begin, like that of Young Ireland, but more profound and personal, and that could we but get a few plain principles accepted, new poets and writers of prose would make an immortal music. I think I was more blind than Johnson, though I judge this from his poems rather than anything I remember of his talk, for he never talked ideas, but, as was common with his generation in Oxford, facts and immediate impressions from life. With others this renunciation was but a pose, a superficial reaction from the disordered abundance of the middle century, but with him it was the radical life. He was in all a traditionalist, gathering out of the past phrases, moods, attitudes, and disliking ideas less for their uncertainty than because they made the mind itself changing and restless. He measured the Irish tradition by another greater than itself, and was quick to feel any falling asunder of the two, yet at many moments they seemed but one in his imagination. Ireland, all through his poem of that name, speaks to him with the voice of the great poets, and in *Ireland's Dead* she is still mother of perfect heroism, but there doubt comes too.

> Can it be, thou dost repent
> That they went, thy chivalry,
> Those sad ways magnificent?

And in *Ways of War*, dedicated to John O'Leary, he dismissed the belief in an heroic Ireland as but a dream.

> A dream! a dream! an ancient dream!
> Yet, ere peace come to Inisfail,
> Some weapons on some field must gleam,
> Some burning glory fire the Gael.

That field may lie beneath the sun,
Fair for the treading of an host:
That field in realms of thought be won,
And armed minds do their uttermost:

Some way, to faithful Inisfail,
Shall come the majesty and awe
Of martial truth, that must prevail
To lay on all the eternal law.

I do not think either of us saw that, as belief in the possibility of armed insurrection withered, the old romantic Nationalism would wither too, and that the young would become less ready to find pleasure in whatever they believed to be literature. Poetical tragedy, and indeed all the more intense forms of literature, had lost their hold on the general mass of men in other countries as life grew safe, and the sense of comedy which is the social bond in times of peace as tragic feeling is in times of war, had become the inspiration of popular art. I always knew this, but I believed that the memory of danger, and the reality of it seemed near enough sometimes, would last long enough to give Ireland her imaginative opportunity. I could not foresee that a new class, which had begun to rise into power under the shadow of Parnell, would change the nature of the Irish movement, which, needing no longer great sacrifices, nor bringing any great risk to individuals, could do without exceptional men, and those activities of the mind that are founded on the exceptional moment.[4] John O'Leary had spent much of his thought in an unavailing war with the agrarian party, believing it the root of change, but the fox that crept into the badger's hole did not come from there. Power passed to small shopkeepers, to clerks, to that very class who had seemed to John O'Leary so ready to bend to the power of others, to men who had risen above the traditions of the countryman, without learning those of cultivated life or even educating themselves, and who because of their poverty, their ignorance, their superstitious piety, are much subject to all kinds of fear. Immediate victory, immediate utility, became everything, and the conviction, which is in all who have run great risks for a cause's sake, in the O'Learys and Mazzinis as in all rich natures, that life is greater than the cause, withered, and we artists, who are the servants not of any cause but of mere naked life, and above all of that life in its nobler forms, where joy and sorrow are one, Artificers of the Great Moment, became as elsewhere in Europe protesting individual voices. Ireland's great moment had passed, and she had filled no roomy vessels with strong sweet wine, where we have filled our porcelain jars against the coming winter.

Notes

1. John O'Leary (1830-1907) was one of the most important political influences on Yeats. He began to edit a Fenian journal, the *Irish People*, in 1863, for which he was imprisoned in 1865; he was released after nine years, and allowed to return to Dublin in 1885.

2. F. W. H. Myers (1843-1901) founded the Society of Psychical Research in 1882.

3. I have heard him say more than once, 'I will not say our people know good from bad, but I will say that they don't hate the good when it is pointed out to them, as a great many people do in England.' [Yeats's note.]

4. A small political organiser told me once that he and a certain friend got together somewhere in Tipperary a great meeting of farmers for O'Leary on his coming out of prison, and O'Leary had said at it: 'The landlords gave us some few leaders, and I like them for that, and the artisans have given us great numbers of good patriots, and so I like them best; but you I do not like at all, for you have never given us any one.' [Yeats's note.]

15
James Stephens, 'The Outlook for Literature With Special Reference to Ireland', 1922

James Stephens (1880-1950) began writing verse for the United Irishman *in 1905, and then for* Sinn Fein *from 1907 onwards. His novel* The Crock of Gold *(1912) is perhaps his most well-known legacy. This essay appeared in* Century Magazine, *October 1922.*

I

It is as easy to foretell next year's weather as to foretell next year's literary orientation, but the laws underlying supply and demand are so curiously perfected that even a demand for prophecy can be met with some kind of goods. There is a great deal known about weather, and although the knowledge does not greatly assist the weather-forecasters in their prognostications, it does provide them with matter upon which they can converse intelligently; and there is a sufficiency of data about art to enable us not only to gossip agreeably, but to speculate upon it, and to draw conclusions from it which we may allow the march of events to prove or disprove or neglect.

In referring to artists I do not here refer to Shakspere or Dante or their peers. Such men stand above comparison or criticism, and possess a technic which lesser men can no more manipulate than they can play marbles with mountains. I speak of the ordinary man who cannot paint, but does, and who cannot write, but cannot be prevented from writing, and who pleases his contemporaries largely because he explains to them that which they already know, than which no explanation is more acceptable. These are the artists and writers, and it is their business, by hook or by crook, to live, and to do the work that people like them to

178

do as well as ever it can be done. Their work is to tell the truth as closely as they can manage it. Ultimate truth cannot properly be required of the artist, but immediate or local truth is his proper business, and this is almost entirely a matter of emotional appreciation. Probably there never was an intellectual artist, and probably there never will be one, for life is being, and the artistic reaction to it is an emotional one.

In immediate terms, truth is that to which we are sympathetically attracted. We may amuse ourselves with intellections, but it is a temperamental loyalty that we give to a person, an art, or an idea, and the intellectual truth of that person or thing is seldom questioned by us and seldom examined; for truth, on the various planes of being, is not an intellection. It is a passion, the passion of life, and it sways us in blind hungers, blind loves, blind loyalties, and blind ambitions. It sways us unconsciously, in other words, and it is always incapable of being expressed or explained or exposed. Art, therefore, can only remind us of something we have done or suffered, and it can convey to no man an experience which he has not personally fathomed. Culture is a conversation between equals, and the artist on every grade is the liaison officer who links that vast diversity together for social purposes. All those bundles of proceeding and digested actions is the thing we call life, and, still speaking in immediate terms, it makes thinking look like nothing at all; for by the side of an action no thought is valid, and the person who truly meditates an action will be withheld by no reasonable consideration, or by any other power than that sense of caution which is only a glyph on fear or incapacity.

This endless succession of deeds that are passions is the stuff that must be translated out of the whirl of movement into the thin quietude of words and paint and speculation, and it can be translated only by a passion that is the equal of itself; for if the artist is not that passion embodied, then art will continue to be an ineffective watering-down of reality until the mind has evolved an inward power that is at least the equal of its outward manifestation.

Everywhere the artist is in revolt against art, for there is a profound cultural discontent on every side, which must have as profound a cause. It is useless to dismiss it, for it will continue despite our displeasure, and it is senseless to try to ignore it, for no cultivated man can afford to be ignorant of anything that is happening in his time, and, be it good or bad, that is happening mainly because of him. You cannot tango or shimmy-shake and think that art will not begin to slip and waggle also; for the only difference between the artist and the ordinary man is that the artist is more sensuously appreciative than the ordinary man is. He often gets and earns a bad reputation by reason of this excessive sensibility. You cannot throw the world into violent and nonsensical war and think that art will register anything but that violence and nonsense. What man does, and thinks about it, is the material of the artist, and he will return exactly that which is furnished to him and which he is familiar with. Inspiration, as it is called, is a passionate recording of exact knowledge, for passion without exactitude is just nihilism; while exactitude without passion is only the labor of a pedant.

What is the ideal attitude toward life for the artist? It is that he should be endlessly sensitive and insensitive. So sensitive that a cruelty or injustice done to other people will set him mad; so insensitive that an injustice to himself will tickle him to death. He is not a self, but a national or communal conscience. His protest is against ugliness and maladjustment. Perhaps one should say, the ugliness that is maladjustment, for it may be that there is no other ugliness; and, so far as his powers go, his own work will be free from all those bad qualities which he has publicly undertaken to criticize and force toward remedy. But it is well for him to remember that in every line he writes and in every picture he paints he presents, with his matter, his limitations. He is always engaged on his own portrait. Even in his choice of a subject, to say nothing of his conduct of it, he is making a definite statement about himself which can be very cruelly read and very contemptuously dismissed. A book is the person who wrote it; there is nothing in it that is not of that person, and it would be an easy thing to name bullies, traitors, and thieves by merely reciting the titles of stories. That is why there should be an ideal attitude toward life for the artist, as there is for the physician, the priest, and the philosopher.

Literature is an ideal expression of the environment; that is, of the human society it is born from. As that society is noble, greedy, brutal, or artistic, so the literature it generates reveals this, that, or the other quality of the time. In my own country of Ireland man is now in the making, and in a very few years our national action will tell us what it is we may hope for culturally, or what it is that we may be tempted to emigrate from. But Irish national action and culture can no longer be regarded as a thing growing cleanly from its own root. We have entered the world. More, the world has entered us, and a double, an internal and external, evolution is our destiny, as it is the destiny of every other race in the world. We shall learn the Irish language: we must. We shall *talk* like Irishmen, or we are done for: we shall *think* like Europeans, or we are done for. There lies our internal and external evolution, and there the gifts we shall give to and accept from the world, and in those concussions and repercussions will be forged our art, our literature, and ourselves.

II

In these days of swift intercourse no country can be regarded as possessing an existence independent of or even removed from the rest of the world, and the artistic, economic, and social repercussions from all quarters are now more unescapable than they have been hitherto. They never could be ultimately eluded, but they might be referred, as it were, to the ides of March, and left till Never came. Never is upon us, and, in this time of quick dissemination of ideas and commodities, action and reaction are to be looked for almost immediately after the appearance of whatever new idea provokes them.

Whoever takes thought for the future of Irish literature must think of Dostoyevsky, of Tolstoy, of Sudermann, of Romain Rolland, of Marcel Proust, and of a host of lesser men, who, although they are not working in his vernacular, are still delving in the very stuff that his thoughts are made of. The music, painting, literature, and economics of today are no longer local or sporadic. They are world inheritances, or, rather, world urges; and for their purposes it is correct to say that there is a universal idea with which every national speech must be saturated if that speech is to continue as a living medium of expression or to represent anything whatever of actuality.

The past is a word to conjure with, it is a word to hypnotize with, but it is not a word to evoke reality. Reality is present action. The past is the memory of actions done, and, as these are incorporated in our present minds, we need not be afraid that we shall greatly depart from them or shed more of our national characteristics than we have no use for. It is certain that Ireland will revisit her past with vast curiosity and reverence, but she will not remain there long enough to eat a railway sandwich. She will return with her booty to the eternally present time of an eternally modern world. The Irish past is not a catalogue of events and personages. The Irish past is the Irish language. Learn that and you will have enough of the past to last you for the entire of your future, and you will have done the one thing necessary to make this nation a nation, and to prepare for a literature, an art, and a culture which will not be an abject imitation or a dishonest forgery.

III

There never was an archaic period in the history of the world. At every moment man is modern, and while his needs do not change except in vast cycles of time, his technic of living requires modification in every few generations. Between the technic of living and the technic of art there is no difference. They are simultaneous expressions of the same thing. Life at present, jazz at present, cubism and dadaism at present, represent the one identical lack of control which is the present technic of life, and it is in this matter of technic that the immediate interest of our time lies, and it is from the same technic that three quarters of our inquiry will be answered. If we could discover a mind of sufficient scope to comprehend the hundred technical adventures and experiments that are now engrossing the scientific and artistic minds of the world, such a mind would draw from them the generalization which is all we need to start our new schools upon; but that critical intelligence has not yet revealed itself, and does seem to be as lacking in every land as is the creative intelligence of the artist, which is also in eclipse.

Art is, in fact, seeking enthusiastically, and at times wildly, for the technic which can be applied to a new order of ideas, and the fact that a technical problem is pressing for settlement implies positively enough that a new order desires to function. This impatience of the old craft and the old craft form is apparent in every department of effort, and it is evident that a vast historic phase, artistically, culturally, socially, and economically, has come to its decline, and that a modified chaos will continue in being until a synthesis is made, and the obvious order is drawn from the apparent disorder in which we find ourselves. In olden days it would have been correct to say, that if you change a road you change a country; but today it would be true to say that if you alter a technic you change a continent, and the statement will register the difference between a psychology that will visit this earth no more and a psychology which is still a matter for speculation.

In painting, in music, in psychology itself, a new conception is struggling into birth, and only a few generations may be necessary to put out of date, as it has already put out of countenance, the culture that we automatically inherited, and which, by mere habit and possession, we are inclined to consider as the only culture that is possible.

The ear and the eye, the instruments with which we investigate external effects, are the veriest slaves of the mind they seem to inform, and should that mind become interested in a different musical scale, our ears would obediently assure us that a sonata by Beethoven is only an ignorant uproar, and that the new thing, which previously had visited us like a toothache, is really a miracle of justness and harmony. So with the eye, a small modification in technic would enable us to regard a picture by Rembrandt with the same incredulous and forlorn inquiry that we now turn on Chinese and Japanese masterpieces. Change technic, and apparently you alter all, and it seems absolutely certain that the world is bent on that great transformation.

It is art that will first bring to consciousness that which the unconscious has motived, for art is less a method of portrayal than a criticism of life, and its explanatory analysis is one of the most valuable facts we know of. Bound up with this mental change are corresponding world changes so vast in their scope that a mind which is still thinking in the old terms will be unable to regard them without fear and unbelief; for there is no such thing as a solitary change or a solitary anything, and one radical alteration in our mode of thought will present us with a new universe, and a new man to cognize it.

IV

Is Ireland doing anything to prepare herself for this tumultuous and engrossing future? It is certain that none but a young nation can deal with it, and I think that no country which, in the scriptural phrase, 'has great possessions', or an ancestral idolatry of them, will be able to deal with it at all; for with this change much more than artistic processes must go by the board.

183

Ireland, I think, can stand it. An act is always truer than a thought, for it is a thought clothed in reality, and during the last five years the national act of Ireland has been so real that it has achieved what older minds considered to be impossible, and has achieved it by methods which the official and logical intellect, if its advice had been sought, could only have considered as infantile. It is the good fact of life that the infant wins always, and I think that Ireland awakens from her profound sleep as the youngest race now active in the world, and the best fitted to accept possible modifications with the curiosity and good humor of a brave young person.

If we search curiously enough for anything, we shall find it, and if we strive to discover the dominant fact in the last hundred and fifty years, it is not beyond the wit of man to place a finger on it. The idea that has dominated the European mind during the later historic period is the idea of speed; and as man transplanted himself from place to place with greater facility, so every other action and attribute of his came under the same dominating idea, and a universal adjustment to new velocities is now part of our unconsidered inheritance.

The steamship tried to keep pace with the railway train, the printing-press tried to go faster. The woolen-mill, the shoe-factory, the baker, the tailor, were paced by the steam-engine. There are no records; they are all abreast. We have speeded up the beehive and the cabbage-patch; we make cows give twice as much milk in half as much time, and we are assisting the domestic hen to provide a weightier egg on less food than she had been accustomed to. It is an actual fact that we are living unconcernedly in a world the velocity of which would have worn our ancestors into rags in less than ten years, and now the aëroplane has come to make us go still faster, and to alter every aspect of the world we know into something that we cannot even conjecture. Do we really consider that the airman, the movie-man, and the psychoanalyst are signs of nothing, or that they have been evolved by nothing from nothing and are going nowhere?

It is a mistake to speak of this as the age of mechanics. It is the age of speeding-up, and that speeding-up is even more ideal than it is material. That is, the process takes place as much in the mind as in outer material. And it is a stupidity to consider that the mind can be more than temporarily dominated by its own inventions. The effect which the mind externalizes is visible to us as this and that invention. The effect of that creative effort on the mind itself is not so quickly appreciable, but it is much more real than any of its toys are.

The person who thinks that we can do a thing and not become it must think again. It is not that our cities, our modes of locomotion, and our social views and actions have changed; the mind itself has undergone the transformations which are visible in our surroundings, and in the examination of that mental change we find the explanation of, and the necessity for, a new psychology, for a new valuation of the values, for a new art, and for a new technic of human conduct, whether in art or morality. We may say, with perfect fitness, 'The world is dead! Long live the world!' for today a new world is born, and is greatly distressing the nurses who are teaching it to walk when it quite obviously ought to be learning to fly. Are not the cubists, the dadaists and the makers of free-verse trying to fly? It is exactly what they are doing, and more power, or more wings, to their elbows!

These ideas may seem fantastic, but all ideas are fantastic until they become accepted, and then, by mere process, they rapidly become ridiculous, in other words unsuitable, and a new fantasy pushes them to the ditch. The thing which has not kept pace in the general acceleration is education, and by that I mean the whole scheme of cultural control, which is framed to make man a subservient instrument of life rather than to equip him as the living being that he is: and it is scarcely too much to say that every idea in the text-books was framed to fit a servile order that has disappeared, and that they are of no help and of much hurt at this period. Has the servile order disappeared? It may be that in this generalization alone the whole modern secret has been uttered.

V

Has all this anything to do with the future of Irish literature? It has everything to do with it, for Irish literature will be a part of world literature, drawing nourishment from the ends and ends of the earth. It will be a description of the ideas and actions of the modern Irishman in a modern world. I say 'ideas and actions'; I place the word ideas before the word action, for unless there are ideas there is no action, there is no literature, there is no art, but only an imitation of these, and that imitation is taken from a cabbage or a cow. Nothing in this modern world is isolated: all things are in concord with one another, or in a discord that is more apparent than real, for they are all fundamentally interrelated and interdependent. Some one has said that any war in Europe is civil war, and it is true, for the European type has been evolved and does contain and override all that is local or peculiar within it. So, in this modern world, we cannot any longer speak in terms of cultural difference of an Ireland, an England, a France, or a Germany. These exist as geographical descriptions, but they are not separated things. There is a European culture and there is an Asiatic one, the world has grown so small! One or other of these gigantic conceptions will emerge from the final struggle for supremacy as the world culture, and it is for that great struggle that the world is set prow on.

But by geography and tradition Ireland will go with her neighbors. If our culture is less than European, it will frankly be nothing at all; it will not be worth attention; it will not be worthy of one man's loyalty or one instant's hope, and at the head or tail of the European procession Ireland must take her place or die. I include America in the term 'European', for she is, in fact, the essence of Europe, and she is present in Europe as a ferment is present in a brew, and she is perhaps the most vital factor in the European future.

I consider that the scepter of artistic dominance began to pass as long as twenty years ago from the nations who then held it — that is, from England, France, and Germany — to other nations whose energy enables them to accept the great legacy. These other nations are America, Russia, and Italy, and it is from their rivalries and co-operations that the new social order and the new art and literature will emerge; with our assistance I hope, for we are younger than they all, and essentially more energetic than the three together. Ireland may never have existed as a political entity, but as a center of essential energy Ireland deserves to be ranked as one of the wonders of the world.

With the decline of the former great nations the art they stood for declines with them, and the question of the future of Irish literature requires an Irish examination and a world examination to resolve it. What is this Irish literature in which we are all interested, and in which, I suppose, we are all experimenting? A hundred years ago our national culture was suppressed so thoroughly that the very memory of it has almost disappeared from our common mind. If one were to make very large generalizations as to world literature, we might say that in the recent period only England and France could be referred to in terms of world-wide approbation, and that in both of these literatures the predominant fact was a brutal idealism, the brutal part of which is now exhausted, leaving the idealistic part without power to function. We could say that German literature disclosed a certain home-loving quality and a dull interest in the domesticities or mechanics of life: it was a well articulated piece of machinery, and of immense dullness. We could say that France was noted for an effort to achieve formal perfection and for an apparently endless sex interest, into which her literature sank as into a bog. The outstanding facts in English literature, on its popular plane, appears to me to be brutality and boyishness. In the first chapter you discover the murdered man, and in the last one you hang the person who didn't do it.

What, even in these hasty terms, does Irish literature in the English tongue stand for? Irish fiction, Irish poetry, with the most pitifully few exceptions, are only timid and ineffectual imitations of the English mode; and our young artists (read their books if utter boredom does not prevent you) can be as cruel, as grimy, and as sentimental as any Garvice or Le Quex of them all. They do not write; they copy and they do it badly, for it is a prime fact in both art and life that a copy cannot be done well. Ask American literature if a copy can be done well. There is no future for us there. We cannot rival them in the tricks of that trade which is all trickery, where the rogue is hero, and the heroine is a fool. Or will any one be temerarious enough to say that Shaw or Moore or Dunsany are producing Irish literature, or that Wilde or Goldsmith or Swift did produce it? We must get back to our own language, which is our psychology, our technic, and our treasure-house; then only shall we know if we have anything to say, and we will learn quickly enough how to say it.

VI

The European technical apparatus went out of date at least fifteen years ago, and there is no longer a standard for art to follow. It has to be recreated and reorganized. Nietzsche and Wagner tried to recreate it by injecting violence into it instead of beauty; and they have failed, as all their militaristic successors have failed.

If any artists have cause to be weary of current technical processes it is surely ours, who have been associated with it so long and so futilely. Are we irredeemably enamoured of the tale of hearty fun, which consists in robbing some one? Of the historical narrative, which sets forth how a strong, silent man was neither strong nor silent, but did manage to get away with everybody's goods that he came in contact with? Of the psychological tale, which succeeds, after Olympian difficulties, in marrying two persons who would really have got married on the dropping of a hat? Are those robberies and murders and marryings of actually permanent interest, and do they truly represent something that nourishes or sustains the spirit of man? The poetic literature of England is one of the mightiest efforts that a national mind has ever achieved, but her prose literature has never grown up. It was written on the playing-grounds of Eton. From the Round Table through Scott and Stevenson to Conrad it is always a boy's tale, with adventures borrowed from the criminal calendar, and a psychology that is taken bodily from the cricket-field; and I think it is today as dead as is the literature of Belgium, of Spain, or of Switzerland.

But what is true of these is generally true of Europe. The models from which they all worked have ceased to apply in the modern world, and there is no hope for art or literature but in the wild men who paint pictures with their eyes shut, and who write poetry with their ears shut.

16
Patrick Kavanagh, from *Collected Pruse*, 1967

Patrick Kavanagh (1904-67) lived in County Monaghan, where he was born, until 1939, when he moved to Dublin. His autobiography, The Green Fool *(1938) and the novel* Tarry Flynn *(1940), complement the achievement of his poetry, best represented by* The Great Hunger *(1942), and* Come Dance with Kitty Stobling *(1960).*

16(a) 'From Monaghan to the Grand Canal'

I have been thinking of making my grove on the banks of the Grand Canal near Baggot Street Bridge where in recent days I rediscovered my roots. My hegira was to the Grand Canal bank where again I saw the beauty of water and green grass and the magic of light. It was the same emotion as I had known when I stood on a sharp slope in Monaghan, where I imaginatively stand now, looking across to Slieve Gullion and South Armagh. An attractive landscape of small farms and a culture that hadn't changed in a thousand years. A hundred yards away from me I could observe primitive husbandry where Paddy Nugent was threshing oats with a flail in a barn.

But something disturbs my imagination.

I am thinking of a term which was much in use in the early days of my life in Dublin. He has roots in the soil, they used to say. I was one of those who had an unchallenged right to claim roots in the soil, but I was an exception and the rooted in the soil theory gave birth to a vast amount of bogusry — in Ireland, writers like Michael McLaverty, and in England, H. E. Bates and indeed Thomas Hardy. Could any man be more remote from the simple, elemental folk of Wessex than Hardy?

Roots in the soil meant that you knew about people living close to nature, struggling for survival on the small farm, and you had a practical knowledge of animal breeding.

But of course roots in the soil have nothing to do with these things. What are our roots? What is our material?

Real roots lie in our capacity for love and its abandon. The material itself has no special value; it is what our imagination and our love does to it.

Lying at the heart of love we wander through its infinities.

The world that matters is the world that we have created, just as we create our friends. In making friends or a myth the material is sometimes of account. Some people will not stay made as friends; you mould them to your heart's desire, and when you are absent they change their shape.

Writers whose gimmick is roots in the soil produce a very violent article. The Seven Deadly Sins of Pride, Covetousness, Lust, Envy, Anger, Gluttony and Sloth loom large in those novels. But real elementalism is a more tawdry thing, resentful, mean and ungenerous. The majority of men live at a very petty level.

The society and place out of which I came was not unattractive. No man ever loved that landscape and even some of the people more than I. It was a barbaric society not appreciably different from an old fashioned Dublin slum. Our manners were the same. But there was the landscape and the sense of continuity with a race that had come down the centuries.

I loved that country very much in spite of its many defects, and I had no messianic impulse to leave it. Everything that I did as regards acting or doing something was done against my natural feelings. Perhaps it is that basically we realize that all action is vulgar, that only the contemplative matters.

Watching the potato buds coming up, living the old pattern, what was there of spiritual values that could not be fitted into that context? And yet, having sown a couple of acres of barley in May, I walked off. I felt that I shouldn't have done it, that I was acting by some untruthful principle that had been created. It is indeed that untruthful principle that besets all of us in most of our activities. We can be taught only what we know. When you try to teach someone something they have not experienced they do not hear.

I think that coming from the society and background that I have come from was disadvantageous to me in some respects.

The worst respect was that one accepted as the final word in painting and letters the stuff that was being produced in Dublin. Another disadvantage was that the basic ingredients of the society in which I grew up were football and the smoky, sweaty dance hall. Football is not too bad but as the dance hall is one's only contact with social life, it was tough on a man of sensibility. It was simply impossible to love a galvanized dance hall and the atmosphere both physical and moral which prevailed there. Literature could not be made out of that material as Carleton made literature out of the many thrilling dances which are to be found in his *Traits and Stories*. Earlier I did find some imaginative and comic material in dances given to celebrate a wedding. The ear caught many of those delectable idiocies that people produce when in a state of excitement.

I remember a neighbour giving such a dance explaining that they weren't going to have any intoxicating drink. 'Their fill to eat and drink of currant bread and tay, and what more do they want?' A phrase like that was sure to gain currency in that ironic country where there were many intelligent and amusing people.

When I came to Dublin the dregs of the old Literary Revival were still stirrable. The Palace Bar was crowded with two or three dozen poets and their admirers. I do not wish now to be satirical about these men. I am speaking about them now as part of my literary pilgrimage. Here the Movement which I thought quite discredited was being talked about. When I came to Dublin, Yeats was dead. Yeats was a poet and he invented many writers. He invented Synge and Lady Gregory and he was largely responsible for F. R. Higgins. As George Moore wrote: 'The Irish Literary Movement began with Yeats and returned to him.'

During my early years in Dublin the virtue of being a peasant was much extolled. This peasant derived naturally from the roots in the soil theory. Knowing nothing better, I accepted it and flaunted my peasantry in their somewhat spivvier genealogies.

Poor Higgins tried hard to play the peasant with bad poems about blackthorn sticks. The ballad was the peasant's poetic form. I suffered sore at ballad-mongering sessions before I realized that this form of torture was no different from the self-expression of any bore from the golf bore to the architect and cricket bore. Ballad singing is all right for the singer, but will he ever stop and give the others an innings?

I was the established peasant poet. Far from the poet being a peasant — if there is such an article outside the Russian novel — he is the last word in sophistication. All his life's activities are towards the final fusion of all crudeness into a pure flame. The keynote of the poetic mind is an extreme subtlety.

All this stuff about roots in the soil, peasants and balladry was no doubt the degenerate family of the pre-Raphaelites, coupled, by the time I came to know them, with the left-wingery of the International Brigade of the Spanish Civil War. I cannot deny that I subscribed my quota of 'working class' jargon. Somebody recently embarrassed me by reminding me of a poem I had printed in *Ireland Today* about a servant boy. Oh my goodness! Well, we live and sometimes learn.

With a small society lacking intensity like this, one needs a coarse formula, if we are to have any body of writing. And that is what we have had for the past fifty years.

I cannot help saying that as far as I can see and as far as I have experienced, there has never been a tradition of poetry in Ireland. One can feel this lack of belief all the time.

And now raising my eyes to the horizon I am again looking across the small fields of South Monaghan and South Armagh, and wondering did any of the Irish writers who claimed to bring realism instead of the old sentimentalities ever express the society that lies within my gaze, with the exception of my own small effort in *Tarry Flynn*?

I am not suggesting that being true to life in a realist way is the highest function of a writer. As I have pointed out already the highest function is the pure flame from the material.

The writers who wrote about Ireland in the new 'truthful' way proved to be no truer than the popular sentimentalizers such as Kickham and Canon Sheehan; they all seemed off-truth. This is not surprising, for most men who attempt to write about a particular society are deluded as to their qualifications for the job. For example, Mr Peadar O'Donnell has written novels about Donegal. It seems at once *his* country, but is it? Similarly there is a group who write about Galway and another about Cork and another about Kerry. Yet another school believe that in Dublin with its unique *clichés* and way of life is a ready-built band wagon on which to ride to literary success. Any critic whether from Dublin or Soho can see that this stuff is just noisy emptiness, completely unfunny.

It took me many years to work myself free from that formula for literature which laid all the stress on whether it was Irish or not. For twenty years I wrote according to the dispensation of this Irish school. The appraisers of the school all agreed that I had my roots in the soil, was one of the people and that I was an authentic voice. I wrote, for example, a terrible piece about —

> My soul was an old horse
> Offered for sale in twenty fairs;
> I offered him to the Church, the buyers
> Were little men who feared his unusual airs.

One can at once see the embarrassing impertinence and weakness of it, the dissolute character whining. But it was the perfect Irish formula and English publishers loved it. Nothing would satisfy them but to put it first in the book. There has always been a big market in England for the synthetic Irish thing. Even Shaw who was a bogus Irishman had to do a bit of clowning.

Another villainous maw opened for things Irish-and-proud-of-it is the American literary market. The stuff that gets published as Irish in America is quite awful. One of the great, roaring successes of American publishing a couple of years ago was a novel by Brian Moore about some Irish girl who had a vast number of illegitimate children. In reviewing this book (and books of this kind) none leaned further back in referring to its compassion, its humour and its many other qualities than the Catholic papers. They seem terrified that they will be outdone in the liberal ethic race. A dreary dust of left-wingery, a formula which excludes all creative thought, lies over the vegetation. They feel, I suppose, that literary and thought politics, like all other politics, is the philosophy of the possible. What's the use in being different if you can't get your words printed? Still.

In Ireland one is up against the fact that very few care for or understand the creative spirit. You can come across by being specifically Irish in manner and spirit, but when you attempt to offer them the real thing it's no go.

When I started to write what I believe is the real thing there was not much response, except possibly from Stephen Spender who described it as 'violently beautiful'.

Previously I had been concerned with Ireland and with my ego, both of which come together often enough. Imagine the dreadfulness of —

It would never be summer always autumn
After a harvest always lost
When Drake was winning seas for England
We sailed in puddles of the past
Pursuing the ghost of Brendan's mast.

When the editors of *The Oxford Book of Irish Verse* wanted something
of mine they worked on me for this poem, and in the end, owing
to my need for money, I let the lines in. But how appallingly this
poem accepts the myth of Ireland as a spiritual entity.

Then one day as I was lying on the bank of the Grand Canal
near Baggott Street Bridge having just been very ill in the hot
summer of nineteen fifty-five, I commenced my poetic hegira.
Without self-pity to look at things.

To look on is enough
In the business of love.

To let experience enter the soul. Not to be self-righteous. To have
a point of view which is a man poised with a torch. Whoever
wants to light a taper may; the torch-bearer does not mind. The
light was a surprise over roofs and around gables, and the canal
water was green stilly.

Commemorate me where there is water,
Canal water preferably, so stilly
Greeny at the heart of summer. Brother
Commemorate me thus beautifully
Where by a lock niagarously roars
The falls for those who sit in the tremendous silence
Of mid-July. No one will speak in prose
Who finds his way to these Parnassian islands.
A swan goes by, head low with many apologies,
The bending light peeps through the eyes of bridges
And here! a barge comes bringing from Athy
And other far-flung towns mythologies.
O memorial me with no hero-courageous
Tomb but just a canal-bank seat for the passer-by.

This sonnet was inspired by two seats on the bank of the Canal
here 'Erected to the memory of Mrs Dermot O'Brien'.

194

The main thing is to be free
From self-necessity.

On the road of my hegira I began to reflect with astonishment
how poor as technicians the Irish school of poets and novelists
have been. Real technique is a spiritual quality, a condition of
mind, or an ability to invoke a particular condition of mind. Lack
of technique gives us shallowness: Colum's

O men from the fields
Softly come through
Mary will fold him
In a mantle of blue.

A charming sentiment undoubtedly, but all on the surface.
Technique is a method of being sincere. Technique is a method
of getting at life. The slippery surface of the *cliché* — phrase and
emotion — causes a light skidding blow.

I discovered that the important thing above all was to avoid
taking oneself sickly seriously. One of the good ways of getting
out of this respectability is the judicious use of slang and of
outrageous rhyming. The new and outrageous rhymes are not to
be confused with the slickeries of Ogden Nash. I draw attention
to my rhyming of bridges with courageous.

Another bad thing about the Irish school was its dreadful
sadness and lack of comedy. People who are unsure of themselves
cannot afford to break out into uproarious laughter or use a piece
of slang. You may find a small number of readers who cotton on
to the technique but large numbers of people will look with
contempt at you and say what a pity it is that he lacks schooling.
This can be depressing.

To write lively verse or prose, to be involved with Comedy
requires enormous physical and mental power. Energy, as Blake
remarked, is eternal delight. The more energy is in a poem or
prose work the more comic it is. Melville's *Moby Dick* is a
tremendous comedy, borne along to its end on the wings of its
author's outgiving faith in his characters. Melville loved
everything on that ship. And what a great poet in prose he was!
We laugh inwardly in our souls with Melville.

Laughter is the most poetic thing in life, that is the right kind
of loving laughter. When, after a lifetime of struggle, we produce

the quintessence of ourselves, it will be something gay and young.

But to be undull is dangerous. Dullness as a cultural asset is most valuable. One remembers that old school friend meeting Johnson after many years and his saying rather sadly that he might have been a great success but 'cheerfulness kept breaking in'.

I have my own trouble with humour. A work that is inspired by the comic spirit has much to contend with, for a work that is inspired by the comic spirit has a sense of values, of courage and rectitude — and these qualities are hated immemorially.

Why they should be hated is not difficult to understand. A man in offering the small unique thing that is the most the greatest possess, eliminates completely the gassy fiction by which the majority live.

The notion of being one of the people is part of the general myth of roots in the soil. Analysing the thing now I see or feel that I always had some sort of kink in me. It is this kink which makes a poet, I believe. As Colette observed, it is not what a poet writes that makes him one, but this other thing. 'Rectitude', Cocteau calls it.

To have absolute rectitude in any field is to be an eccentric. You are not in step. Perhaps it is a form of pride and selfishness born of the realization that telling lies is a bore. In high company or low pub this rectitude is a constant quality with a poet. Being fated to live with this terrible tyrant of truth has often driven the possessed to violence, rage and, as in the case of Dylan Thomas, drink.

I am not sure if this kink of rectitude is on the whole beneficial to the man possessed by it; it makes a poet of him, but is it really necessary? It is this kink which makes people say, 'why are you so damned difficult? We are anxious to help you.' And so on.

A trouble with the poet is that he is not a professional writer in the usual sense. Most of his hours are spent living. He can gulp out all he has to say in a short time. After a lifetime of experience, as Rilke pointed out, we find just a few lines. It is because of the minute quantity of that poetic essence that is in the best men that I do not regret having developed late and very slowly. If you read about English poetry you will find that the poets spent most of their time in taverns — Ben Jonson at the Mermaid, Dryden in Will's Coffee House. It takes a lot of living to produce a little experience. We remember Tennyson's remark, quoted by Carlyle, 'I am the greatest poet since Shakespeare;

unfortunately I have nothing to say.'

The poet is a poet outside his writing as I have often argued. He creates an oral tradition. He does something to people. I am not sure that that something is always good, for it is a disruptive, anarchic mentality which he awakens — and if we pursue him far enough we will be inclined to agree with Plato that the poet is a menace.

There is however not much danger of his menacing Dublin or, I imagine, Ireland generally.

Voltaire said that doing a thing was the only reward worth while and Cézanne put that idea into practice when, having painted a picture, he left it behind him in a cottage or perhaps flung it into the bushes.

It was a long journey for me from my Monaghan with my mind filled with the importance-of-writing-and-thinking-and-feeling-like-an-Irishman to the banks of the Grand Canal in nineteen fifty-five, the year of my hegira.

16(b) 'The Irish Tradition'

For a man in Ireland to have the label 'poet' attached to him is little short of a calamity. Society, when it has established a man as a poet, has him cornered within narrow limits. If he looks like having too much scope in his little corner he will be still further narrowed by having an adjective in front of 'poet' — such as Country poet, Catholic poet and so on. He becomes a sort of exhibit, not a man in and of the world.

If he happens to be a dilettante without a passionate faith he will enjoy this position, but if he is a genuine poet it is an indignity and something much worse. Therefore, I announce here and now that I am speaking as a journalist. I have resigned from being a poet and I hope that my resignation will be accepted.

In so far as the poet is thought of in Ireland, the idea is that he is either an uproarious, drunken clown, an inspired idiot, a silly school-girl type, or just plain dull. He is in no way to be taken seriously.

The Irish ideal of a literary genius — weak, charming and a challenge to nobody — is in the image of that celebrated synthetic tramp, Padraig O Conaire, with his goat tethered outside the Bailey Restaurant. I find it hard to pass from this image without saying that O Conaire, choosing the disreputable life, is the direct opposite of my idea of the poetic genius. The poet does not seek misfortune; the poet does not pursue experience — experience pursues him. The poet does not go searching for beauty or intensity; these things happen to him. But that is a long story.

The logical collateral of these ideas regarding the poet is that poets are quite common in Ireland. They are never mentioned except in batches of a dozen or more. Fourteen hundred are reputed to have been present at the famous Assembly at Drumceat, and not so long ago, in one of the Irish papers, I saw a list of modern Gaelic geniuses, which for a moment deceived me into thinking it was the list of chief mourners at the funeral of some noted patriot or industrialist.

It was a patriotic gesture, for patriotism does include belief in the importance of literature. For those of us who believe that the poetic spirit is of some value, this patriotic enthusiasm is a bad thing, for it sets up as admirable, from motives that are not pure, something that cannot possibly be the authentic thing. The authentic thing, if it happened to appear, would be crushed.

Even allowing for unfavourable circumstances, it is remarkable that in a thousand years Ireland has not produced a major poet or, indeed, a good minor poet. There was no audience for the poet's high dignity. I will return to this theme later but, in the meantime let us consider what a real poet is.

The poetic view of life is a view based on a true sense of values and those values must be of their nature what are called unworldly. Furthermore, a man may be a poet in prose as well as in verse, or in merely talking to the people. To narrow the poetic spirit down to its expression in verse is equivalent to narrowing religion down to something that happens on Sundays.

A good idea of the nature of the poet is to be found in E. V. Rieu's introduction to his translation of the Four Gospels. He remarks of St. Luke: 'St Luke was a poet. I do not mean by this that he embroidered his narratives, but rather that he knew how to distil truth from fact.' Rieu goes on to refer to Luke's 'poetic insight into reality' and to his realization of the part played by Woman in the revelation of the Divine Idea.

That is the poetic mind.

If I happened to meet a poet — and I have met poets — I would expect him to reveal his powers of insight and imagination even if he talked of poultry farming, ground rents or any other commonplace subject. Above all, I would expect to be excited and have my horizons of faith and hope widened by his ideas on the only subject that is of any real importance — Man-in-this-

World-and-why.

He would reveal to me the gay, imaginative God who made the grass and the trees and the flowers, a God not terribly to be feared.

It is a curious and ironical fact that for a man to show himself at all seriously concerned with the one thing that matters is to have himself looked upon as somewhat eccentric — unless, of course, he keeps that seriousness in an air-tight compartment. Society generally is suspicious of the imaginative sense of values because, as Professor Whitehead pointed out, of the anarchic nature of the speculative mind. Yet it cannot afford to be openly barbarous, and so you have the worship of false gods of the imagination — people who believe in what they call Art, art of the film, art of the ballet. But one must not allow oneself to be inhibited by too precise definition.

Roughly, two classes of people abhor the imaginative sense of values. There is the sound businessman whose solid worth finds expression in the trivialities of the newspaper, and there is the literary mediocrity who must deny the existence of Parnassus if his little dust-heap of biographies and novels are to mean anything.

The sound man of the world never reflects. Not to reflect is what is considered sanity. Yet, without this reflective centre man is a savage and will not be long in revealing his savagery if you touch the hollow beneath the conventional dress of respectability. And that touching or stripping of the hollow heart is what the poet willy-nilly does, and is the thing which makes him hated by the world. In every poet there is something of Christ writing the sins of the people in the dust.

As I have said, one of the Irish ideas of the poet is of the uproarious clown. I have hardly ever heard an Irish admirer of Gaelic or of any poetry speaking of the poet that he didn't give the impression that he thought it all a great joke.

Another idea of the poet is of a man who at the drop of a hatpin would run off with another man's wife. In the Gaelic mythology it is the priest's housekeeper who gets abducted, and this gives rise to terrible heresy which rocks Christendom. Now, I do not say that some geniune poets have not lived the wild life, have not run off with the other men's wives, but I do say that it is entirely contrary to the poetic nature. It is a *bourgeois* concept of rebelliousness.

The note of the poetic mind is a moral one, and it is this moral quality which the world cannot stand, for it is a constant reproach to inferior men — and inferior men, let me explain, are men who are committed to inferior things, who lack the courage to pronounce a judgement in defiance of their own petty vanity. The world loves the wild, uproarious fellow who is made in its own image and will (when it comes to the test) take him to its bosom and confer upon him all the wordly privileges. Display a touch of this kind of irresponsibility and you're home and dried. The world knows it is not genuine.

To some extent this view of the poet is mediocrity fighting back, trying to establish a corner in commonsense. As I suggested, it is not confined to Ireland.

Perhaps it may be said that I have been labouring this Irish idea of the poet too hard, that there does exist in this country a public which accepts all I have to say, a public which has goodwill and a sincere, moral point of view. The fact that I believe there is such a public is the reason I am saying these things; for we can only preach to [the] converted. In other words, the poet is himself no more than the voice of the people. It is the pressure of a people's need for a voice which is his power.

After all these high claims for the poet you might be pardoned for expecting him to utter high and stupendous truths. But that is not the way of truth. Truth is very disappointing; we expect it to come transfigured and are inclined to ignore it when it comes simple and humble.

16(c) 'Nationalism and Literature'

Let us start with naming. Naming things is part of a poet's function. I did some naming once. It was an exhibition, or rather collection of copper jewellery. Several people looking at the pieces of jewellery commented on the aptness with which the artist had faithfully interpreted in the work something called...I have forgotten...perhaps 'The Temple of Romance'. The remarkable thing is how the article that precedes a name comes to look like its name, for an unnamed thing has little life in the mind.

Regarding myth making and myths in general, I note that a well-known French scholar priest is coming here to demolish the Anglo-Saxon myth. According to this man's theory the whole legend of an Anglo-Saxon culture is nothing but legerdemain. The legend is there just the same. It cannot be demolished, any more than that singular Gaelic figure St Patrick, as portrayed on banners and cards, can be demolished. A myth is necessary, for a myth is a sort of self-contained world in which one can live. As literary critics live in theirs, discussing family intimacies.

Ireland as a myth which could protect and nourish a body of creative artists is rather unique. One of the reasons why it has failed again and again is that nationalism is seldom based on those sincerities which give any truly spiritual force its power. Good work cannot survive in an angry atmosphere, and without being too boringly insistent on the value of truth, I can only say that it is the most entertaining type of communication.

The reasons why work produced by a Celt receive praise or blame have on the whole had little or nothing to do with aesthetics or truth. As I have said myths are indestructible, but what I should like to point out is that myths do not work and the Irish myth is one of them. Of course the Russians had a myth. Dostoevsky in exile at the casinos of Europe is never done lamenting his absence from Russia. But of all patriotic myths the only one in my opinion that came alive and worked for the author was Joyce's myth of Dublin. Why it sustained him is that he never stopped to think. Once we stop to think the illusion is gone. In the case of a poet's mythology the all-embracing fog must remain impenetrable. We must not be able to escape from it. In certain circumstances the only way to succeed in this is to accept failure and by so doing realize that failure is something in the mind.

I know a few writers who live in Ireland who have not cottoned on to the fact that Ireland as a myth is no use. When Dr Johnson said that patriotism was the last refuge of the scoundrel, he was once again right on the mark. In all formal patriotic activity there lies the seed of something that is not the seed of virtue. There have been many fine patriots but there must be some inherent defect in the whole business, seeing that men of little or no principle can readily weigh in with it and be accounted fine men.

Regarding the mighty corpus of English literature, this seems to me largely divorced from England the nation, the often scoundrelly nation. Some poets have praised Cromwell and a great one was his secretary and another one his cousin, but for all that the protective atmosphere which fed the English poetic world had little to do with politics or patriotism. Love of the land and landscape is of course a different kettle of potatoes altogether. Constable, Wordsworth, Clare, most of them were great patriots in that sense. It seems at first blush that English poetry grew to its splenditude in a myth void, that it was entirely individual.

But there was a myth and a true one.

This curious myth has to do with faith in one's own judgement and the courage to pronounce it. Wherever there are a number of men with that faith and courage you have a myth-making society. Even today in London a man may be talking to another in a pub. As they speak they are accompanied in their consciousness by many others who are not present at all. It is this sort of family thing that alone can make a society happy. For some reason or other this source of strength has never been lost in England. It goes on quietly unconcerned, undeceived by the latest reports on anything. As one goes on in the country, knowing exactly who is down in the valley sowing turnips or levelling the potato drills and who is not, and what they are all thinking about.

It is this kind of parish myth regarding literature that has been totally lacking in Ireland. Instead we have this national thing which is no use to anyone. Is Synge the voice of Ireland? Has Ireland a voice? I believe it has a faint, odd voice, difficult to establish. Indeed Carleton is our native voice. And I am always so glad that notwithstanding anything one may say nobody will ever read Carleton. You can praise or blame this great writer without involving anyone.

The thing is that here in Ireland we have a Celtic hinterland of Festival towns deeply committed to the national myth. At these festivals you have...well you ought to know what you have. But a man is the worst in the world if he ventures any criticism. And what can one do? It is all the great days of the Abbey, *Cradle of Genius* was what a film on those great days was called. If one says that Synge wasn't a genius and so on you are instantly up against patriotism. I believe that the 'Theatre' is largely a journalistic property. You have only to glance at the space devoted to amateur theatricals in the papers to understand this. Not that I mind myself. My ambition was at one time to get on to the amateur stage in some play by perhaps J. B. McCarthy. I was full of Ireland then. And when all is said and done one might be full of worse things. Particularly down in the country you just cannot postulate high and mighty ideas. There was a time when my great ambition was to get published in the *Weekly Independent* or *Ireland's Own*. On one occasion there was a prize of half a guinea, and here I was routed by an effort sent in from a Care of address. This was:

I think that I shall never see
A poem lovely as a tree

202

I mention this to fix the Irish position. It was indeed a great day for me when I had a piece accepted and printed without any address and needless to say unpaid for by the *Dundalk Democrat*. I was quite convinced that everyone in Ireland would see it. I feel this may possibly have something to do with that voice of Ireland mentioned before. I don't suppose we have produced many poets of the best talent, but there was something and that something was not unconnected with the ballads and poems that used to get printed in these local newspapers. Those old Gaelic poets, by the way, of whom we hear quite a lot were as genuine as one could expect them to be. There was no doubt the usual percentage of true poets amongst them. But I fear there was no proper society in which they could flourish. There was no faith.

However to return to the Irish myth, the unworkable one, this only got going properly about fifty years ago. Keegan Casey for instance with his Rising of the Moon:

O then tell me Shawn O'Farrell
Where the gathering is to be
In the old spot by the river
Right well known to you and me...
I bear orders from the captain
Get you ready quick and soon
For the pikes must be together
At the rising of the Moon.

Or such anonymous songs as

It was early early in the Spring
The birds did whistle and sweetly sing
Changing their notes from tree to tree
And the song they sang was old Ireland free.

It is odd that we got a myth like that going here, much as America got one in which literature could flourish a century ago. You had Longfellow, Melville, Bret Harte and so forth all derived, I regret to admit, from the English tradition as spread from New England. Today you have a sort of International writing crowd, not involved in myths indigenous or otherwise. And yet...

I suppose that judged in the cruel light of top-class literary criticism, a poet like Mangan comes out pretty badly. But to those involved with the local sentiment Mangan made a profound appeal. At one time Mangan immensely moved me with

> I walked entranced
> Through a land of morn
> The sun with wondrous excess of light
> Shone down and glanced
> O'er fields of corn
> 'And lustrous gardens aleft and right
> Even in the clime of resplendent Spain
> Beams no such sun upon such a land
> But it was the time
> 'Twas in the reign
> Of Cahal Mor of the Wine-Red hand.

I almost begin to believe in the myth of Ireland as a spiritual reality.

16(d) 'The Parish and the Universe'

> To have the deep poetic heart
> Is more than all poetic fame.
> > *(Tennyson)*

A man should not want to be an artist. To want to be anything is the sure way to drive the impulse away. A man wanting to be in love cannot contract the disease.

None of those whom the world calls creative ever thought for a moment about Art, though I admit that I am over-stating the case here: there have been art for art's sake periods.

The purpose of all expression is happiness. If you have something to express, then the expression of it will relieve you, produce a catharsis: but if you have nothing to express you will endure the agonies of a man whose stomach is empty, retching with sea-sickness.

Art is never art. What is called art is merely life.

This is particularly true of literature which is hardly ever art. Whenever an architect tries to be an artist as is happening every day, he becomes vulgar.

Beautiful things are made by people who enjoy doing them. If you are not enjoying yourself it is a bad sign.

If you stand outside any position however dreadful it seems you are not at its mercy; this is true of all tyrannies including that of class.

Men are forever seaching for a formula which is not dependent on inspiration, a formula for making a poet without his having to be born. The majority will on all occasions root hysterically (and with hatred in their eyes at the smallest criticism) for any form of art which is within the reach of a hard-working chap.

I do not think that ever before were so many people convinced that art in some form is necessary to life, liberty and the pursuit of happiness. The Hitler war gave a great lift to this feeling, but it is a constant human emotion.

Hence you have armies whose private soldiers may take it in no happy spirit if you think that their interests are crude sex and sexy journalism. They may well feel affronted at you putting them back in the ghetto of their class. They may be expecting a lecturer on Whitman or a member of a symposium on the ballet, or interested in a Gramophone Society.

Listening to music up to this has provided the majority of these people with their art. But listening to music is not enough; it is a poor form of self-expression. They don't want to be an audience always, though they are willing to be some kinds of audience. They want some sort of orgy. In England the tradition was better. The England idea was to keep the masses from getting a taste for something that would only make them unhappy. The vast hinterland of anonymous masses has made for the greatest of English literature. In America you have millions of highly conscious folk and very little poetry.

The masses of men are no longer — not even the English manual labourers — willing to live lives of quiet desperation. They may be desperate but they will let you know about it.

There is yet another need for a formula for synthetic poetry. As I think Auden did remark in a wireless talk the faith basis for the poet is breaking down. In society's enthusiasm for the creative imagination is the desert of consciousness.

Parochialism and provincialism are opposites. The provincial has no mind of his own; he does not trust what his eyes see until he has heard what the metropolis — towards which his eyes are turned — has to say on any subject. This runs through all activities.

The parochial mentality on the other hand is never in any doubt about the social and artistic validity of his parish. All great civilizations are based on parochialism — Greek, Israelite, English.

In Ireland we are inclined to be provincial not parochial, for it requires a great deal of courage to be parochial. When we do attempt having the courage of our parish we are inclined to go false and to play up to the larger parish on the other side of the Irish Sea. In recent times we have had two great Irish parishioners — James Joyce and George Moore. They explained nothing. The public had either to come to them or stay in the dark. And the public did come. The English parishioner recognizes courage in another man's parish.

Advising people not to be ashamed of having the courage of their remote parish, is not free from many dangers. There is always that element of bravado which takes pleasure in the notion that the potato-patch is the ultimate. To be parochial a man needs the right kind of sensitive courage and the right kind of sensitive humility.

Parochialism is universal; it deals with the fundamentals.

It is not by the so-called national dailies that people who emigrate keep in touch with their roots. In London, outside the Catholic churches, the big run is on the local Irish papers. Lonely on Highgate Hill outside St Joseph's Church I rushed to buy my *Dundalk Democrat*, and reading it I was back in my native fields. Now that I analyse myself I realize that throughout everything I write there is this constantly recurring motif of the need to go back. Why do we always need to go back? What is it we want to return to? Freud says, the womb, and there is something in it too. We are never happy from the moment we leave the womb. The Mother is the roots. The Mother is the thing which gives us a world of our own. The Mother is the basis of romantic love.

Far have I travelled from the warm womb.
Far have I travelled from home.

So it is for these reasons that I return to the local newspaper. Who has died? Who has sold his farm?

17
Thomas Kinsella, 'The Divided Mind', 1973

This essay appeared in Seán Lucy (ed.), Irish Poets in English *(Cork, 1973). Thomas Kinsella (b.1928) has recently edited the* New Oxford Book of Irish Verse *(1986); he is one of the most distinguished of the present generation of Irish poets.*

There is no great disagreement about the term 'Anglo-Irish poetry' and what it covers: poetry written in English by Irishmen, or by someone in Ireland, or by someone with Irish connections. Some will take it in its broadest sense — as in the 1958 *Oxford Book of Irish Verse* — and include Emily Bronte; others — like Russell Alspach, in his book *Irish Poetry from the English Invasion to 1798* — will take a narrower view and exclude, say, Swift as being simply an English poet. The trouble is that, however we take it, the term imposes a restriction on our view of Irish poetry. It tends to stop us thinking of poetry in the Irish language. It suggests that poetry written in English in Ireland has nothing to do with our poetry in Irish; that it is instead an adjunct to English poetry — important perhaps, but provincial or colonial.

The two languages, and their poetry, may never have had much to do with each other — may even at times have been unaware of each other's existence; and certainly our poetry in English has never been isolated from English poetry, much to the benefit of poetry in general. But the separation between the two languages was never complete, and neither was the connection between the two literatures. If we realize this we may become aware of a vital reality — one that has everything to do with the 'divided mind' of the modern Irish poet, which is my allotted subject.

A modern English poet can reasonably feel at home in the long tradition of English poetry. No matter what his preoccupations may be, he will find his forebears there, and he apparently feels free to conscript an Irish or an American poet into the tradition if that seems necessary. As he looks back, the first great objects in view might be Yeats and T. S. Eliot, then Matthew Arnold, Wordsworth, Pope — and so on through the mainstream of a tradition. An Irish poet has access to all of this through his use of the English language, but he is unlikely to feel at home in it. Or so I find in my own case. If he looks back over his own heritage the line must begin, again, with Yeats. But then, for more than a hundred years, there is almost total poetic silence. I believe that silence, on the whole, is the real condition of Irish literature in the nineteenth century — certainly of poetry; there is nothing that approaches the ordinary literary achievement of an age. Beyond the nineteenth century there is a great cultural blur: I must exchange one language for another, my native English for eighteenth-century Irish. Yet to come on eighteenth-century Irish poetry after the dullness of the nineteenth century is to find a world suddenly full of life and voices, the voices of poets who expect to be heard and understood, and memorized. They are the almost doggerel end of Gaelic literature, but they are at home in their language and tradition; it does not occur to them to question the medium they write in. Beyond them again is Aogán Ó Rathaille,[1] the last major poet in Irish, and beyond him the course of Irish poetry stretching back for more than a thousand years, full of riches and variety. In all of this I recognize a great inheritance and, simultaneously, a great loss. The inheritance is certainly mine but only at two enormous removes — across a century's silence and through an exchange of worlds. The greatness of the loss is measured not only by the substance of Irish literature itself, but also by the intensity with which we know it was shared; it has an air of continuity and shared history which is precisely what is missing from Irish literature, in English or Irish, in the nineteenth century and today. I recognize that I stand on one side of a great rift, and can feel the discontinuity in myself. It is a matter of people and places as well as writing — of coming from a broken and uprooted family, of being drawn to those who share my origins and finding that we cannot share our lives.

When Yeats looked back over the same stretch of time, he saw it very differently. He valued what he could in Gaelic literature and used it, as we know. But his living tradition was solely in English; and it had its high point, not its tragic last gasp, in the eighteenth century. Its literature and its human beings are specialized and cut off, an Anglo-Irish annex to the history of Ireland. He yoked together Swift, Burke, Berkeley and Goldsmith for his writers, and chose for his people a race of 'swashbucklers, horsemen, swift indifferent men'. It is English literature, not Irish, that lies behind them; and their line — as he sees it — is ending in his own time. Yeats is *in* the tradition of Irish literature; he gives it most of its body and meaning for us. But he is *isolated* in it. Early in his career, in an essay in *Ideas of Good and Evil*, he wrote of the people on the Galway plains that 'One could still, if one had the genius, and had been born to Irish, write for these people plays and poems like those of Greece. Does not the greatest poetry always require a people to listen to it?' But he is partly isolated from these people: their language is not his, and therefore he cannot completely touch their lives. The separation is incomplete, but he is wounded by it. He is wounded also by the incompleteness of his identification with English poetry — indeed, by the whole historical reality that underlies these divisions. Writing in 1937, in one of his last essays, 'A General Introduction for my Work', he dramatizes his isolation, remembering the past persecutors of the Irish people:

> there are moments when hatred poisons my life and I accuse myself of effeminacy because I have not given it adequate expression...Then I remind myself that though mine is the first English marriage I know of in the direct line, all my family names are English, and that I owe my soul to Shakespeare, to Spenser and to Blake, perhaps to William Morris, and to the English language in which I think, speak, and write, that everything I love has come to me through English; my hatred tortures me with love, my love with hate.

For an Irish writer examining his traditional position, therefore, it doesn't seem to matter what view he chooses, or is forced to take. There can be no great difference for a writer in Irish, separated linguistically from the great majority of his fellow countrymen: what he sees and feels is division, a division so fundamental as to form a considerable part of his actual imaginative substance.

There is nothing necessarily fatal in this for poetry. It is not in itself a diminishment, something that must automatically reduce the quality of the poetic response. Yeats was in no way diminished, for example, by his 'torture'. Its nature and its cause needed to be recognized; he recognized them, and turned them into subject matter. A strong writer may benefit from the support of a living tradition, but he won't be kept from major achievement by the lack of it — though his achievement will be of a more solitary kind.

Things go harder with the weaker spirits, though they are seldom aware of their exact handicaps, and may never know what they lack in not having a full tradition — even to fight against. Such talents spring up in the usual profusion, like the poetic impulses of youth, but they are likely to grow stunted or wither away quickly, or fail in some way to grow to their full capacity, not being strong enough to drive their roots where they must for imaginative nourishment. These individual failures, by courtesy of time's cruelties, don't really matter — nothing matters but excellence. Yet taken all together, as we have the chance to see them in 'Anglo-Irish poetry' so called — a few struggling poetic souls in a bleak climate, and a host of failures — they give a certain baleful tone to our recent poetry — I mean our poetry in English since about 1800.

If we look at that poetry without sentimentality, and apply standards of poetic judgement only, what remains from the nineteenth century? My own first finding, I repeat, is dullness: a huge supply of bad verse and, amidst their own contributions to this supply, a few tentative achievements by Moore, Ferguson, Mangan and (I am sometimes tempted to feel) Allingham. From Moore: a sampler of songs and witty pieces, distinguished for their expertise and athletic lightness, but without imaginative depth, either 'serious' or 'light': 'a master in fancy', as Stopford Brooke diagnoses the case...'full of that power which plays with grace and brightness on the surface of Nature and man but which never penetrates...' Despite the extraordinary esteem in which his contemporaries held him it is close to Moore's own modest judgement on himself. Callanan[2]...nothing. Thomas Davis, Thomas D'Arcy McGee,[3] Speranza[4]...rhetorical fluency, savage indignation, high purpose. If pure human intensity could produce great poetry it would have done so here. But it isn't enough. The strong spirit of nationalism which seems to give their work cohesion is, for poetry, just as shallow a force as Moore's desire to 'charm' his audience. A spirit of nationalism is too simple a thing to survive for long intact — or at any rate to continue being simple — in a maturing poetic career.

From Mangan...for the first time we are in touch with real

poetry, in which from time to time the profoundest personal depths are sounded in an investigation of life, and in which language itself comes to life. Yet there are scarcely half a dozen poems that don't ask us to make allowances. For the mastery of the recurring refrain in 'Dark Rosaleen' we have to pay dearly in the exclamatory deadliness of the same device in an otherwise good poem 'The Karamanian Exile'. For the piercing images of 'Siberia', and their accurate economy, we must pay very dearly indeed in the bulk of Mangan's exotic verse, with its frivolous wastefulness. Yet I believe that those half-dozen are among our 'indispensable' poems ('Siberia', 'Dark Rosaleen', 'O'Hussey's Ode to the Maguire', 'The Lament for the Princes...' and perhaps 'The Nameless One'). They are the vessels of a continuous creation; their living language pours out, continually in need of refreshment to cope with the complexity of its statements, and continually finding it. But they are only the remains of a squandered future, of 'genius wasted' as Mangan himself confesses in 'The Nameless One'.

With Ferguson we are again in the presence of the real thing; his nature, against Mangan's, may seem dispassionate and slow, but it is almost as deep. And again the whole process is characterized by waste and randomness, by the funneling away of great energies. If Mangan spent his frivolously, it seems to me that Ferguson spent his solemnly — and just as lavishly — in the service of an imposed plan. It is a great artistic temptation to impose order or purpose on one's work, and if the temptation is yielded to the price can be great. Ferguson pays the full price in his epic poems 'Congal', 'Conary' and the others, which are part of a heroic attempt to recreate Ireland's past in modern verse. Yeats has said of these historical poems that their author is 'the greatest poet Ireland has produced, because the most central and the most Celtic...' This bears more investigation than there is time for now — the relationships, for example, between greatness and centrality and nationality — but presumably poetic excellence was being taken for granted. I can't help suspecting, ungenerously perhaps, that it is gratitude rather than strict judgement that is involved, Yeats's gratitude to Ferguson for a great personal poetic debt. While I hesitate over Yeats's estimation of the historical poems, I think Ferguson's ballads are another matter — some of them, at least: 'The Burial of King Cormac', 'The Welshmen of Tirawley' — and the inspired 'Lament for the Death of Thomas Davis', this too one of our indispensable poems, of a simple and stubborn structure and a loose rich rhythm that equals anything by Mangan.

After these...One might delay a moment over names like John Todhunter or Aubrey de Vere or Alfred Percival Graves...but no more than a moment. A little longer over William Allingham, for a kind of passive wisdom — though it rarely comes to life in his verse, except in flashes of sudden concern, sudden power and economy, as in the eviction scene in *Laurence Bloomfield in Ireland*. But then all sinks again into mood-setting and description — description in the service of nothing.

Waste is the distinguishing mark in all of these careers (as it is to mark most of our poetry so far in the twentieth century as well). If ever poets might have benefited from a living tradition these would have been among them. But they *are* heroic figures: what they are doing is what Yeats said of Ferguson — providing the 'morning' of the truly great and national literature that might come. They and all the Irish poets of the nineteenth century are in the first wave, where casualties are heaviest, and they are the ruined survivors.

Before I go further, I should return to a limiting phrase I found myself using a moment ago, when I described the major achievement of recent 'Anglo-Irish poetry' as solitary — more solitary than it might have been if it had had a living tradition to rise from. I dwell on the phrase 'solitary achievement' because if I had to choose a single phrase to characterize *all* the good poetry of the last fifty years or more — in Ireland or anywhere else — that would probably be it. So that the 'divided mind', as a function of rootlessness, of historical or social deprivation or alienation, may not be the exclusive property of the modern Irish poet...One has only to say this to see that it is true — to see that 'Anglo-Irish poetry' is in a way a useful model of the whole of modern poetry. Remembering Yeats, his 'torture' and his solitude, is it not possible that we are enduring now in our lives the culmination of what he sensed in its beginnings, and endured imaginatively, in his time? The falling apart of things...

In the best pioneering poetry of the twentieth century, that of Yeats and Eliot and Pound, we have the first full articulation of the world as it is now becoming, the world that has replaced the essentially nineteenth-century world of sensible perfectibility. In the fifty short years since Yeats's prophetic poem 'The Second Coming', that Second Coming has been accomplished; externally, in the physical chaos of extermination and race slaughter, internally in a sense of precariousness and disorder in the spirit. The random horrors of the First World War may have begun the process, and possibly provided Yeats with his first images of basic upheaval. But it is one thing for Yeats to have foreseen such an upheaval as inevitable, in a schematic way, and even to have given body to his idea as the rough beast slouching toward the place of rebirth, destroying one state of order in the emergence of another. It is another thing to have participated in the second coming itself, even remotely, as my own generation did, coming to consciousness during the Second World War, in Ireland — to have breathed in the stench and felt the dread as the rough beast emerged out of massed human wills. It was no news that the human mind was an abyss, and that the will, just as much as the imagination, was capable of every evil. But it was something new that creatures out of Hieronymus Bosch should have materialized in the world, formally inflicting and enduring suffering beyond all reason, in obedience to a diabolic logic; it is something new to have had the orderly but insane holocausts imagined by Leonardo da Vinci set loose on the earth in an act of logical but monstrous choice. The coming to reality of these apparently fantastic images is an inner catastrophe; we have opened up another area of ourselves and found something new that horrifies, but that even more intensely *disappoints*. The realization of this disappointment seems to me the most significant thing in contemporary poetry: it is the source of that feeling of precariousness which is to be found in the best poets now living.

Among the first things to go down with the destruction of the old order was the great poetic stance of Romantic isolation — isolation of the artist from a more or less unified society. After the catastrophe the poet is still isolated, of course; but so now is every man. The repeated checks to reasonable hope which the world has suffered have destroyed the cohesion of the modern social organism. The organism continues to function but the most sensitive individuals have long ago been shaken loose into disorder, conscious of a numbness and dullness in themselves, a pain of dislocation and loss. Everywhere in modern writing the stress is on personal visions of the world, in which basic things are worked out repeatedly as though for the first time.

Again, as with the special mutilations which are a part of the Irish experience, there is nothing ruinous for poetry in all of this. The poetry is in the response, and these national and general calamities have to do with the quality of the ordeal, not of the response. The ordeal is around us and in us — the ordeal of mankind and the ordeal of each man. Its qualities do not change: the same high hopes, the same disappointments, the same hideous discrepancy between what one might and what one can and does. In the private context, as the ordeal bears down on us one by one, the weight may be lightened by the experience or the ideal of love. There seems little likelihood that love — or even decency — will ever amount to much in social affairs or in the world as a whole. But that is another matter...

So, it appears to me that for a modern writer, Irish or not, his relation to a tradition, broken or not, is only part of the story. For any writer there is also the relationship with other literatures, with the present, with the 'human predicament', with the self. This last may be the most important of all, for certain gaps in ourselves can swallow up all the potentiality in the world. But say that we are not crippled in this way, then we inherit all the past one way or another. A writer, according to his personal scope, stands in relation to what he can use of man's total literary tradition. Eliot and Joyce could use much, Dylan Thomas very little. But Thomas's relationship with the self was — or was beginning to be — adequate for great poems. A man in his life shares more with all men than he does with any class of men — in eating, sleeping, loving, fighting, and dying; he may lack the sense of tradition, almost, and still share most of human experience.

Is there any virtue then, for literature, for poetry, in the continuity of a tradition? I believe there is not — just as its discontinuity is not necessarily a poetic calamity. A continuous tradition, like the English or French, accumulates a distinctive quality and tends to impose this on each member. Does this give a deeper feeling for the experience gathered up in the tradition, or a better understanding of it? Again, I doubt it. It is not as though literature, or national life, were a corporate, national experience — as though a nation were a single animal with one complex artistic feeler. This may be true for brief periods that have 'unity of being', like those that produced Greek or Elizabethan drama: there is probably some truth in it, ultimately, for mankind as a whole. But for the present — especially this present — it seems that every writer has to make the imaginative grasp at identity for himself; and if he can find no means in his inheritance to suit him, he will have to start from scratch.

To look at it more remotely still: pending the achievement of

some total human unity of being, every writer in the modern
world, since he can't be in all the literary traditions at once, is
the inheritor of a gapped, discontinuous, polyglot tradition. But
any tradition will do: if one function of tradition is to link us
living with the significant past, this is done as well by a broken
tradition as by a whole one — however painful, humanly speaking,
it may be. What matters for poetry, to say it once more, is the
quality of the response.

To summarize, therefore, I believe that it is a series of flaws
in the responses of nineteenth-century Irish poets that makes their
poetry not matter very much. I have suggested that their primary
disadvantage was the lack of an available tradition — that in the
traumatic exchange of one vernacular for another a vital sustaining
force was lost. But underneath all that, as I have suggested also,
there is the fundamental matter of the individual talent. It is the
lesser talents whose art suffers by such human deprivations. Major
talents are neither diminished nor set astray by these things. Yeats
and Joyce take leave, with a vengeance, of the gloomy
circumstances of nineteenth century Irish literature. And we are
free to do so with them, if we can.

Have we done so? What of our twentieth century so far? As to
Yeats's contemporaries, my own impression is of a generation of
writers entranced, understandably, by the phenomenon of Yeats
among them, and themselves mainly going down in a welter of
emulation and misunderstanding of his work. Among the more
disappointing are Seamus O'Sullivan, Joseph Campbell, F. R.
Higgins, and James Stephens (I am speaking only of his poetry).
On the positive side there are distinct achievements in single
poems here and there, and in the ballads in Pádraic Colum's first
book of poems, *Wild Earth*. In the first generation after Yeats's
death there is no shortage of poetic activity, but a great deal of
it is intermittent or fumbling, with much of the energy misdirected
or squandered. It is a repetition, in short, of some of the
characteristic shapes of the nineteenth century in Ireland, and of
poor verse in general: the capering entertainer, with one eye always
straying from the work to assess the effect he is making; the 'plain
blunt man', confusing vigorous assertion with intensity; the serious
career wasted, or gapped, in one way or another. It would be
impossible to demonstrate this in a sentence or two, or to deal
with the few advances — and the many throwbacks — in
contemporary Irish poetry; and I am not going to try on this
occasion. A good critic is really needed for that thankless task,

and Ireland has not produced one yet who is able and willing. An anthology is also needed, one that will contain only good poems — nothing that is merely representative or historically important: the result could be very interesting. In the meantime it seems proper to say that two talents have risen above the general level — those of Austin Clarke and Patrick Kavanagh. Each has produced notable poems, each has established a valid individual poetic voice over the heavy reverberations of Yeats's. Not the least of their achievements is to have stood for discrimination in a poetic community that seems always in danger of falling back into self-excusing, self-congratulatory ease. When Patrick Kavanagh introduced a broadcast of *The Great Hunger* some years ago, and confessed with his usual forthrightness that the work'...is not completely born...You must have technique, architecture...' his self-knowledge was punishing, and his self-judgement heroic. They are both a reproof to those (touching in their indiscrimination) who would still call *The Great Hunger* a great poem. To do so is a disservice not least to the set of truly fine short poems that Kavanagh wrote during the middle Fifties. We must discriminate where we can — where our best writers have shown — or we may find ourselves, again, unable to discriminate at all.

What of the future? Is there a way for a modern Irish writer to fight this danger — a danger he is more vulnerable to the more isolated he is content to be? I think there is: there is always a way...It will not be found in rigid opinion or verbal gesticulation; we have had more than our share of these. But it may be found in a willingness and determination to investigate one's self and one's world, to make relentless comparisons, and to remain open at all costs to the teaching that life inflicts on us all.

Notes

1. 1670-1726.
2. Jeremiah Joseph Callanan (1795-1829) was one of the first to collect and translate the ballads and legends of Munster.
3. McGee (1825-68) wrote poems for the *Nation*.
4. Lady Jane Francesca Wilde (1826-96), mother of Oscar, used this pseudonym for her contributions to the *Nation*.

Select Bibliography

Alspach, R. K. *Anglo-Irish Poetry from the English Invasion to 1798* (Philadelphia, 1943; 2nd edn, 1960)

Beckett, J. C. *The Anglo-Irish Tradition* (London, 1976)

Brown, M. *The Politics of Irish Literature: from Thomas Davis to W. B. Yeats* (Seattle and London, 1972)

Brown, T. *Northern Voices: Poets from Ulster* (Dublin, 1975)

—— *Ireland: A Social and Cultural History 1922-79* (London, 1981)

Carpenter, A. (ed.) *Place, Personality and the Irish Writer* (Gerrards Cross and New York, 1977)

Costello, P. *The Heart Grown Brutal: The Irish Revolution in Literature from Parnell to the Death of Yeats, 1891-1939* (Dublin and New Jersey, 1978)

Cronin, J. *The Anglo-Irish Novel: the Nineteenth Century* (Belfast, 1980)

Dawe, G. and Longley, E. (eds.) *Across a Roaring Hill: the Protestant Imagination in Modern Ireland* (Belfast, 1985)

Deane, S. *Celtic Revivals: Essays in Modern Irish Literature, 1880-1980* (London, 1985)

—— *A Short History of Irish Literature* (London, 1986)

Dunn, D. (ed.) *Two Decades of Irish Writing* (Cheadle Hulme, 1975)

Fallis, R. *The Irish Renaissance: An Introduction to Anglo-Irish Literature* (Syracuse, 1977)

Flower, R. *The Irish Tradition* (Oxford, 1947)

Foster, J. W. *Forces and Themes in Ulster Fiction* (Dublin, 1974)

Gwynn, S. *Irish Literature and Drama* (New York, 1936)

Hogan, R. *After the Renaissance: a critical history of Irish drama since 'The Plough and the Stars'* (Minneapolis, 1967)

Jeffares, A. N. *Anglo-Irish Literature* (London, 1982)

Loftus, R. *Nationalism in Modern Irish Poetry* (Madison and Milwaukee, 1969)

Longley, E. *Poetry in the Wars* (Newcastle upon Tyne, 1986)

Lucy, S. (ed.) *Irish Poets in English* (Cork, 1973)

Lyons, F. S. L. *Culture and Anarchy in Ireland 1890-1939* (Oxford, 1979)

McCormack, W. J. *Ascendancy and Tradition in Anglo-Irish Literary History from 1789 to 1939* (Oxford, 1985)

Martin, A. *Anglo-Irish Literature* (Dublin, 1980)

Maxwell, D. E. S. *Modern Irish Drama 1891-1980* (Cambridge, 1985)

O'Connor, U. *Celtic Dawn: A Portrait of the Irish Literary Renaissance* (London, 1984)

Welch, R. *Irish Poetry from Moore to Yeats* (Gerrards Cross, 1980)

Index

Abbey Theatre 16
AE *see* Russell, George
Aeschylus 63, 87, 89, 97
Allen, Michael 31n31
Allingham, William 9, 15, 23, 91, 92, 172, 210
Arnold, Matthew 9, 13, 22, 23, 24, 61–8, 85, 94, 107, 108, 109, 110, 114, 115, 123, 208
Auden, W.H. 15, 27, 31n26, 205
Augustine, Saint 135, 137n1

Balzac, Honoŕe de 128
Banim, John 71, 73n1
Banim, Michael 71, 73n1
Bates, H.E. 189
Belfast Harp Festival 10
Bell, The 27–8
Béranger, Pierre-J. 162
Berkeley, Bishop 104, 209
Blake, William 22, 90, 91, 195, 209
Blavatsky, Helena Petrovna 18
Brontë, Emily 207
Brooke, Charlotte 10, 14
Browning, Robert 89
Bunting, Edward 10
Bunyan, John 172
Burke, Edmund 209
Burns, Robert 158, 162, 174
Burton, Sir Frederick William 52
Butt, Isaac 146, 170n2
Byron, George Gordon, sixth Baron 9, 88

Callanan, J.J. 15, 210, 216n2
Campbell, Joseph 215
Campbell, Thomas 162
Carleton, William 52, 103, 104, 191, 202
Carlyle, Thomas 101, 173, 196
Casey, Keegan 203
Cézanne, Paul 197
Chaucer, Geoffrey 87, 89
Clare, John 201
Clarke, Austin 6, 7, 27, 216

Cocteau, Jean 196
Colette, Sidonie Gabrielle Claudine 196
Colum, Padraic 19, 195
Conrad, Joseph 188
Constable, John 201
Curran, John Philpot 52
Curry, John 71, 73n1

D'Annunzio, Gabriele 117
Dante Alighieri 8, 49, 55, 63, 97, 99, 101, 116, 159, 178
Davis, Thomas 13–15, 16, 17, 18, 23, 25, 26, 44–53, 61, 82, 91, 93, 104, 134, 141, 171, 173, 174, 210
Deane, Seamus 30, 61
Degas, Edgar 160
de la Villemarqué, Theophile Hersart 58, 60n2
De Vere, Aubrey 23, 91, 104, 212
Dickens, Charles 130
Dillon, J. B. 13, 44, 146, 170n3
Dostoevsky, Fyodor 181, 201
Dowden, Edward 130, 131n1
Dryden, John 196
Dublin University Magazine 11, 12
Duffy, Sir Charles Gavan 13, 18, 20, 44, 53, 69–73, 174
Dunsany, Lord 187

Edgeworth, Maria 71, 73n1, 104
Eglinton, John (William Kirkpatrick Magee) 19, 118–23, 124, 125
Eliot, T. S. 208, 212, 214
Ellis, Edwin 135, 137n2
Ellman, Richard 16, 21
Emerson, Ralph Waldo 123
Emmet, Robert 10, 101, 163

Farquhar, George 98
Fenianism 15, 16, 79, 171